Self-Coaching

Self-Coaching

*The Powerful Program to Beat
Anxiety and Depression*

Completely Revised and Updated Second Edition

Joseph J. Luciani, Ph.D.

BICENTENNIAL
1807
WILEY
2007
BICENTENNIAL

John Wiley & Sons, Inc.

Published by John Wiley & Sons, Inc., Hoboken, New Jersey
Published simultaneously in Canada

The first edition of this book was published by Wiley in 2001 under the title *Self-Coaching: How to Deal with Anxiety and Depression.*

Design and composition by Navta Associates, Inc.

The information contained in this book is not intended to serve as a replacement for professional medical advice. Any use of the information in this book is at the reader's discretion. The author and the publisher specifically disclaim any and all liability arising directly or indirectly from the use or application of any information contained in this book. A health care professional should be consulted regarding your specific situation.

For general information about our other products and services, please contact our Customer Care Department within the United States at (800) 762-2974, outside the United States at (317) 572-3993 or fax (317) 572-4002.

Wiley also publishes its books in a variety of electronic formats. Some content that appears in print may not be available in electronic books. For more information about Wiley products, visit our web site at www.wiley.com.

Library of Congress Cataloging-in-Publication Data:

Luciani, Joseph J.
  Self-coaching : the powerful program to beat anxiety and depression / Joseph J. Luciani.—Rev. & Updated 2nd ed.
     p. cm.
  Includes bibliographical references and index.
  ISBN-13 978-0-471-76828-9 (pbk.)
  ISBN-10 0-471-76828-6 (pbk.)
   1. Depression, Mental. 2. Anxiety. 3. self-talk. I. Title.

RC537.L78 2007
616.85'2706—dc22

2006042609

Printed in the United States of America

10 9 8 7 6 5 4 3 2

I would like to dedicate this book to all my patients and readers and to members of my Self-Coaching.net community. You have been my inspiration, my encouragement, and my motivation to continue on my path.

Contents

Contents

Preface

In the summer of 2001, when *Self-Coaching: How to Heal Anxiety and Depression* was released, I had no idea of the turbulent times that would befall our country in a matter of days. On the morning of September 11, 2001, I was driving into Manhattan on the George Washington Bridge. Suddenly the music I was listening to on the radio was abruptly interrupted by frantic and conflicting reports about an explosion at the World Trade Center. I glanced down the Hudson River shoreline, observing what was to become the most disturbing sight of my life. In that frozen moment, as the impossible expressed itself in the form of a black-orange plume of smoke wafting against an azure sky, I, like so many others, was confronted with a horror that continues to reverberate in my mind even now, years later.

During the months following 9/11, I was kept very busy with TV and radio interviews; everyone was clamoring for advice on how to handle their feelings of grief, fear, anxiety, and depression. As a nation, we were trying to cope. I hope that my message of Self-Coaching was able to offer solace during those impossible days. As a psychologist and author, I was deeply gratified by the response I received from readers and listeners all over the world letting me know that Self-Coaching had given them a new perspective, a way out of their suffering and struggle.

It never occurred to me that years later I would have so much more to say about healing anxiety and depression. As with so many things in life, growth and change are inevitable. The more I incorporated Self-Coaching into my practice and the more I lectured and wrote, the more I made refinements to my philosophy and my techniques. In 2003 I wrote *The Power of Self-Coaching: The Five Essential Steps to Creating the Life You Want.* This, my second book in the Self-Coaching series, applied my Self-Coaching techniques to a wider range of struggle than just anxiety and depression.

It was around this time that I created my Web site, www .self-coaching.net. Through the Web site and numerous translations of *Self-Coaching* into other languages, I was able to reach people around the world. Those who wrote to me were curious about how and why Self-Coaching would be different from the many approaches they had tried. Many wanted to know if there was hope, legitimate hope for living their lives without anxiety, depression, or panic, and so many were looking for something they could do on their own to effect change in their lives.

Answering the thousands of posts on my Web site has allowed me to grow along with my readers. This daily ritual has also forced me always to be on the lookout for new ways to expand and improve my message of empowerment. There was the man from Seattle who thought he would never be free of panic attacks; the woman from Jordan struggling with depression and afraid her husband would find out; and the recent widow in New York, suffering from a chronic disability, who asked, "Why should I go on?" In order to help all these people, I knew that I had to continue to simplify my Self-Coaching message.

I've taken the accumulated insights from the past five years and written this revision. The program outlined in this book reflects countless hours spent helping patients understand that anxiety and depression aren't illnesses, diseases, or conditions that you *get*; they're nothing more than habits, habits of faulty, insecurity-driven thinking. And as with all habits, if you feed them, they will grow. If you learn to starve them instead, they will wilt and die. It's no more complicated than that.

The heart and soul of Self-Coaching is my technique of Self-Talk. Self-Talk is your *how-to* method to liberate yourself from anxiety or depression. In this edition I offer a completely updated and revised Self-Talk section.

For those of you who are new to Self-Coaching, welcome. For those who are joining me once again, thank you for becoming part of the growing Self-Coaching community.

Acknowledgments

In the years since *Self-Coaching* was first released I have had the good fortune to meet and communicate with many people from all over the world. Through my Self-Coaching.net community, I have developed a much deeper appreciation for the torment and confusion that shrouds anxiety and depression. To all the good people who have joined me as part of my Self-Coaching community, I want to thank you for your courage and willingness to insist on living a more liberated, empowered life. It is primarily because of you that I have been encouraged and fortified to take this next step.

In the years that I've worked with my agent, Jean Naggar, I've come to recognize that had it not been for her faith in me and my writing, this dream would not have been realized. Jean has been a driving force behind the development and success of Self-Coaching from its inception. Her uncanny instincts, unwavering support, and vision have been my source of confidence these past five years. I want to thank Jean and her wonderful staff—Jennifer Weltz, Alice Tasman, Mollie Glick, and Jessica Regel—for all they've done.

My editor at John Wiley, Tom Miller, was pivotal in this project. It was Tom who first suggested this revision. He has been a friend, an editor, and a shoulder to lean on during the process of putting together this, my third book with Wiley. From the start, Tom has demonstrated his unique ability to synthesize, organize, and reshuffle a manuscript in a way that continues to amaze me.

My relationship with Jane Rafal goes back to darker times when I was questioning whether I would ever get published. If it weren't for Jane, I don't think I would have persisted. She was nothing less than my editorial coach. She was always there in a pinch, pointing me in the right direction, motivating me, and offering sage and sound advice. Without hesitation, I know that my evolution as a writer can be traced directly to Jane's expert tutelage. I want to thank her for being my literary center, but mostly I want to thank her for her friendship these past ten years.

A special thanks to my yoga instructor and mentor, Perinkulam Ramanathan. Rama has taught me many things. Most of all, he has allowed me to grasp the essential, wonderful simplicity of life. My practice of yoga and meditation has had a profound influence on my life and work. *Om shanthi.*

Finally there is my family. My daughter and fossil buddy, Lauren, is now a beautiful young lady attending the University of Delaware. Lauren, like her mother, will one day be a gifted elementary school teacher. I predict that Lauren's magnetic personality and innate charm will garner her bushels of apples from her admiring students. My son, Justin, has now graduated from Princeton and has put his heart and soul into developing HealthylivingNYC.com, a health and wellness publication for New Yorkers. Justin doesn't climb mountains; he moves them. Last, but certainly not least, is my wife, Karen. Karen has been my support since I was an aimless teenager floundering for a direction in life. She encouraged and believed in me then, and she continues to be my inspiration and strength now. Her unselfish, undying love and loyalty have made her an equal partner in all my success. As I said five years ago in my acknowledgments, she is my gift.

Introduction

As far back as Joe could remember, he worried. When he was very young, about five or six, he mostly worried about his parents dying. An only child, Joe couldn't imagine life without them. He worried in school, too. What if he got into trouble or didn't do well? Some things, such as his parents dying, he couldn't control. Other things, such as school, he could.

At least he thought he could—until fourth grade. One morning, Joe's teacher saw him slouched over his desk and told him to lift his head up. Joe was caught completely off guard. Hearing a few giggles, he got upset. Then he panicked. If he raised his head to please the teacher, the kids would surely see the tear that was rolling down his cheek. So Joe did nothing—he froze.

The teacher stalked to Joe's desk and yanked his head up. Unfortunately, Joe's jaw clenched—right through his tongue. His mouth began to bleed. The teacher, seeing the blood, lost control and violently dragged Joe out of the classroom, tearing his shirt, screaming, and slapping him along the way.

Panicked and terror stricken, Joe ran from the building. The bottom had fallen out of his world. His worst nightmare had come true: his teacher obviously wanted to kill him, his classmates saw him crying, and his parents would surely be upset with him for messing up. (This was, after all, the 1950s, when parents viewed schools as ultimate authorities.) It was lunchtime. Joe ran all the way home and managed to slip into his room unnoticed. He changed out of his torn shirt, rinsed off the blood, and combed his hair. He would have made it back to school if it hadn't been for his cousin, who was in Joe's class and, traumatized by the whole incident, arrived in tears at the front door.

Although what happened next was a blur, Joe does recall his parents being upset. His father was so enraged that he had to be physically held back from going to the school. A day or two passed, and when Joe returned to school, his teacher had been replaced. It didn't matter when someone told Joe the teacher had "snapped" and needed to go for help. As far as Joe was concerned, this was all his fault, and he had a lot of trouble living with that realization.

Joe, already a cautious, worrisome child, vowed to become even more vigilant, more in control. Somehow he would manage never to be caught off guard again. He would see to it. Unfortunately, it never occurred to Joe that he had done nothing wrong. Nor did anyone else make that clear to him.

Joe thought long and hard. He knew he wasn't perfect—far from it. Thankfully, he didn't have to *be* perfect; he only had to *act* perfect. Although he had always been rather finicky, it was different now. In the past he liked getting things just right. Now he felt he had no choice: He *had to* get things right. If, for example, he were building a model airplane and happened to smudge some glue on it, he couldn't go on; the model was ruined. If he had to make a correction on his math, instead of erasing the wrong answer, he would redo the entire assignment. Perfection became his shield against vulnerability.

Socially, it took a long time for Joe to feel comfortable. After all, he had been seen at his weakest moment. He gradually developed an acute sense of what any social exchange called for and managed to deliver it. He could be entertaining, silly, interesting, or serious—whatever the situation required. He became a chameleon, a very good chameleon. As one teacher was fond of telling him, "You're a good little soldier." No doubt about it, Joe not only knew how to follow orders, but he also anticipated them.

In spite of all his newfound success, Joe's self-esteem never gained solid footing. In fact, the more success he had, the more convinced he became that he had to work harder to maintain the whole charade. After all, he had a lot more to hide. Everyone thought he was so cool that the truth of just how uncool he was would certainly be a traumatic revelation. He was depleted, always looking over his shoulder, wondering what might go wrong, always fearing the "what-ifs."

It wasn't easy for Joe. I ought to know—I'm that Joe.

Finding the Answer

I lived those early years of my life fighting and clawing to keep in control. It never occurred to me to ask why I needed to be in control; it only mattered that I was. By the time I reached high school I was a veteran manipulator. I joined the football team so the kids would see me as a tough guy—even though at 102 pounds, I was scared to death. I joined clubs, got elected to student council, and eventually was voted most popular. I had figured out how to be what people wanted.

No doubt about it, I controlled how people saw me. I never felt I had a choice; everyone had to like me. At the time it made common sense: make people like you and they're not going to hurt you. I began to feel like one of those houses in a movie: a two-dimensional façade built to fool the audience. That's what I had become: an illusion, a house without insides.

By the time I was in college, I had had enough. My life had become tormented; I longed for relief. All the "what-iffing," the "shoulds," and the "have-tos"—I was truly driving myself crazy. I worried about everything: grades, dates, money. Most of all, though, I worried about losing control—screwing up, getting into trouble, being in any situation where I would be floundering at fate's mercy.

I decided to major in psychology. Don't laugh; psychological torment makes for a good therapist. I once heard this phenomenon referred to as the theory of the wounded healer. I'll admit that my initial motive was more self-serving than altruistic. I had become desperate enough, anxious enough, and depressed enough that studying psychology appeared to be the brake pedal I was looking for. Maybe, just maybe, there was a way out.

Self-Coaching: Opening Your Fist

My studies of psychology, as well as the years I spent in both group and individual training analysis, were helpful, but both of my hands still tightly clenched life's steering wheel. I still worried and occasionally beat myself up. I gave Freud a chance, then Jung, but nothing changed. I still worried. Once again I heard myself saying, "I've had enough!" I was hungry for an insight.

I didn't have to wait long. One night, on the way home from work, a very simple thought floated through my mind: "There's no reason to be so miserable!" Let me tell you, something very startling happened in that moment. It's hard to convey the magnitude of this seemingly innocent and altogether elementary revelation, but for me it started a revolution in my thinking. *Nothing* was stopping me from feeling better! *Nothing* was making me worry except the way I was thinking. The truth was that I *could* choose not to be miserable! Finally, I had the insight that I had longed for. I realized, for example, that even a stubborn mood, if challenged by a shift in thinking, quickly tumbles.

I had always considered feelings, moods, and thoughts to be infused with unconscious roots. Was it possible that feeling good could be as simple as letting go of negatives? One day, while having a root canal, I had an interesting revelation. While drawing hard on the nitrous oxide to avoid a little pain, I was trying to understand just why this torturous procedure was not generating more anxiety. What I discovered was that the nitrous oxide caused me to forget. A jolt of pain would get my attention, causing a rush of anxiety, but the very next nanosecond I was completely relaxed, separate from the previous painful memory. In contrast, my normal, non–nitrous-oxide thinking would have been the opposite experience.

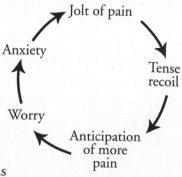

What if you could learn to let go of needless worry and anticipation of negatives, even without the aid of nitrous oxide or other drugs? What if you could actively change the channel from distressful rumination to healthier, more constructive thoughts? What would happen to your anxiety, your depression? They would vanish. Just as the amnesiac effects of nitrous oxide will pull you away from anxiety and worry about a dental procedure, Self-Coaching will pull you away from the thoughts that bury you. What's more, once you learn how to liberate yourself from insecurity-driven thinking by replacing it with self-trust, you will have beaten anxiety and depression.

It Doesn't Have to Be Complicated

In my twenty-five-plus years of private practice, lecturing, and writing, I knew that all my insights were wasted unless I had an adequate means of delivering those insights to others. As far as I was concerned, traditional therapy had become too complicated and stale, but many patients still felt comforted by traditional therapy's all-knowing therapist. I often heard from patients, "You're the doctor; tell me, what's going on? What should I do?" My patients expected and sometimes demanded that I not disappoint them by being a mere mortal.

Bret, a retired high school teacher, came to me dissatisfied with the years he had spent in traditional analysis. He wasn't dissatisfied with Dr. So-and-so, only with the fact that he didn't seem to be getting any better. Bret held Dr. So-and-so in the highest esteem and felt somewhat ashamed to have been such a poor patient. Bret couldn't understand why he hadn't profited from his analysis. Had his doctor not been retiring, Bret was sure he would have eventually figured it all out.

At first, no matter what I said, all Bret wanted to know was how his problems tied in with his Oedipal complex and repressed libidinal instincts. He was convinced his problems would one day be explained away by some arcane theory. His problems weren't, after all, simple problems. His torment was worthy of only the masters, Freud or Jung (and of course Dr. So-and-so). The straightforward, problem-solving approach I was presenting seemed too simple.

I asked Bret whether he had ever heard of William of Occam, the English philosopher. Bret hadn't, but he was delighted that I was finally bringing in one of the masters. Sir William, I explained, postulated the law of parsimony, commonly referred to as Occam's razor. I told Bret, Occam's razor states that you should prefer explanations that are no more complicated than necessary for any given situation.

I wanted Bret to know that for both patient and therapist, complicating things is often nothing more than a case of vanity. The only reason Bret fought my explanation was because he wanted his problems to be anything but ordinary.

Bret isn't unique. You may have similar ideas about why you suffer and what you need to feel better. Perhaps Self-Coaching doesn't sound as exciting as psychoanalysis, analytical therapy, or transactional analysis. In fact, Self-Coaching doesn't sound much like a psychological approach at all. Chapter 1 will provide you with a more grounded and formal explanation, but for now I'll just say this: put aside your old ideas. I will prove to you that there's a simple, direct way to beat anxiety and depression. My way isn't the usual path of traditional psychology. It's a more direct path, using simple and practical psychological tools combined with coaching and motivational strategies.

As Sir William of Occam might agree, if you want to be free from anxiety and depression, why not choose the simplest, least complicated way to do it? That way is Self-Coaching. Furthermore, once you rid yourself of anxiety and depression, you can keep using Self-Coaching to maintain a healthy, spontaneous life. Once you get in shape—psychological shape—you'll never want to go back to your old ways again.

PART I

What Is Self-Coaching?

1

A New Self-Therapy

Why are you reading this book? Maybe you worry too much, or perhaps lately you've been struggling with panicky, out-of-control feelings that leave you anxious and frustrated. You may snap at others. Perhaps your sleep isn't what it used to be, and you always seem to be in a bad mood. Maybe you've become depressed; you feel tired, hopeless, or just plain defeated. Sometimes you just want to give up.

You may feel confused, but you're sure of one thing: life's not supposed to be this hard. You want answers—now! The last thing you want is to waste more time.

So let's get started. The following self-quiz will show you how you can benefit from this book.

Is Self-Coaching for Me?

Identify each sentence as either mostly true or mostly false:

T   F   I often start my thoughts with "What if."

T   F   I usually see the glass as being half empty.

T   F   I worry too much.

T   F   I'm often fatigued.

T   F   I have difficulty concentrating.

T   F   I have trouble meeting deadlines.

T   F   I worry about my health.

T   F   I generally feel as if I'm on edge.

T   F   I'm often sad.

T   F   I have trouble falling asleep.

T   F   I have trouble trusting my perceptions (for example, Did I lock that door? Did I talk too much?).

T   F   I have too much doubt.

T   F   I would say I'm insecure.

T   F   I wake up too early.

T   F   My worst time of the day is the morning.

T   F   I dread having things go wrong.

T   F   I'm too concerned with my looks.

T   F   I have to have things done my way.

T   F   I can't relax.

T   F   I'm never on time.

T   F   You can never be safe enough.

T   F   I exaggerate problems.

T   F   I experience panic.

T   F   I feel safest when I'm in bed.

T   F   I'm too sensitive.

T   F   I often wish I were someone else.

T   F   I fear growing older.

T   F   Life is one problem after another.

T   F   I don't have much hope of feeling better.

T   F   I constantly fidget.

T   F   I'm prone to road rage.

T   F   I have phobias (for example, intense fear of closed spaces, bridges, open spaces, or social encounters).

Total your "true" responses. A score of 10 or fewer suggests that you are a relatively well-adjusted individual. Self-Coaching can teach you to shake off life's setbacks. You can expect your social and personal effectiveness to improve as you begin to become less tripped-up by emotional interference. Mostly, you can expect to enhance your already healthy personality with a more dynamic approach to life.

A score between 11 and 20 suggests that you have a moderate degree of personality erosion. Self-Coaching can quickly and simply teach you to get beyond the self-limiting effects of anxiety or depression and realize a more spontaneous, natural way of life.

If your score was above 20, you have significant difficulty with anxiety and/or depression. For you, Self-Coaching needs to become a priority. With patience and practice, you can learn to live your life symptom free.

As beleaguered as you are, I don't expect you to be convinced easily. For now, just recognize that regardless of how anxious or depressed you are, something in you is managing to read these words. That something, the part of you that hasn't quit, that healthy part of your personality that's still willing to try to solve the riddle that has become your life—that's the healthy person in you whom Self-Coaching wants to reach.

Self-Coaching, the Program

It took me twenty-five years of clinical work to write this book. That's not because I'm particularly slow or lazy (far from it), but because it takes a long time, a really long time, to see through the deceptive mist that shrouds anxiety and depression. One reason for this deception was my myopic view of psychology. Like so many other mental health professionals, I had been taught to view therapy as a relatively passive process, requiring a thorough, often painstaking, exploration and dissection of the past. The rationale is that unless you get to the underlying, unconscious reasons why you struggle, you can't expect to be healed.

It wasn't until I broke ranks with this traditional mind-set and started relying on my intuition and instincts that I began to see things differently. What I saw was that anxiety and depression weren't mysterious or obscure maladies; they were nothing more than the unavoidable outcome of misguided, faulty perceptions—perceptions that, in time, wind up depleting and victimizing you. What's interesting, once you understand the nature of these faulty perceptions, is that anxiety and depression actually begin to make sense. As irrational as your particular symptoms may feel, when you learn the punch line, the riddle becomes clear. You'll see. These insights were the catalyst for a new form of therapy I developed to teach patients what they could do to make themselves better. (I dislike the term "patient," but I like "client" even less, so I'll use "patient" throughout the book.) I call my method Self-Coaching (Self, with a capital S).

Before telling you about the specific origins of my program, let's look at a few common misperceptions about anxiety and depression. Everyone gets a bit anxious or depressed once in a while. It's a normal part of everyone's life. Getting uptight if you're late for an appointment or feeling down and upset over an argument with a friend are inescapable parts of life. Contrary to what most people think, it's not life's challenges (or our genetics) that lead to what we call clinical depression or anxiety (more about this in upcoming chapters), but how we react to these challenges. When insecurity is allowed to embellish difficult life circumstances—such as a tax audit, not getting a raise, or a fight with your spouse—with unnecessary doubts, fears, and negatives, then you're being driven not by facts but by fictions, fictions perpetrated by insecurity. You tell yourself, "I'll never get through this!" or "I can't handle this."

As Shakespeare wrote, "The fault . . . is not in our stars, but in ourselves." It's not life that victimizes us and brings us to our knees, but how we interpret and react to life. And when insecurity is steering your life, the effect is like rubbing two pieces of sandpaper together; it's friction, psychological friction. And make no mistake, psychological friction will wear you down just like sandpaper on wood, creating the clinical conditions we commonly refer to as anxiety, panic, or depression.

Intuition

The talent I value most as a psychologist is my intuition. Intuition is the ability, as Carl Gustav Jung once said, to see around corners. In contrast to the intellect, intuition is much less deliberate; it just happens. When it comes to psychology, strong intuitions are about as important to you as a telescope is to an astronomer. Just as the surface of the moon turns into a landscape of pockmarked craters under a telescope's magnification, intuition can begin to reveal the hidden aspects of anxiety or depression.

Once I magnified my view of anxiety and depression, I found myself reacting to my patients differently. Instead of treating them in a traditionally passive way, I responded to them in an active, rather spirited way. This wasn't a conscious or deliberate strategy. I just allowed my intuition to guide me. With depressed patients, for example, I sensed that they were missing a vital energy necessary to combat their difficulties. Using my energy, my optimism, and my enthusiasm, I modeled the attitude necessary to conquer the negativity, despair, and inertia. Essentially, I created what I perceived to be lacking in my patients.

With anxious patients, I followed my intuition, too. For these patients I became the voice of calm, encouragement, and conviction. I pushed hard for courage and risk taking against life's worries and fears. Anxiety-prone people are overthinkers and worriers who need to learn to overcome self-doubt by learning to risk trusting life and self.

Both anxiety and depression are weeds that grow from the fertile soil of insecurity. In order to challenge the powerful influence that insecurity has on our lives, I knew that not only did I need to have a "can-do" attitude, but I also needed to challenge the sanctity of anxiety and depression.

I suspect that most people consider anxiety and depression to be forms of mental illness; some might use the word *disease*. What we call something is very important. Words shape the way we think and feel. Mark Twain once said, "The difference between the right word and the almost right word is like the difference between lightning and the lightning bug." To me, mental *illness* is not "almost" the right word, it's the wrong word! When I think of an illness or a disease, I think of something you catch, a sickness that infiltrates your body leaving you its victim—you catch a cold or the flu. If you step on a rusty nail, you contract tetanus. You don't catch or contract anxiety or depression. You generate it!

Why is this important? With a cold, a flu, or tetanus, you're nothing more than a passive victim of some outside nefarious biological agent. And by definition, a victim is someone who is helpless and powerless. If you think of anxiety and depression as illnesses, than you can't help but feel victimized. So let's change the language. Instead of calling anxiety and depression illnesses or diseases, I'm going to suggest the rather heretical notion that anxiety and depression be seen as habits—habits, fed by insecurity, that wind up depleting your chemistry (which is why medication works) while distorting both your perceptions and experience of life. Habits that *you* generate. Anxiety, just a habit! Depression, just a habit! Granted my approach may seem radical, if not capricious, but its effect on my patients was undeniable: "You mean I'm not mentally ill?" "Can it possibly be as simple as you say?" It can be. It is.

It was obvious to me that my new approach was a dramatic departure from the more traditional therapeutic methods I usually employed, yet because my insights were more of an evolution than a revolution, it took me a while to put my finger on exactly what it was that I was doing. One day, while working with a young man who had been struggling with anxiety and panic attacks, I heard myself telling him, "You keep looking to me to make your anxiety go away. I can't do that for you. What I can do is give you a new way of seeing why you're suffering. I can fire you up and tell you exactly what you need to do to eliminate anxiety from your life. But I can't change you. Only you can do that. Instead of thinking of me as your psychologist, think of me as your coach." There it was. I was *coaching*, not analyzing, not passively listening, not reflecting. I was coaching to bring out strength, confidence, and a sense of empowerment. My patient quickly and easily related to this simple concept. Rather than seeing me as parent-authority-healer, he clearly understood my new, revitalized role: I was coaching *his* efforts, *his* determination, and most important, *his* need to overcome anxiety and depression.

The ease with which my patient and I progressed convinced me that healing problems as a coach rather than as a therapist could have far-reaching implications. But wait, let me stop myself here. Rather than using the word *healing*, let me replace it with a more precise word: *change*. From the start, it's important for you to know that I'm not trying to promote healing, because there's no illness. And if you're not ill, then you don't need to be healed. If you're anxious or if you're depressed, you need to *change*.

So what I do is coach change—changing insecurity to security, distrust to self-trust, depression and anxiety to a liberated life of empowerment. In order to challenge these entrenched habits, I recognized that an easy-to-follow, commonsense technique was needed. So I created a technique I call Self-Talk. Self-Talk is a straightforward, three-step technique that ensures change. I first introduced this method in my book *Healing Your Habits*, where I called it Directed Imagination.

Self-Talk provides a powerful formula, capable of stopping anxiety and depression where it begins—in the thoughts that precede and fertilize these conditions. Self-Talk replaces faulty, destructive, insecurity-driven thinking with healthy, liberated living. Notice I say "liberated living" and not "liberated thinking." When you remove the clutter of overthinking, rather than filtering everything through your mind ("I should tell him how I feel, but maybe I shouldn't be so bold, or maybe . . ."), you'll begin reacting to life in a more direct and spontaneous way.

Insecurity leads to attempts to control life: "If I can't trust, than I have to figure out how to be safe." In time, you become reliant on *figuring out* life rather than living it: "If he asks me where I was, I'll say I was sick, and then if he wants to know . . ." and so on. Figuring life out before it happens seems much safer than living unrehearsed. In fact, living life more spontaneously may feel downright reckless. But it's not reckless at all; it just *feels* that way. You have six million years of instinctual, intuitional hardwiring that's not going to let you down, not once you learn to trust. And this is one of Self-Coaching's essential goals: to reconnect you with your innate capacity for intuitional self-trust. Only with self-trust will you be willing to risk living your life more naturally, more spontaneously, and less rehearsed. And when you do, it will be without anxiety and depression.

Self-Coaching Reflection
Anxiety and depression depend on your inability to trust.

It doesn't matter whether you're exercising to lose a few pounds, working to improve fitness through power walking, or preparing as a serious athlete for a big race: effective training always involves following a program of repetition and progressive effort. Psychological training is no different; it requires repetition and progressive effort. Self-Talk will become the core of your training program, demanding a similar commitment. There's no magic, no gifts, no abracadabra insights, just plain old hard work—hard work that pays off.

Training

As I continued to develop my program, I found that the concept of training was particularly appealing to my highly motivated anxiety-prone patients. They usually struggle with traditional therapy's passive approach, especially when they aren't seeing results. A well-thought-out training program was clearly something they could sink their teeth into.

Depressed people face a different challenge. Depression makes it hard to muster the energy to do anything. How could I motivate depressed patients to want to train? Depression is like driving a car with one foot on the gas (that is, healthy desires) and one foot on the brake (that is, negative distortions); you're forever feeling stuck, frustrated, and discouraged. I knew that if my method was going to be successful, the training program had to offer release from the braking effects of depression—and that's exactly what happened. By replacing negative thoughts with more objective, reality-based thinking—separating facts from fictions—Self-Talk, in combination with a coached attitude of optimism, made the difference. Once patients got a taste of being unstuck, the necessary motivation for continued training was no longer a problem.

This training approach to therapy also explains why results are contingent not on therapeutic insights and aha! experiences, but on consistent, daily workouts using my Self-Talk approach. If you walked into a gym expecting that ten minutes on the treadmill would take two inches off your waist, no doubt you'd be very disappointed. In contrast, what if you approached the treadmill with a more realistic attitude, combined with a genuine desire to begin training? First off, you'd realize that one treadmill session is just that: one treadmill session. Only after repeated training sessions over time would you begin to reap the accumulated benefits of your efforts, but the benefits would come. Whether in the gym or in therapy, a training approach both requires and teaches three essential things:

1. Patience
2. A realistic understanding of the dynamics of change
3. Self-reliance

This coaching/training program, using my Self-Talk technique for breaking destructive thought habits, became the heart and soul of the book you hold in your hands, with, of course, one major modification: rather than having me be your coach, you become your own coach, directing your own liberation. Understand that the potential for healing, real healing, always resides within you. Remember, the best psychologist in the world can't make you better. No one else can. Only you can, and Self-Coaching will teach you how.

Noticing how quickly and easily my patients responded to coaching, I wondered how effective this method would be in a self-help format. Could what I was doing for my patients be presented in a book? Had it not been for a cousin who asked me what she could do for her anxiety, I might not have pursued this possibility. I discussed my technique of Self-Talk with her and gave her a number of the handouts I had prepared for my patients, describing a few simple strategies and exercises. When she called me a few months later reporting that her anxiety was gone, I was more convinced than ever that coaching could, in fact, make the transition to Self-Coaching. It didn't take me long to make my final decision to start writing, but what finally convinced me wasn't my cousin's success.

I Think I Can, I Thought I Could

Somewhere back in my late thirties I had an inexplicable urge to run the New York City Marathon. I couldn't tell you why I wanted to run it. Maybe I did because it just sounded so impossible—26 miles! Perhaps I just wanted to know whether I had it in me. Whatever the reason, I decided to give it a shot. I didn't give my training much thought. After all, I had been a recreational, couple-of-miles-a-day jogger for years, so what could be the problem? You just run longer and longer distances, right?

Fast-forward six months.

The first couple of hours of the marathon were terrific. I was high-fiving the kids along Brooklyn's Fourth Avenue, enjoying the crowd, my adrenalin, and the race. Why hadn't I done this before? By the third hour, however, more than halfway through the race and chugging through Queens, my high-fiving long since abandoned, I began to notice a deepening fatigue. Four hours into the race, the Bronx began to fade as all my attention became focused on the squish, squish of blisters. The fatigue that began ten miles earlier had become all-consuming by the fifth hour as I entered Central Park. My mind was taken over by a survival instinct that sought only to stop the pain and cramping. Somehow, I hung on and finished, five hours and twenty minutes after I had started. I shuffled through the chutes at the end of the race, trying not to think about the preceding three hours of my life.

After recovering for a few months (months in which I vowed never, ever to entertain the notion of running another race), I began talking to a friend who had run the same marathon at a much more respectable pace. He couldn't believe that I did all my training on the track. "What, no hill work? No speed work?" he asked. I realized how terribly flawed my training had been. I also realized that some things in life aren't apparent—at least not at first.

More months passed. I came across a great book written by two former coaches and marathoners, *The Competitive Runner's Handbook*. The book explained and analyzed elements of training in a comprehensive program. In spite of my resolve never to think about another marathon, I found myself devouring the book. I began to understand why my legs had become stiff, why I had cramped, why I had fallen apart the last half of the race, and even why my feet had blistered. These problems, I learned, could all be eliminated by proper training. Given the right program to follow, it should be possible to overcome the breakdowns that I had experienced. What had been a humiliating and chaotic experience could actually be deciphered, anticipated, prepared for, and, most important, conquered. I liked that. I was eager to put my Self-Coaching to the test. To date, I've run three marathons, and I'm currently training for my fourth. My times have dropped, not by minutes, but by hours.

If I say so myself, I've learned a lot about Self-Coaching. My Self-Coached marathon experiences proved invaluable as I pondered the possibility of putting my experience coaching patients into a Self-Coached format. I began to pay particular attention to the way I worked with my patients, what I told them, how I advised them, and specifically what I was doing that coached success. In this book, I have distilled this information in such a way that a reader wanting to change will be able to succeed. Interestingly, when working with patients, I often hear myself repeating sections from this book word for word. Although I would hate to make myself obsolete, the truth is that there are fundamental aspects of Self-Coaching that lend themselves quite well to a self-help format. In certain ways, such as self-reliance and self-empowerment, there are distinct advantages to managing your own Self-Coaching program of change. These, then, were the goals that I set out to accomplish when I first introduced my book a few years ago, and from the countless responses I've received worldwide, I know that my goals have been realized.

Whether you're anxious or depressed, Self-Coaching can teach you how to do what's necessary to eliminate your problems. Our minds, as well as our bodies, deteriorate if we allow ourselves to follow destructive patterns. That's what anxiety and depression are. They are patterned, negative, self-defeating habits. Self-Coaching teaches you two things: (1) how to break the destructive patterns that distort your thinking and leave you vulnerable to depression and anxiety, and (2) how to replace these thoughts of insecurity with self-trust. Remember, it is the loss of trust with self and with life that underwrites anxiety and depression.

Self-Reliance

There are obvious advantages to having a personal coach (aka therapist), but keep in mind the distinct advantage of Self-Coaching. From the start, you have only yourself to rely on. You either work hard or you don't; you either improve or you don't—and this is as it should be. Trust me on this: with anxiety and depression, it is absolutely critical to believe in your own resources to heal yourself. The sooner you take full responsibility for your program of change, the sooner you take back your life. Anyone who insists on looking for a guru, a shrink, a pill, or even a book to do their work will ultimately fail, because no one but you can ever topple your destructive habits. When you look for someone to heal you, to take care of you, to make you better, then, like a child, you remain without the full potential power of your maturity. It is exactly this power of personal maturity and trust that Self-Coaching promotes.

At first, relying on yourself for what you need may seem like a daunting proposition, especially if you're depressed. I understand this concern clearly and have made every attempt to anticipate your inertia. Ever try to push a car that's stalled? You put your back into it, straining every muscle, pushing until finally you begin to feel a slight movement. Then you push a bit more, and the car goes a bit faster, a bit easier. You've been straining against inertia. Objects at rest—and people, and anxiety, and depression—resist movement. Your initial efforts will be the most difficult, but with proper encouragement, motivation, and direction, inertia can, and will, yield to momentum. Momentum is that glorious feeling of movement—movement that becomes easier and easier once you get started. You'll see.

✦ ✦ ✦
TRAINING SUGGESTION

Inner Experience–Outer Experience:
Learning to Get Out of Your Head

Periodically throughout the day, begin to listen to your "inner talk." Whatever your thoughts are, for now, don't judge or criticize; just be aware of your thinking.

Once you've followed your thinking for a few moments, see whether you can switch from following these thoughts to participating in your world. This could be any activity: listening to music, looking at a flower, or twiddling your thumbs. Whatever you try, do it as completely as you can. If, for example, you decide to wash a dish, wash it with complete attention. Feel the soapy water, the squeak of the dish as you scour it, the dragging of the towel against the damp plate as you dry it. Rather than thinking about what you are doing, try to just feel it. Try to get out of your head and into your experience.

This exercise is an important prelude to the eventual ability of learning to let go of destructive thinking.

2

The Seven Principles of Self-Coached Healing

The heart and soul of Self-Coached healing can be condensed into seven basic principles. Although you've already had an overview of these ideas in chapter 1, now, as your training gets underway, you will consolidate them into specific principles to support all your training efforts. With practical, daily use, these truths will become more apparent. For now, in preparation for the training that's ahead, it's important that you gain a feel for these principles. I recommend that you write down these seven principles on a slip of paper and keep them in your wallet or purse. Occasionally, just read through the list, allowing yourself to absorb them and reflect on them. As soon as you have a casual, working awareness of them, you're ready to begin part 2, which addresses the problems Self-Coaching can eliminate.

Principle 1: Everyone Has a Legacy of Insecurity

Since no one grows up in a perfect world with perfect parents, being human means growing up with some degree of insecurity. It's inevitable. Children are ill equipped to cope with—much less make sense of—early traumas, conflicts, misunderstandings, or losses. When children feel out of control and vulnerable, they resort to any strategy that offers relief: tantrums, whining, sulking, hiding, whatever works. These are primitive tactics designed to reduce vulnerability by gaining more control.

Over time, these rather diffuse tactics become solidified into familiar personality patterns such as worry (Worrywarts, chapter 12), perfectionism (Perfectionists, chapter 16), avoidance (Turtles, chapter 14), manipulation (Chameleons, chapter 15), or hostility (Hedgehogs, chapter 13). Although intended to protect you from insecurity, control patterns such as these wind up doing just the opposite: they become the seeds that predispose you to anxiety and depression. What began as random attempts to ward off insecurity wind up becoming habits that alter your natural personality while diminishing the quality of your life.

When you find your mind spinning out fears, doubts, and negatives— "I can't handle these children!" or "Why go on, what's there to live for?"— you need to ask, "Who's talking, me or my insecurity?" The moment you recognize that insecurity has a distinct *voice* is the moment you begin to understand that you have a choice: you can choose not to listen! Differentiating your voice of insecurity from your healthy thinking is the first step to a more mature, liberated, healthy life.

Chapter 8 will introduce you to a technique called Self-Talk, which will teach you how to break the habit of listening to insecurity's primitive, childlike attempts to control your life. Insecurity is what feeds anxiety and depression, and Self-Talk is what starves them.

Principle 2: Thoughts Precede Feelings, Anxieties, and Depression

When it comes to feeling anxious or depressed, most people see themselves as victims: "She called me a jerk, so of course I'm depressed. Wouldn't you be?" or "See, now you got me upset. Are you satisfied?" or "How could you stay out so late? I was worried sick." Victims feel they have no choice; someone or something is always "making" them worry, panic, get upset, or be unhappy: "How can I stop worrying? With my crazy job, I have no choice!"

Sometimes, when a mood or anxiety seems to appear without rhyme or reason, you feel like a victim of fate: "I wasn't doing anything; I was just driving to work and I got this panic attack." When you're feeling

23

like a victim, it never occurs to you that you can do anything about how you feel.

Once you realize that thoughts precede feelings, you can understand that you're not powerless. There is something you can do. You can change how you think and simultaneously discover that you're beginning to feel better. Self-Coaching can teach you how to take responsibility for your thoughts and change that victim attitude, especially the thoughts produced by insecurity. If left unchallenged, insecurity will ruin and rule your life. Learning to challenge insecurity's primitive attempts to control life with worry, rumination, perfectionism, and the like is how you'll reclaim your life.

Principle 3: Anxiety and Depression Are Misguided Attempts to Control Life

When insecurity leaves you feeling vulnerable and helpless, anxiety and depression are nothing more than desperate attempts to regain control. You've probably heard of the fight-or-flight reaction. When humans are confronted with danger, we instinctually either fight back or flee. This is a part of our psychological hardwiring, which over the course of our evolution has proven itself to be an effective survival strategy. Anxiety can be seen as a form of fight, depression a form of flight. Anxiety (fight) does this through an expenditure of energy (worry, panic, rumination, anticipation, "what-iffing," and so on). Depression (flight) acts by diminishing energy (isolation, fatigue, avoidance, not caring, and the like). Unfortunately, rather than helping solve problems, anxiety and depression *become* the problems.

It may seem strange to view anxiety and depression as coping strategies trying to protect you from perceived harm. Rather than viewing them as coping strategies, it's more accurate to think of them as "controlling strategies." Anxiety mobilizes all your remaining anticipatory resources and employs them in a maneuver that attempts to brace (that is, control) you for a perceived collision. Depression, on the other hand, controls through disengagement—by shutting down, withdrawing, even suicide—from what you perceive as a threat. Whether you wind up depressed or anxious really isn't important; either way, you lose. Either way, you're being duped by the shortsightedness of reflexive, insecure thinking.

Principle 4: Control Is an Illusion, Not an Answer

Insecurity creates a feeling of vulnerability. When you feel vulnerable, wanting to be in control seems like a natural, constructive desire. It may start out as a constructive desire, but a controlled life always invites anxiety and depression. Insecurity is greedy: the more control you have, the more you seek. Nothing ever makes you feel secure enough. You're doomed to chase control's carrot. As you grow desperate and pursue your "carrots" with increased agitation, you can't help but notice that depression and anxiety are becoming permanent fixtures in your life.

The truth is that life cannot be controlled. What confuses most people is the fact that control does give temporary relief. If you've managed to manipulate or cajole life into appearing tamed and controlled, you do feel relief—for the moment. When you're desperate, this temporary relief is spelled with a capital R. If you're honest, however, you know that control is only and always an illusion. Like the eye of a hurricane, it's a false sense of calm before the remainder of the storm.

If controlling life is an impossibility—nothing more than a dangling carrot—then what's the answer? The answer is to resurrect a feeling of self-trust and confidence so that instead of controlling life, we are courageous enough just to live it.

Principle 5: Insecurity Is a Habit, and Any Habit Can Be Broken

You weren't born insecure; you learned it. Because children are ill equipped to adequately cope with early traumas, conflicts, misunderstandings, or losses, some amount of insecurity is inescapable. We learn self-doubt and self-distrust, and if these destructive attitudes are reinforced, they become habits. Habits are difficult to break because, as with any muscle, when given enough exercise, they grow in strength.

Self-Coaching will give you the strength, technique, and willpower to break your habits of insecurity. Start convincing yourself now that what you learned can be unlearned. No question about it: any habit can be broken. All that's needed is a plan, a little patience, and Self-Coached determination.

Principle 6: Healthy Thinking Is a Choice

You may not realize it (not yet), but you have a choice not to be hammered by anxiety or depression. Perhaps you can't control thoughts from popping into your mind, but you don't have to follow them around like an obedient puppy. If, for example, you think, "I can't do it; I'm going to fail," you're obviously being challenged by insecurity. Here is where you have the choice. Do you continue with the thought, "What if I fail? What will I do? This is terrible," or do you stop insecurity in its tracks? If you realize you have a choice, then you can insist, "This is my insecurity talking, and I refuse to listen. I *choose* not to be bullied by these thoughts." Self-Talk will make it crystal clear how you build the necessary muscle to choose healthy thinking.

Principle 7: A Good Coach Is a Good Motivator

The best coach in the world must also be a good motivator. Technique, skill, and conditioning will get you so far, but without proper motivation, your results will be disappointing. Nowhere is this more important than in Self-Coaching. If you're suffering from anxiety or depression, then your insecurity has all the muscle (the habit strength). This puts your emotional health at a grave disadvantage, because your insecurity has been constantly undermining your attempts to feel better. In order to turn the tide—building healthy muscle/habit to resist the distortions of insecurity—you must keep yourself pumped up for the challenge.

You're going to learn to disregard your insecurity's resistance, using Self-Coaching tools to bring out the best in yourself. Fighting the good fight requires two things: the right attitude and proper motivation. Attitude is simply having the right, positive frame of mind, and motivation is infusing this can-do attitude with energy. Motivation is what allows you to sustain your efforts and go the distance. Start shifting that attitude right now. Begin with a positive affirmation: "I'm going to beat this."

TRAINING SUGGESTION

Because anxiety and depression have a tendency to confuse and disorient you, be sure to write down these seven principles on a slip of paper.

You might find it helpful in moments of stress or struggle to read through the list. These principles will become your mantra for success. Read and repeat them to yourself often.

❖ ❖ ❖

PART II

The Problems Self-Coaching Can Heal

3

Getting to the Root
of Your Problem

Most people think of anxiety and depression as two totally separate, unrelated problems. They're not. Although anxieties and depression are very dissimilar experiences, they are in fact closely related. Once you see this relationship, you will understand your problems more fully.

Anxiety can exist alone, as can depression. At other times, anxiety can lead to depression, or a depression can be mixed with anxiety components. I have had patients who could be frantically anxious one moment, and then shut down with depression the next. They were filled with worry, self-doubt, rumination, insecurity, fear, apathy, and fatigue. The question remained: How could these very different experiences have so much in common? Rather than attempting to describe these apparent dissimilarities, I will first illustrate them. Take a look at the figure on page 32. What do you see, a vase or two faces? If you saw a vase, go back and see whether you can find the two faces. If you saw two faces, go back and find the vase.

This illustration highlights what psychologists call figure and ground. What catches your eye first—what you see in the foreground—is called the figure. The background is the field on which *your* figure (whether the vase or the faces) rests. If you saw the vase first, you probably didn't see the two faces in the background. Now go back and look again. Try seeing the vase, then switch to seeing the two faces. Notice how whatever you're seeing seems to come forward and what you're not seeing seems to recede.

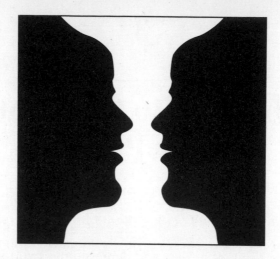

If you're anxious, then anxiety is in your foreground. It's what you see. Although you may not suspect that depression can be a background contributor to your difficulties, it can still be part of the overall, less than conscious, picture. On the other hand, if depression is in your foreground, suspect anxiety lying behind it. Why? Both anxiety and depression come from the same underlying source of insecurity. They're two different strategies that attempt to protect you from harm. Anxiety does this through an expenditure of energy, depression by a withdrawal of energy.

Ken, a forty-year-old lawyer, experienced an anxiety-depression cocktail just a few days after he landed a high-profile court case. After weeks of intense suffering, Ken was desperate to know what was going on. He'd been waking up each morning feeling shaky and nervous. "My skin felt like it was crawling. I had this terrible feeling of apprehension and panic. The panic was always followed by this 'down' feeling. I mean really down! I began staying home, going back to bed. I only wanted to be left alone."

Ken had been waiting all his professional life for this kind of break. Now, he would finally be in the spotlight. But some old insecurities began to percolate, and what would have been the challenge of a lifetime turned out to be his undoing. It began with crippling doubts about his abilities and quickly escalated into a hornet's nest of panicky "what-ifs." His anxiety and depression were last-ditch efforts to control a situation that Ken's insecurity had labeled hazardous.

It may seem odd that anxiety and depression are actually attempts to attain control, but Ken's reaction clearly supports this notion. If he couldn't leave his house, then he would have to resign from the case (which he did, unfortunately), and once he was off the case, there was no longer any danger of losing control. Because Ken did resign from the case, thereby eliminating any chance of public embarrassment (that is, loss of control), we could say that his anxiety and depression did, in fact, protect him from his fears. The end of the case was not the end of his anxiety, however. In fact, he became more depressed, and he came to me for therapy.

Self-Coaching Reflection
If you allow insecurity to steer your life, then
don't expect to have a life.

Whether you suffer from anxiety, depression, or symptoms of both, you—like Ken—are simply trying to survive what you perceive as a threat to your security. However, you don't need to rely on primitive, ineffective, destructive strategies any longer. Self-Coaching will not teach you to control your problems; it will teach you to live without them.

Misguided Helpers

How you see the world, how you interpret your experiences, and even your philosophy of life are all the result of your unique background. Just as the path of a mountain stream reflects the land it traverses—a boulder, a rise, a stand of trees—your background experiences, positive and negative, have shaped, bent, and ultimately decided the course of your psychological life. A child who experiences rejection, trauma, family discord, neglect, or divorce may develop an anxious or depressed view of life. For this child, there is never enough safety. In contrast, a child brought up with only minor mishap in the loving embrace of family and friends may develop a gregarious appetite for stimulation and adventure. For this secure child, there ain't no mountain high enough; it's the same world but with different interpretations.

Early wounds, whether physical (accidents, illnesses, hospitalizations, and the like) or psychological (rejections, frustrations, broken homes, neglectful or abusive parenting, and so on), are unavoidable. From these wounds, insecurity sends its roots deep into your psyche, setting the stage for destructive patterns of thinking and perceiving. Over time, these patterns of insecurity can whittle away at your psychological stamina, leaving you feeling out of control and susceptible to emotional problems. When you find yourself floundering in life, anxiety and depression are natural—albeit misguided—attempts to handle this perceived loss of control.

As far as defenses go, anxiety and depression may be ugly, but when you're caught off balance, without any suitable alternative, well, any port in a storm will do. If you suffer from anxiety or depression, you've run out of constructive alternatives—until now, because Self-Coaching *is* the alternative.

Self-Coaching Reflection
Life doesn't create anxiety or depression; you do.

Stress: It's All in the Eyes of the Beholder

Touch a hot stove, and you reflexively recoil in pain. Similarly, anxiety and depression seem more like simple reflex reactions to stress than defenses designed to ward off insecurity. If life presents you with a traumatic experience, isn't "life," like that hot stove, creating your anxiety and depression? Isn't a trauma just as traumatic for everyone? Sometimes, but not always. Most people would find an IRS (Internal Revenue Service) audit traumatic, but not everyone reacts the same way. The same is true of a car accident or the loss of a job. Even though you may have been quick to react reflexively in the past, Self-Coaching will teach you that life isn't a hot stove, and getting caught up in destructive emotions isn't automatic. Before you go around feeling victimized by anxiety and depression, learn an important lesson from Tom's story:

> Tom, a middle-aged man who had lost a hand in an industrial accident only months before, came to therapy for marital advice. He and I had had a few sessions dealing with some frustrations he felt with his wife. When Tom made no mention of his accident, I felt he might be in denial, trying to avoid facing his tragedy. I asked him how he felt about his loss and he told me, "It doesn't bother me, I've got another one." As it turns out, he wasn't kidding! Months later, therapy confirmed that the loss of his hand had little to do with his problems. As you may suspect, when it comes to such a traumatic loss of control, Tom is truly the exception to the rule. In contrast to Tom was a patient who became depressed over the loss of a *molar*.

Tom is living proof that what constitutes a trauma has more to do with what you tell (or don't tell) yourself about what happens than what actually happens. Granted, Tom is an extreme example, and most people would be profoundly traumatized by the loss of a hand, but keep in mind that it's not *what happens* in life that traumatizes you; it's *how you interpret* what happens. No one but you decides what's good or bad, friend or foe, dangerous or safe, difficult or devastating.

Depression and Anxiety Are Choices

Make no mistake, anxiety and depression, whether mild or severe, will always diminish the quality of your life. Many people just shrug their shoulders, accepting their plight as inevitable, "Nothing ever turns out right for me, so why bother?" they say. Others may frantically look for some control over their lives: "If only I had that job (car, promotion, boyfriend, degree, house), then I'd feel better." Some do nothing, as they passively try to adjust, but who adjusts well to a life of frustration and torment? Maybe you've come to recognize that you're living only half an existence, but what choice do you have?

The operative word here is *choice*. Let me explain.

Once established, insecurity dictates not only how you see the world, but also how you see yourself. It's not uncommon for us to identify with our problems. You might, for example, start believing that you're a nervous person, or perhaps a moody person, or irritable, or inadequate. When a new patient tells me, "I'm depressed," I waste no time setting things straight: "No, *you* are not depressed, a part of you is. You are not your depression!" This simple distinction—separating you from your symptoms—is the first step in realizing that you have a choice. When you're caught in a blinding maelstrom of psychological struggle, it may seem impossible to believe that depression, anxiety, and panic are nothing more than trespassers on your otherwise healthy nature. Although it may seem impossible to disengage from your struggle, it's not. Lucy's post at my Web site is typical of this confusion:

> I'm completely overwhelmed with the chatter in my own head. I try not to worry, but those voices in my head insist, "You have no reason to be calm and happy now," and "What if something terrible happens?" I do attempt to tell myself that these thoughts are ridiculous, but they feel so real. Worrying is what seems real, and ignoring worry feels like I'm living in a fantasy.
>
> Since the worry in my mind feels like reality, it seems irresponsible for me not to listen to it. I seem to be hell-bent on sabotaging my own peace and happiness! Does this make any sense? I'm so consumed with anxiety, it's becoming difficult to function in my day-to-day life.

I responded:

> No, *you're* not hell-bent on sabotaging your happiness, but your habit of anxiety and worry is! You've become so identified with your anxious thinking that it's hard to separate what's healthy from what's

unhealthy. Many years ago when I quit smoking, I was so identified with my habit of smoking that, to this day, I'm embarrassed to talk about some of the wild thoughts that ran rampant through my mind. I actually asked my wife to explain to me why I should want to live. I wasn't depressed or suicidal, not at all; I was just confused because everything pleasurable was associated with my habit. My habit was ruling my perceptions, my fears, and me—I was totally disoriented. This is what happens when you become identified with a habit—whether it's cigarette smoking, unhappiness, anxiety, or depression—you lose perspective.

Because of the typical confusions associated with anxiety and depression, I developed my Self-Talk technique to train others to disengage from the distortions brought about by insecurity. Once you realize this distinction between you and your struggles, the truth will begin to become apparent. Then, using Self-Talk, it's merely a matter of choosing the peace and happiness you seek.

Chances are, you never realized that you have a choice not to be depressed or anxious. Just as a dog constantly feels its desires frustrated by the tug of a leash, your thinking has frustrated you into accepting a lifestyle of distress. Self-Coaching will teach you that you have a choice. Regardless of how long you've been besieged by your habits of insecurity, once you learn to exchange insecure, reflexive thinking for more mature, responsible thinking, your anxiety and depression will no longer be able to contaminate your life.

"Me, think differently!" Sound impossible? That's how my daughter, Lauren, felt about running the mile when she was on her eighth-grade track team. The first few times she and I went out for a jog, she developed a side stitch and had to walk. Discouraged, she questioned whether she could ever race a mile. I tried to reassure her, discussing the importance of proper training and letting her know that it was only natural for her body to resist being pushed to such extremes of exhaustion. In order to run that mile, she would have to train her body to do something that, at first, felt very unnatural.

She began training. We analyzed her efforts carefully, and within a couple of weeks, she was running a nice, easy-paced mile. In order to develop more respectable times, she needed to build both endurance and speed, two more aspects to be addressed in her training. Using my own experience from marathon running, we put together a program adding longer workouts, some hill work, and some speed work. Through training, we began shaping her body into handling what, only a few weeks earlier, seemed impossible. As her first track meet approached, she was nervous, but she was ready and well trained. The trophy she won that day still rests proudly on her bookshelf.

Self-Coaching's training program will provide the winning formula for you, too. Sure, it's going to feel unnatural to do things differently. "What, you want me to be more trusting? I've always been suspicious!" Nonetheless, your persona, your image, what you're identified with is nothing more than habit, a habit that reflects the sum total of your entire life experience. Because your persona was learned, then according to Self-Coaching, it can be challenged, unlearned, and replaced with more healthy alternatives.

Neurotic self-perceptions are shaped during your early, formative years. That's why your anxiety or depression often reflect such primitive and childish characteristics. Take a look at Eric's fears:

> I'm driving myself crazy! All I do is worry. If someone has a cold, I'm afraid I'm going to catch it. If I hear about a celebrity getting cancer, I start feeling anxious. I worry about my boss criticizing my work. I don't want to get yelled at. I feel so vulnerable, so scared. I just want to be safe. It seems like the world is a big ugly place and I'm no match for it. I feel I'm going to get chewed up and spit out. I'm such a baby. If my wife heard me talking she'd die. I hide my fears from her. She thinks I'm just this normal guy. The truth is, I'm anything but normal!
>
> When I was young I had this serious kidney disease and had to stay home from school for my whole third grade. After my illness, my mother continued to worry about me. She made damn sure no

one was going to hurt me. You should have seen her go after my Little League coach when he yelled at me for flubbing a play. Once, when a bully at school said he was going to beat me up, she demanded—and got—a written apology from the boy and from his parents! I'll admit, I was overprotected, but I never had to worry, either. I know it's sick, but I long for that safety. I didn't have a care in the world; it was great.

Sometimes, when things get really upsetting and I find myself getting into a panic—I've never told anyone about this—I find myself sucking my thumb! I feel really sad admitting this; I feel like crying right now. It just seems like I was never meant to grow up.

Eric is what we call a Puer Aeternus, a grown man who never grew up.

Look at your own anxiety and depressive expressions. How childish are some of your reactions? They're childish because they were designed by a child—you, way back when. Although you've grown and changed in many ways, when it comes to your habits of insecurity, nothing's changed. They're just as primitive and distorted today as they were years ago. You've become so used to living with your outdated insecurities, you never think to challenge or update them. You live your life clinging to insecurity because it's never been any other way. It actually feels natural being neurotic, but it's not pleasant.

Considering that habits of control and insecurity are deeply ingrained, and it's a fact that habits aren't easy to break, then what's the prognosis for change? The prognosis is *excellent* because of a secret weapon at your disposal: truth. It's really quite simple. Anxiety and depression are based not on truth but on false and distorted perceptions that are fictions, not facts. Perceptions such as "I'm unlovable," "I'll never succeed," or "I'm a loser" may feel like the truth (as you bite off the head of anyone who disagrees with you). If you want to free yourself from anxiety and depression, you must stop the motor of insecurity. You do this by cutting off the fuel supply and replacing your child's view of reality (the fictions) with facts. You may have many distorted reasons for loathing yourself or your life, but there's only one truth: there's nothing wrong with you, and there never was.

Learning the truth about your life and living your truth is a major goal of Self-Coached training. It may seem unnatural at first, but trust me: living according to your truth will quickly replace your old, worn-out destructive habits and perceptions. You'll find that living effectively in the present is a completely natural and comfortable experience. Skeptical? I assure you that all the patients I've ever worked with, once they move from insecurity's childish thinking to mature living, have never wished to go back to their old habits.

Ruling Out Physical Causes

The next two chapters discuss anxiety and depression in detail, but before moving on to this discussion, there's one caution I should mention. Although the majority of these problems are psychological in origin, some depressions and anxieties can be triggered by physical problems. These include hyper- and hypothyroidism, hypoglycemia, endocrine disorders, cardiovascular conditions, respiratory conditions, metabolic conditions, neurological conditions, viral infections, fatigue, reactions to medication, and the abuse of alcohol, caffeine, and other drugs.

Before beginning any self-help program, you should first rule out the possibility that your anxiety or depression may have a physical/biological basis. One simple test is to see whether your symptoms are accompanied by distorted, negative thinking, recent trauma, loss, or a chronic stressor. If this is not the case, the possibility exists that your problem may have a physical origin, and you should consult a physician. If you have any doubt, by all means, arrange to have a thorough physical.

❖ ❖ ❖

TRAINING SUGGESTION

Before learning about anxiety and depression in the next two chapters, take a few minutes to go through some of your more disturbing behaviors or feelings. Decide whether your struggles are rooted in anxiety or depression or a combination of the two. As a simple guideline, remember that anxiety is a defense of excessive psychic energy, and depression is a defense based on the withdrawal of energy. You may want to make a chart like the one below. After reading the next two chapters, see how accurate your intuitive perceptions were.

Describe Troublesome Behavior or Thinking	Depression	Anxiety	Anxiety and Depression
1. I found myself sulking all day. Why did she treat me that way?	☑	☐	☐
2. I couldn't get to sleep last night. Maybe he really doesn't love me. What will I do? I'm such a loser.	☐	☐	☑
3. I can't believe I actually said that to him! What's wrong with me? What if he thinks I was serious? What if he's told everyone . . . ?	☐	☑	☐

❖ ❖ ❖

❖ ❖ ❖

TRAINING SUGGESTION

Follow Up

After filling in your chart, take a second to look at your troublesome behaviors. See whether you can notice any primitive childish tendencies. This recognition will eventually be very important to your Self-Coaching program.

❖ ❖ ❖

4

Depression

Mention that you feel depressed, and anyone will know what you're talking about. Feelings of being down in the dumps, miserable, negative, overwhelmed, or worthless are all symptoms of what we commonly refer to as depression. Certainly, we've all shared these symptoms from time to time. That's because getting depressed is a normal, inescapable part of being human. Getting depressed is not the same as clinical depression.

Traditionally, *clinical depression* refers to any depression that meets specific, clinical criteria described in the *Diagnostic and Statistical Manual* published by the American Psychiatric Association. Far from being something imagined or "all in your head," clinical depression is a whole-body problem, with both biochemical and emotional underpinnings. With symptoms such as sadness, crying, fatigue, appetite disturbances, decreased sexual desire, worry, fear, concentration difficulties, and feelings of hopelessness, it's obvious that clinical depression can be a serious problem if left untreated. Yet, as devastating as clinical depression can be, it's often left untreated.

The reason depression often goes untreated is that for some, "depression" is a shameful label. They feel embarrassed and humiliated because they feel they can't cope or because they're just too weak. They say, "I should be able to handle this," or "There's no reason for me to be depressed. If I wait long enough, I'll just snap out of it." Yet for others, it's just a matter of ignorance, as they perceive their depression to be an inevitable part of life. Take a look at Peggy, a thirty-four-year-old stay-at-home mother of three who was depressed. Because she functioned adequately, she didn't realize she needed help:

> I've been feeling kind of blah for a long time. At first I thought it was the routine—getting up, getting the kids off to school, cleaning, shopping, cooking, homework. Every day, never a break. Lately I've been more fatigued and just feeling down. I never gave it much thought. I just felt that I had no choice. I saw my life as a burden and, well, that's life! It's funny, but that old song by Peggy Lee "Is That All There Is?" keeps popping up in my head. Guess it's not that funny.
>
> Lately I've had a few crying episodes. They come from out of the blue. I'll just find myself crying. I put on a show for the kids and my husband, but lately it's become more difficult—especially with my husband. I have absolutely no interest in sex. The things I used to enjoy—reading, going out to dinner, having friends over—are all too much of an effort. I just want to be left alone. But that's impossible. I'm beginning to feel more and more detached. The one thing that scares me most is that my kids don't bring any joy to my life. That kills me!

Peggy is obviously depressed—right? Well, it wasn't obvious to her. It took her more than six months of suffering to realize it. Another common reason that depression is often overlooked is that we have a tendency to adapt to our declining mood—our habit of depression. It begins to feel natural—crummy, but natural. It's similar to how after you have sunglasses on for a while, the darkened view becomes natural. At first, Peggy thought she was just one of those ineffective people. She, unlike other mothers, was too weak to handle the demands of motherhood. This distorted shameful self-perception was enough to solidify her already formidable insecurity and push her into clinical depression.

How Depressed Am I?

When Peggy started counseling, her functioning had deteriorated substantially. Because of the pressing responsibilities she felt at home, she was eager to explore the possibility of antidepressant medication. Within a month of starting medication, Peggy began to feel more tolerant and optimistic. Her functioning improved significantly, as did her overall effectiveness.

Feeling less pressured, Peggy was able to use counseling to finally stop the erosion caused by her insecurity. She learned that she had allowed herself to become a victim of circumstances. Overwhelmed, out of control, and too insecure to explore her needs, Peggy had capitulated. She also learned that once you surrender, it's almost impossible to avoid feeling depressed. She felt hopelessly trapped, never realizing she had choices. Her first step toward health was the realization that she was, in fact, depressed and in need of help. Self-Coaching, along with the relief she experienced from medication, quickly allowed Peggy to start making healthy choices.

Like Peggy, you need to accurately evaluate how depressed you feel. If your functioning is deteriorating and you find your thoughts growing darker and yourself overwhelmed, you should explore the possibility of medication. If, on the other hand, you find yourself holding your own and managing your life in spite of a mild or even moderate depression (as long as you're managing), then by all means, a self-managed program may be all you need to begin to turn the tide of your malaise.

Because depression can be a serious, life-threatening condition, let's begin with the following self-quiz to assess whether you might be struggling with clinical depression. Take a look at the following checklist. Put a check mark next to any symptom that you've experienced for more than two weeks.

☐ I feel depressed, sad, and/or irritated most of the day, nearly every day.

☐ Things that once gave me pleasure don't interest me any longer.

☐ I've noticed a decrease or increase in my appetite, with a change in my weight.

☐ I sleep either too much or too little.

☐ I'm fatigued and drained all the time.

☐ I feel worthless or have intense guilt most of the time.

☐ I can't concentrate like I used to, and I find it difficult to make decisions.

☐ I feel restless, agitated, or slowed down physically.

☐ I think of death often. I've thought of or tried to commit suicide.

If you've experienced four or fewer of the preceding symptoms, you may be dealing with a mild depression (assuming you didn't check the last box and aren't suicidal). Keep in mind, however, that even a mild depression needs your attention. A dysthymic disorder, for example, is one particularly troublesome form of low-grade depression that can last for years, with chronic feelings of sadness and hopelessness. Another, rather elusive form of mild depression, called atypical depression, can be difficult to evaluate because you may feel fine one day and down the next. Self-Coaching alone or Self-Coaching along with counseling can make a real difference in these struggles. In some cases, antidepressant medication may also be helpful. If you choose a Self-Coaching approach, retake this quiz periodically to make sure your depression is, in fact, subsiding.

If you checked five or more of these symptoms, you may be experiencing a major depressive episode and should consult a mental-health professional or your physician. The need for antidepressant medication should be explored, especially if you've had suicidal thoughts or fantasies.

If you've had suicidal thoughts and feel out of control, you should call a health care professional immediately. Don't hesitate! If you don't know who to contact, go to your nearest hospital emergency room or call 911.

Pinning Down Depression

The exact cause of depression is unknown. What is known is that there are some common factors that may trigger depression and depressive symptoms. The following five factors may be related to your depression:

1. *Physical illness* can be associated with depression. Diabetes, thyroid disorders, cancer, congestive heart failure, Parkinson's disease, and chronic, incurable, and painful conditions (spinal cord injury, acquired immunodeficiency syndrome [AIDS], and so on), or even a simple virus can contribute to your becoming depressed. Because many medical conditions may contribute to a depression, should you have any physical concerns, arrange to have a complete physical.

2. *Medications, over-the-counter drugs, and illegal drugs* can all have side effects associated with depression. Prescription drugs (including hypertensive medications, tranquilizers, steroids, and codeine), alcohol and other drug intoxication, and alcohol and other drug withdrawal can all cause depression. If you think your depression is caused by medicine you are currently taking, you should not hesitate to call your physician.

3. *Family history* can contribute to depression. Depression is 1.5 to 3 times more common among siblings, parents, or other close relatives. Discuss the importance of this information with your relatives, encouraging them to be candid with you.

4. *Environmental stress* can contribute to depression. Losses such as death, divorce, or breakup of a significant relationship, or job loss, as well as difficult living conditions such as poverty, danger, or uncertainty, can all provide significant stress and precipitate a depression. Some current research shows how stress—environmental or social—actually changes the shape, size, and number of neurons in the brain. Keep in mind, it's not just the stress that affects us; it's how we

interpret and handle stress in our lives. (Self-Coaching can teach you how.)

5. *Psychological factors* also influence depression. Most depressions are triggered by stress and anxiety. Research suggests that early childhood experiences set the stage for a sensitivity and susceptibility to depression. Simply stated, this means that insecurity sets the stage for distorted, negative thinking. It's this habit of insecure thinking that supports your depression. Depression is predominantly a recurrent problem. Eighty percent of those having one episode will eventually have another—*unless* they change the habit of distorted thinking that feeds and sustains a depression. (Self-Coaching can change that habit for you.)

Self-Coaching Reflection
Unless you change your habit of insecure, negative thinking, you will remain susceptible to depression or to a recurrence of a depression.

Natural and Destructive Depression

As you can see, depression has many faces and can be the source of much confusion. Self-Coaching can help by simplifying the problem. We do this by using only two broad categories of depression: natural depression and destructive depression. A third depression is listed here, but this is merely a designation for a natural depression that progresses into a destructive depression.

Natural Depression   A natural depression is a proportionate reaction to loss, frustration, or tragedy. Natural depression dissipates in a timely manner. The death of a loved one, for example, can certainly bring on a debilitating depression with such symptoms as intense sadness, insomnia, poor appetite, inability to concentrate, and a general malaise. As difficult as these symptoms may be, because they're a normal and expected part of bereavement, I wouldn't ordinarily suggest that the grieving person seek therapy.

If your reactions are consistent and proportionate to a stressful or traumatic life circumstance, then depression can be seen more as a coping mechanism, one that should dissipate on its own in time.

Destructive Depression   A destructive depression may be precipitated by a trauma or a stressor, but it's fueled and sustained by insecurity's destructive thinking. Because your thoughts can change your brain chemistry, destructive depression can easily degenerate into clinical depression. In the upcoming chapters, you'll learn how depression is often a feeble attempt at controlling life.

Natural/Destructive Depression   If people suffering from natural depression begin to fuel their depression with thoughts of insecurity, then destructive depression can develop. In the example of a widow, if her insecurity were to begin to create symptoms not associated with her bereavement—such as guilt, worthlessness, prolonged functional impairment, or thoughts of suicide—we might conclude that her natural depression is progressing into destructive depression.

Relatively Speaking, Just How Depressed Am I?

To evaluate depression, aside from assessing your mood, we also need to assess any change in your behavior. Mild depression, for example, may be experienced as an apathy toward your job: "I can't explain it, I just don't have the desire to go to work anymore." Using the same example, moderate depression may cause you to miss work, call in sick more often, or just take off for no reason. In moderate states of depression, some functioning is sacrificed. In severe depression, functioning is markedly impaired. Again, using our example, not only would work become impossible, but so too would simple day-to-day tasks such as grooming, relating, or even eating. Severe depression is obviously a serious problem both emotionally and functionally.

If you have a virus and your temperature reads 99 degrees, you're less likely to be concerned than if it's 102 degrees. Another common problem with depression is deciding—as objectively as possible—just how depressed you are. Because there's no depression thermometer, I've put together a severity continuum to help you visualize the intensity of your depression. As you progress from left to right along the continuum, notice that the symptoms are cumulative—that is, moderate depression can include any or all of the mild symptoms, whereas severe depression can include any or all of the mild and moderate symptoms. Take a look at the continuum and estimate at what point you would place your depression.

Depression: A Severity Scale

1 2 3 4 5 6 7 8 9 10		
Mild	**Moderate**	**Severe**
Depressed mood, apathy, lethargy, decreased performance, decline in interest or hobbies, reduced spontaneity, "blah" feeling, occasional depression, functioning may be strained but remains mostly unimpaired	Intensification of all mild symptoms, occasional bouts of crying or tearfulness, worry, mildly impaired general functioning, fatigue, anxiety, social difficulties, some appetite disturbances possible, disturbed or excessive sleep, difficulty with concentration and memory likely, diminished interest in sex, depressed most of the time with occasional periods of distraction, susceptibility to illness, low frustration tolerance, feelings of hopelessness	Intensification of all mild and moderate symptoms; functioning is minimal or completely shut down; thoughts of suicide; depressed all the time

The Not-So-Blue Blues

Are moods a form of depression? From time to time, we all find ourselves feeling down—nothing critical, nothing earth shaking, just blah. Because of their transient and reactive nature, moods are not depressions. They're no fun, but they're not serious.

Self-Coaching Reflection
For a depressed or anxious mood, nothing works better
than high-calorie snacking—until you swallow!

In contrast, destructive depression habitually saps your vital energy in an attempt to handle insecurity. The key word here is "habit." Moods are only occasional and mild skirmishes, not ongoing habits.

How did I know that the depressed mood I had an hour ago, when I was buried knee deep in paperwork and miserable from the heat, wasn't a depression? I knew it wasn't because it lifted in a timely manner. If you're not sure, simply wait and see. If, after a few days, your mood doesn't improve, then you may suspect depression.

What about Medication?

As previously discussed, clinical depression can become a major disruption to your normal, day-to-day functioning. With any severe depression, antidepressant medication may be indicated. Considering the low-side-effect profile of the newer selective serotonin reuptake inhibitor (SSRI) medications, which can provide an efficient, safe, nonaddictive intervention, there's no reason to struggle with this consideration. Medication alone, however, is not an effective treatment choice. The combination of medication and counseling has been shown to be the most effective strategy for working with moderate to severe depression. Remember, unless the perceptions and insecure thoughts that support your depression are removed, the chance of your depression recurring is high.

For many, the concept of taking antidepressant medication conjures up many negative reactions: "Guess I'm really screwed up if I need medication." "Medication—I'm that sick?" This is unfortunate, because anyone (not just you), given enough stress, anxiety, or depressive symptoms, is going to wind up disrupting his or her natural biochemical balance. Your emotions are very sensitive to any depletion of the brain chemicals serotonin, dopamine, and norepinephrine, known as neurotransmitters. Antidepressant medication can restore this biochemical depletion. It may seem unnatural to take a pill to feel better, but consider this: antidepressant medication isn't going to get you high or just cover up a depression. It's going to allow you to reestablish a more natural balance. Once you're physically more fortified, your efforts, whether they be Self-Coaching alone or a combination of Self-Coaching and professional counseling, can be optimized. Look at antidepressant medication as a "therapy facilitator" capable of jump-starting your ultimate goal of self-reliance through Self-Coaching.

What if you're experiencing only a few of the foregoing symptoms, or feeling them only occasionally. Are you depressed? Do you need medication? If you're functioning adequately and emotionally holding your own, then you may have a mild depression, in which case medication is probably not necessary—but change *is* necessary. Self-Coaching will teach you to live your life free from insecurity, thereby stopping the depressive psychological and chemical drain on your system. Once you stop the leak, you'll be able to restore your chemical reserves naturally.

Beating depression with Self-Coaching requires that you have:

- A working understanding of what you're doing that's fueling the habit of your depression

- A progressive training program to follow

- A capacity (determined by the intensity of your depression) to maintain your ongoing training

If you can manage these three goals, then you can realistically expect to beat depression.

Types of Depression

I mentioned previously that one reason we tend to overlook being depressed is that we adapt to our declining mood. Another reason is ignorance. Depression (especially mild and moderate forms) can be deceptive, mistaken, or excused away: "I'm just bored," "Leave me alone; I just want to stay in bed. I'm tired," or "There's nothing wrong, I'm just out of sorts." The following list of more common depressions will further assist you in appreciating depression's many faces: major depression, dysthymic depression, seasonal affective depression, bipolar depression, atypical depression, and postpartum depression.

Major Depression

Major depression is one of the most serious forms of depression and is characterized by one or more major depressive episodes (see the symptoms listed in the self-quiz on page 45). Major depression is typified by a profound state of despair, hopelessness, worthlessness, dejection, loss of interest in usual activities, and so on. This type of depression is also associated with a high suicide rate. It's not uncommon for substance abuse, panic disorder, or obsessive-compulsive disorders to occur with major depression.

Major depression, although more frequent in women, can occur in any group of people, affecting one out of every ten of us. With this type of depression you should contact a mental-health professional immediately. Although medication and psychotherapy are essential, Self-Coaching can be an ongoing adjunct to your treatment, as well as a long-term strategy for preventing or minimizing future occurrences.

Dysthymic Depression

A dysthymic depression is characterized by a chronically depressed mood, usually described as being always sad or down in the dumps. Dysthymia usually persists for a period of years and doesn't disable a person's functioning, but it does greatly inhibit it. Typically, there are low-level depressive symptoms that include poor self-esteem, low energy, sleep disturbances, poor appetite or overeating, general feelings of inadequacy, and so on.

Dysthymic depression is generally more frequent in women than in men. Although individual counseling and medication are helpful with dysthymia, Self-Coaching is an extremely valuable and effective technique for helping you get out of your "blahs."

Seasonal Affective Depression

Seasonal affective depression (SAD), often referred to as "winter blues," is a relatively common form of depression. Although the specific cause is unknown, lack of sunlight during the low-light months of winter seems to be a major factor. In fact, the latitude at which you live is an important variable. Symptoms vary from mild to severe and develop in late fall and clear up in early spring.

Phototherapy (full-spectrum fluorescent light therapy) has been proven an effective treatment. Self-Coaching can be very effective in controlling the negativity, guilt, and inertia of SAD.

Bipolar Depression

Bipolar depression (formerly referred to as manic depression) is characterized by alternating cycles of high-energy periods of wildly unrealistic activity, lasting from several days to months, followed by a severe depressive phase consisting of feelings of inertia, low self-esteem, withdrawal, sadness, suicidal risk, and so on. In either phase, there is a susceptibility to alcohol or other drug abuse. These episodes are not precipitated by a clear-cut environmental or situational cause.

Heredity and psychological factors seem to play a major role in bipolar depression. There is a higher incidence in patients with relatives who have suffered from this disorder. A mental-health professional should be consulted as soon as possible. Self-Coaching, used in conjunction with professional treatment, can be a valuable tool for achieving long-term stability.

Atypical Depression

This type of depression is described as not having the usual, steady down reactions of other depressions. A person may be fine one day and then down or depressed the next, often without any obvious trigger or incident. Self-Coaching can be of great assistance with atypical depressions.

Postpartum Depression

Mild moodiness isn't uncommon after childbirth. If, however, these symptoms become more severe and last for more than a few days, postpartum depression must be suspected. Postpartum depression can be severe, threatening both mother and child, and it appears to be caused by hormonal imbalances.

Help should be sought immediately. Self-Coaching, along with formal therapy, can be particularly helpful in fighting off distorted perceptions and feelings and maintaining an optimistic outlook.

TRAINING SUGGESTION

Using the descriptions in this chapter, see how many depressive symptoms you recognize in your day-to-day struggles. Make a list of these symptoms, then use the depression severity scale to estimate the severity of your depression.

The reading from this severity scale will serve as a baseline for your training. When you begin your more formal training, once a week, you may want to repeat your listing and evaluation of your symptoms. One reason for this exercise is to make sure that your depression isn't progressing. Your results will also serve as a useful source of feedback and encouragement.

✦ ✦ ✦

5

Anxiety

I'm going to have a heart attack. Trust me, I know I am. Sometimes you just know certain things, in your gut. Lately, I've been afraid to go to work. When I do go, I'm constantly looking for any opportunity to rest and not get my heart rate up too high. I went for a physical and was told that my pressure was mildly elevated. Listen, if it were that mild the doctor would have told me to lose a few pounds, not prescribe medication! I think he's trying not to alarm me. He started me on some beta blockers, and now all I'm thinking about is that my heart is going to explode.

I was worried before I knew about my high blood pressure, and now I worry about how much damage has been caused. They call high blood pressure the silent killer, but I'm telling you mine isn't silent. I can actually feel my blood pressure! I feel like a balloon that's been overinflated and about to burst.

My doctor says to relax, that I'm "healthy as a horse." I know he wouldn't tell me the truth because he knows how much I worry. And anyway, doctors can't tell what's going on from a few tests. I'm telling you I feel my heart is going to explode! I'm afraid to have sex because of the exertion. My wife thinks I'm crazy. My kids want to know why I won't play catch with them anymore. I'm getting more nervous; I'm not sleeping. Lately, when I'm trying to go to bed, I can feel my heart racing, and that's where I really panic . . . I start sweating. Last night I actually hyperventilated. My heart can't take much more of this. I should be relaxing, but instead I'm driving myself to the grave.

Maybe I need to be in a hospital. I'm worried all the time. It's all I think about. I can't stand thinking about it, but I can't *not* think about it. I'm driving myself crazy. All I see is me riding in an ambulance, the pain. I don't want to die.

Sal was suffering from anxiety and panic, a terrible, terrifying combination. Essentially, his insecurity wouldn't permit him to trust life. The organ most associated with life is the heart, and this became Sal's hook for projecting his insecurity. Because he couldn't trust his heart, he couldn't trust life. His only choice was to live in chronic dread. Self-Coaching was able to teach Sal to challenge these distortions. It wasn't life or his heart that was the problem; it was his long-standing habit of insecurity and distrust that had to be challenged. With the insights we established in counseling, Sal began to fight back.

Sal never had a bad heart. In fact, Sal's monologue came from what he said to me more than five years ago. I recently saw Sal at a local baseball game. He was managing the team and was walking off the field after infield practice. He saw me and approached me with a big smile, telling me, "Hey, Doc, guess you could say the old ticker's doing well, huh?" We laughed. If only Sal could have seen this result five years earlier.

Anxiety, whether mild or as severe as Sal's panic attacks, can have profound effects on your body. Some of the possible effects of anxiety are

- A rise in blood sugar
- Muscular tension
- Dry mouth

- Rapid heartbeat or palpitations
- Headaches
- Fatigue
- Impotence
- Colon spasms
- Diarrhea or constipation
- Insomnia
- Poor concentration
- A general feeling of apprehension and dread

Blame It on the Saber-toothed Tigers

Anxiety is a vestige of what scientists call the fight-or-flight response. During our evolutionary past, this response would have been a crucial reason we survived as a species. Let's face it, as humans, we're not equipped with lightning speed, daggerlike teeth, sicklelike claws, or even protective coloration. The truth is we're pretty vulnerable; we needed all the help our genes could muster in order to avoid extinction.

The fight-or-flight response is a generalized protective strategy that quickly pumps up your body with energy by releasing hormones and other chemicals. Thus fortified, we are in a much better position to fight off danger or to flee from it. Either way, your juiced-up body is prepped and ready. Your genes don't care whether you're a coward or a hero, just that you survive.

Quicksand and Other Life Challenges

Throughout human history, the fight-or-flight response made sense. It still makes sense today—particularly in moments of crisis. I remember being alone on a fossil dig at a phosphate mine in North Carolina. I accidentally found myself sinking in a marl-like quicksand. When I was up to my thighs and sinking, everything about my usual consciousness shifted. Aware only of my very shallow (oxygen rich) breathing, I spread my upper body flat on top of a digging rake I had fortunately taken

57

along. With strength I have never felt before or since, I used my upper body muscles to remain splayed out on my rake while simultaneously pulling my legs free from the marl's incredible suction. Slowly I advanced. After about a ten-minute struggle, which seemed like ten years, I reached more stable ground and collapsed, completely exhausted. I gulped down the remains of what water I had left, while frantically unwrapping a candy bar I had luckily packed with my lunch. I was famished, absolutely depleted, and for quite some time unable to slow down my pulse or my breathing.

What did I learn from my near-death experience? A few things. For one, the body is a magnificent machine. My instincts knew it was do or die (in this case, my only option was to fight in order to flee). Every system in my body cooperated to pull me free from a rather horrific ending. All this expenditure of instinctual energy was necessary to survive. Afterward, I felt as if I had run a couple of marathons, and it took a good night's rest before I felt like my old self again.

Here's my point: as intense as my experience was, I can tell you I've had patients who, suffering from intense anxiety, panic, or phobias, describe virtually the *same* reaction—without the quicksand. The reason for this is really quite simple: anxiety doesn't differentiate between real danger and imagined danger. If, for example, you interpret an IRS audit as the end of the world, then your body will respond in the only way it knows how—fight-or-flight, all or nothing, do or die. All it takes is distorted, insecurity-driven thinking to get your adrenal glands to start pumping stress hormones into your bloodstream, and once anxiety begins, it can become one hell of a steamroller.

Natural and Destructive Anxiety

As with depression, I divide anxiety into two general categories: destructive anxiety and natural anxiety. Sal's panic was a clear example of destructive anxiety. *Destructive anxiety* is driven by insecurity, disproportionate to the circumstance, always exaggerated, and persistent. Its purpose is to try to control life with an intense flurry of mental gyrations (worrying, ruminating, obsessing, and the like).

Natural anxiety, unlike destructive anxiety, is normal, proportionate to the circumstance, not exaggerated, and time limited. Like depression, natural anxiety is an inescapable part of life. What my wife and I went through a few years ago anticipating her surgery serves as a good example. We found ourselves worrying about lots of things—the anesthesia, the outcome, the physical therapy—but finally (at my wife's insistence), we decided to put our faith in the hands of God and the surgeon. We actively chose—and struggled—to let go of our worries. Up to this point, though, I remember a few sleepless nights, headaches, ruminations, worries, difficulty concentrating at work—all anxiety symptoms, yes, but all natural anxiety (that is, proportionate concern, not exaggerated, and time limited).

Just because natural anxiety is a normal part of life doesn't mean you can't deal with it. Self-Coaching can help you know when enough is enough, and how to let it go. Why suffer needlessly, even if it is natural?

Negative Patterns

Although Self-Coaching can be a useful tool for dealing with transient, natural anxiety, when it comes to wrestling with destructive anxiety, it's indispensable. Let's take a look at the most common destructive patterns: general anxiety disorder, panic attacks, obsessive-compulsive disorder, and social anxieties and phobias.

General Anxiety Disorder

General anxiety disorder (GAD) is characterized by the following symptoms:

- Excessive worry and anxiety
- Feeling restless, keyed up, or edgy
- Fatigue
- Difficulty concentrating or forgetting
- Feeling irritable, testy, or grouchy much of the time
- Muscle tension
- Sleep difficulties (difficulty falling or staying asleep, restless, non-restorative sleep)

People with GAD worry all the time. They're not picky about what they worry about. Big problems, small problems, it makes no difference. Someone with GAD is always feeling out of balance and out of control. Worry is an ongoing, persistent attempt to figure out how to regain control and avoid vulnerability. Unfortunately, worrying, rather than lessening vulnerability, generates more anxiety, which increases feelings of vulnerability. A vicious cycle begins:

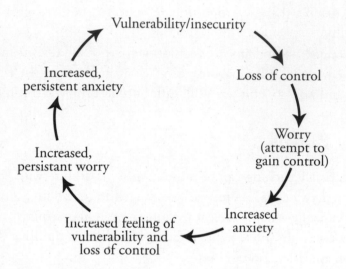

Panic Attacks

Panic attacks are characterized by the following symptoms:

- Palpitations
- Sweating
- Trembling or shaking
- Shortness of breath
- Chest pain or discomfort
- Nausea
- Lightheadedness or faintness

- Fear of losing control
- Fear of dying
- Numbness or tingling
- Chills or hot flushes

People who suffer from panic attacks experience periodic, intense rushes of uncomfortable physical symptoms combined with thoughts of impending disaster and doom. Panic attacks are usually unpredictable and disorienting. These attacks can be so traumatic that a person begins to live in dread of future occurrences.

Panic usually occurs in two stages: (1) an *anticipation stage* of mounting anxiety, where insecurity begins to dominate the thinking, and (2) a *fight-or-flight stage* of physical reactivity. This experience is so intense and disorienting that many people report feeling crazy or losing control.

Obsessive-Compulsive Disorder

Obsessive-compulsive disorder (OCD) has two components: recurrent, persistent, intrusive thoughts that cause an increase in anxiety, and repetitive behavior or thoughts that the person feels compelled to perform in order to regain a sense of control.

OCD sufferers are victimized by ruminative, exaggerated worry. The thought "Did I turn off the stove?" may generate a momentary bit of concern for most of us, but for someone with OCD, it's never this simple. People with OCD are driven to ruminate and obsess, on and on, "Did I set the alarm? I think so, but I can't remember. Did I? I can't be sure. I remember going into the kitchen. I think I did. Maybe I didn't."

OCD is insecurity driven. It's the inability to trust yourself, your actions, or your thoughts. Because you can't trust yourself, then you can't possibly trust your recollections. Never feeling safe (in control) is what generates the anxiety.

Compulsions are an attempt to reduce the anxiety generated by obsessions. In the example "Did I set the alarm?" this question would be followed by checking to see whether, in fact, the alarm was set properly. Unfortunately, it doesn't stop there. Because of the basic distrust, a person with OCD must then question once again, "Am I sure I set it?" Again the alarm will be checked, not once, not twice, but sometimes countless times before it can be left. OCD sufferers get some anxiety relief from their compulsions, but little, if any, satisfaction.

Obsessive-compulsive behavior is closely related to superstitious behavior. Both have to do with controlling some aspect of behavior in order to feel more in control (knocking wood, not stepping on cracks, and the like). OCD rituals are, in fact, superstitious attempts at warding off insecurity by controlling fate. A seventeen-year-old OCD patient of mine had just begun driving. She told me, "If I tap my car door handle six times before getting in the car, I won't have an accident. I tried not giving in to this 'silly' behavior, but my anxiety went through the roof when I tried to drive. I had to stop the car, get out, and do my six touches!"

Having a set number of repetitions is a rather common aspect of these compulsions (three taps on a door before entering, buckling and unbuckling a seat belt five times before driving off, and so on). Over time, a very exacting sequence can develop, with very rigid demands.

OCD sufferers are not crazy. They will, in fact, tell you that they know their compulsions are silly, even ridiculous, but because these rituals reduce anxiety by ostensibly controlling fate, they're reinforced.

Social Anxieties and Phobias

Social anxieties and phobias are characterized by a persistent, excessive fear that is unreasonable and connected to the anticipation of a specific object, situation, or experience.

Some people experience specific situations that bring on anxiety and panic. Fear of bridges, tunnels, public speaking, elevators, and flying are all examples of phobic responses. Essentially, social anxieties and phobias are anxiety and panic attacks that are connected to a hook experience. Any experience that has been imbued with a projection of insecurity (such as "I can't breathe in this elevator") can become a hook for future anxiety and panic. The excessive fear and anxiety usually produces avoidant reactions (referred to as phobic avoidance), as the person tries to avoid any circumstance that will produce this intense, debilitating reaction. With social anxiety, the fear/hook has a social link. For example, fear of disapproval, public speaking, and public bathrooms can all be seen as possible catastrophes.

Physical and Medical Considerations

Although anxiety is typically an emotional disorder, it's important to rule out any medical condition that may be causing it. Problems with your adrenal gland or thyroid gland, heart disease, respiratory disease, or hypoglycemia are all possible underlying physical causes. If things are going well in your life and you can't identify any stressors or reason for concern, and especially if you suspect there may be a physical problem, it can't hurt to have a thorough physical examination. Also keep in mind that many prescription medications, over-the-counter medications (especially nasal sprays and stimulants to lose weight), and other chemicals (caffeine, illicit drugs, and so on), can also cause anxiety. Ask your physician about whether any medications you're taking may cause anxiety.

The issue of whether you need to consider antianxiety medication requires a close look at your functioning. If the intensity of your anxiety or panic is significantly interfering with your ability to work, relate, and relax, then exploring the possibility of medication is usually a wise choice. Don't struggle alone with this evaluation. If you're in doubt, any mental-health professional can help you decide whether medication is an appropriate choice.

Many medications are available for anxiety and, depending on the type of anxiety you suffer from, some may have specific benefits. The benzodiazepines, beta blockers, tricyclic antidepressants, MAO inhibitors, SSRIs, mild tranquilizers, and anticonvulsants have all been successfully employed in the treatment of anxiety. As with medication for depression, keep in mind that medication alone is not nearly as effective as medication along with a therapeutic program.

Whether you're in counseling for intense, debilitating panic attacks, taking medication for a general anxiety disorder, or just curious about handling day-to-day natural anxieties, Self-Coaching will significantly reduce or eliminate the anticipatory, insecurity-driven anxiety that is the base of all anxiety disorders.

✤ ✤ ✤

TRAINING SUGGESTION

Using the descriptions in this chapter, see how many anxiety symptoms you can recognize in your day-to-day struggles. Make a list of these symptoms, including both destructive and natural anxieties. Keep this list for future reference. Periodically throughout your training (about once a month), update this list to monitor your progress.

Use a simple chart like the one suggested here to record your symptoms. Your goal is to eventually eliminate or minimize all entries under the "Destructive Anxieties" heading. Under the "Natural Anxieties" heading, you'll always have a few symptoms; this is normal. Eventually, however, you'll want to see whether you're falling prey to certain patterns of anxiety. Understanding these patterns will help you know when enough is enough.

Destructive Anxieties	Natural Anxieties
1. Intense fear of talking to the opposite sex	1. Feeling a bit anxious about getting your wisdom teeth pulled
2. Heart palpitations, sweating, or panic while caught in traffic	2. Nervousness when a man walks up to your car asking for money
3. Inability to fall asleep, worrying about whether you are going to succeed	3. Worry about your loved one's illness

6

The Control-Sensitive Personality

Rather than prejudice your thinking, let's start out with the following short quiz:

T	F	I tend to be compulsive.
T	F	I get very upset when things go wrong.
T	F	The more chaotic a situation, the more anxious and tense I feel.
T	F	I worry a lot.
T	F	I've been accused of being a black-and-white thinker.
T	F	I'm always in my head, figuring, thinking, ruminating, and so on.
T	F	I find it hard to trust.
T	F	I tend to be suspicious.
T	F	I like for things to be done just so.
T	F	I can't say no.
T	F	I typically have trouble being on time.
T	F	I like to be the one driving the car.
T	F	I'm often rigid and inflexible.
T	F	I'm a doer.
T	F	I go out of my way to avoid confrontations.

T	F	I'm often too sensitive.
T	F	I like to have the last word in any argument.
T	F	I always have a reason or excuse for what I do.
T	F	I would say I'm a better talker than a listener.
T	F	I'm very impatient with other people's mistakes.
T	F	I always feel that I'm right.
T	F	I'm too vulnerable.

Total your "true" responses. A score of 10 or fewer suggests that you are not overly control sensitive. Self-Coaching can teach you to cultivate an even deeper sense of self-trust and spontaneity.

A score between 11 and 16 suggests that you have a moderate degree of control sensitivity. For you, control is a more limiting aspect of your life. Self-Coaching can make a noticeable difference in your overall feeling of well-being and sense of personal security.

A score of 17 or more suggests that you are particularly sensitive to control. For you, life is significantly compromised by a need to maintain control. Self-Coaching is going to change your perspective. You don't need more control; you need more self-trust.

When Control Gets Out of Control

Most people like being in control. It's normal and healthy to want to be in control of life. Avoiding injury, anticipating danger, dressing for inclement weather, or learning to get along with people are all aspects of healthy control. From an evolutionary standpoint, the desire to maintain control certainly seems to have adaptive significance. Losing control, particularly in our ancestral past, would almost certainly have led to personal, familial, or tribal harm. Survival depended on *not* being vulnerable. It made sense to want to be in control during the Ice Age. It still makes sense. We human beings just hate to feel out of control.

Obviously, the desire for a less vulnerable, more controlled life isn't a problem. On the other hand, when you're dealing with a trust muscle that has atrophied, insecurity, doubt, distrust, or fear can cause you to see danger in safe places, to anticipate only what can go wrong in life, or to feel convinced that you are doomed to failure. When this happens, the need for control changes from a healthy desire ("I want Mary to like me") to a compulsive declaration ("Mary has to like me!").

Depending on the level of self-trust, people vary in their sensitivity to a perceived loss of control. On one end of the continuum we have people who are not only insensitive to a loss of control, but even totally oblivious to it. Remember Tom, the man who lost a hand in an industrial accident? You can't get more insensitive than not missing your own hand.

Assuming you're not like Tom, and you do struggle with anxiety or depression, chances are you're what I call a *control-sensitive person*. Simply put, a control-sensitive person reacts strongly to any loss of control, or perceived loss, with symptoms of anxiety or depression (fears, apprehensions, worries, and the like). This sensitivity may be learned or it may simply be part of your nature: your predisposition.

A psychological predisposition is an innate tendency toward certain reactions or behaviors. Have you ever spent an hour at a nursery school? If so, you probably noticed a whole array of psychological dispositions: leaders, followers, talkers, thinkers, introverts, extroverts, criers, pouters, all destined to one day shape one another's eventual adult personality. We know, for example, that children of parents with panic disorder are seven times more likely to be anxious themselves. These children may have an inherently lower threshold to anxiety, which makes them more susceptible to insecurity and depression. They are predisposed to anxiety. This is not to say that learning isn't a big factor; an anxious parent, for example, because of worrisome, controlling behavior, will certainly set the stage for anxiety to find root. But even in families where siblings are reared apart from parents, we still see a tendency toward certain inherited predispositions.

Similarly, children of parents who have suffered from a major depressive episode are 1.5 to 3 times more likely to develop depression. You don't need a predisposition to anxiety or depression to find yourself struggling, however. Stressful life circumstances, especially loss, chronic pain, or ongoing struggle can initiate the same reaction. According to

Self-Coaching, a predisposition alone isn't enough to cause anxiety and depression, nor is it enough to cause a control-sensitive personality. Given enough insecurity, anyone is susceptible to these developments.

Whatever their origins, however, anxiety and depression can be stopped where they begin, in the insecure thoughts that *you allow* to float unchecked in your head. Keep in mind that adversity, loss, even a psychological disposition, aren't necessarily life sentences; they're only tendencies toward certain behaviors. Whether you know it or not, it's up to you to decide whether you're going to fan the flames of insecurity. It doesn't matter if it's a predisposition, a learned pattern of reflexive thinking, or unwieldy life circumstances; there's always a choice. You'll see.

Self-Coaching Reflection
A genetic predisposition isn't a life sentence;
it's only a tendency toward certain behavior.

In the list that follows, you will find some typical strategies for control. The list is far from complete, but it does give you a flavor of control's diversity. The tendencies listed on the left are usually more associated with anxiety, while those on the right are more typical of depression. In the chapters that follow, you will find a full explanation of how these and other similar tendencies, rather than establishing control, wind up making you feel more out of control.

- Worry, rumination—recklessness, not caring, disregard for life circumstances
- Rigid, opinionated thinking—indecisiveness, excessive doubt
- Overcommitment—avoidance of life circumstances
- Social isolation—excessive dependence
- Excessive frugality—overspending
- Perfectionism—slovenliness
- Workaholism—lethargy
- Lack of emotion—excessive emotionality
- Excessive ambition—apathy

- Excessive risk taking—excessive fear
- Arrogance—low self-esteem
- Distrust—blind trust

An Exhausting Way to Live

Without adequate self-trust, you turn to control to combat your insecurity, thus ensuring a life of torment. That's when, instead of living spontaneously moment to moment, you become congested by such thoughts as "What if I lose my job?" "I know he's not going to like me," "I'll never get ahead," or "Why go on?" Instead of mental clarity, what you wind up with is an opaque world, clouded and distorted by perceptions of insecurity.

Anticipating life's potholes may sound appealing if you want to feel invulnerable, but don't be surprised if you become so intent on avoiding potholes that you don't see the stop sign at the intersection. I remember my very first therapy session. I was an intern, and I was nervous. Although I was in casual California, I nevertheless opted for my three-piece blue suit, white shirt, and somber tie. I entered that session feeling very "psychological." Things seemed to go well, and I was more than pleased when the hour finished. As I stood up to escort my patient to the door, something white against a dark blue background caught my eye. My first session was delivered with my fly open! So much for control.

Control requires effort, maintenance, and vigilance, which is an exhausting way to live. So why do it? There are two reasons: First, without adequate self-trust, you've come to feel that you can't handle life's challenges, not without an arsenal of controlling strategies. Second, by attempting to eliminate, or at least minimize, the risks of embarrassment, failure, and rejection, control-sensitive people feel that they, not fate, control destiny. It's this heady notion of controlling destiny and side-stepping life's anxieties that becomes so habit forming. You get hooked into a treadmill-like belief that your ultimate salvation depends on having just a little more control, and more, and then more.

Let me tell you about Jerry, a good friend of mine who was convinced that the future could be controlled.

Jerry owned a very successful restaurant. His home was built above the restaurant. Jerry was in control—compulsively in control—of every facet of his business. When the snowplow showed up at four in the morning to clear out the parking lot, Jerry would be out there directing the driver. If there was a problem with the plumbing, Jerry would be right there making sure things were handled properly. When it came to running his business, Jerry left nothing to chance.

Jerry and I were on vacation a few years ago. As we walked along the beach, I asked him if he felt burdened by his compulsive lifestyle. He said, "It's the only way I can be sure about my future. The way I see it, I'm eliminating chance." Jerry felt that he could ensure (control) a successful life and happy retirement by compulsively attending to every detail of running a restaurant, thereby eliminating chance.

While walking the beach that day, Jerry got a call on his cell phone from his brother. The restaurant and Jerry's home had burned to the ground. Only the chimney remained standing. Jerry lost everything. As you might imagine, it took a while for Jerry to recover from this tragedy, but he did. If you were to talk to Jerry today, he would be the first to tell you that control isn't what it's cracked up to be. He thought he could control fate, but what he learned was that fate isn't something that you control; it's something you inherit.

Self-Coaching Reflection
The key to eliminating anxiety or depression isn't
more control; it's cultivating a sense of trust that
you can handle life's challenges as they unfold.

Traps to Avoid

When the need for control becomes too important, you become particularly susceptible to certain traps—that is, thinking traps. Unless you are aware of them, these traps can quickly become habits, contributing significantly to your difficulties. Recognizing these traps can alert you to danger as you proceed with your Self-Coaching.

Take a look at these common traps and begin to develop an awareness and sensitivity to these very common pitfalls: should statements, what-iffing, tunnel vision, mind reading, have-tos, black-and-white thinking, and name-calling.

Should Statements

"I should be a better daughter," "I should be more successful," "I should be smarter," "I should lose twenty pounds." "Should" statements evoke a sense of guilt and failure. By undermining who and what you are, these statements generate anxiety and depression. While it may be true that you can improve yourself in some way, when you tell yourself you "should" improve, you're telling yourself a negative: you're not good enough right now, and you can only be good enough if you do this or that.

The healthy alternative is to avoid should statements by replacing them with more positive assertions such as "It would be a good idea to be more attentive to my mother," "I want to be more successful," "I would like to know more; perhaps I'll take that course at the night school," "Maybe I'll join the gym and quit eating all that fast food." These alternatives don't negate who you are now. They support growth and improvement based on who and what you are and not at your expense.

What-Iffing

Another insecurity trap is what-iffing. "What if he asks me for my opinion?" "What if I don't get the job?" "What if I get too attached?" What-iffing is an attempt to anticipate problems before they happen, because you believe that if you know what's coming around that corner—before the fact—you can be braced and ready to handle yourself.

So what's the harm in anticipating danger? Nothing, if your thinking could be limited to a few legitimate attempts at problem solving. What-iffing, unfortunately, seems to spiral quickly out of control, jumping from one "what if" to the next. Every possible solution presents you with another crisis. You wind up living with chronic worry that generates chronic anxiety, and chronic anxiety will ultimately deplete you. It's this depletion that explains why anxiety and depression are so often experienced together.

A better response to life is your natural, unrehearsed spontaneity. It's the lack of self-trust that encourages what-iffing. The healthy alternative is to realize that what-iffing undermines your self-confidence by insisting that you can be safe (in control) only if you can anticipate life before it happens. Self-Coaching teaches you to be safe, not by worrying and what-iffing, but by courageously trusting your ability to handle life.

Tunnel Vision

Both anxiety and depression cause a narrowing of our perceptual field. Rather than seeing the whole picture, we see only selective aspects of a situation. For example, a depressed man may see only his own faults, overlooking his positive qualities. "I'm just a cranky old man," or "I can't do anything right." These are tunnel-vision statements. Although they may contain a grain of truth, the reality is that these gross exaggerations wind up keeping you off balance and feeling out of control.

The healthy alternative is to realize that life is rarely limited to one point of view, one option, or one solution. A more expansive view requires some practice. Depersonalization is a valuable tool that can help you see beyond your own narrow view. By asking yourself how someone else (think of someone you feel has a healthier perspective) might respond to your situation, you can experience a totally different perspective. The key is to speculate on how so-and-so would react to a situation, not how *you* think the person would react.

Mind Reading

"I know she hates me," "He does that because he doesn't care about my feelings," "People think I'm boring." Mind reading is an attempt to interpret other people's actions *as if* you know what they are thinking. You're trying to eliminate vulnerability by never being caught off guard.

When you consider how easy it is to misinterpret your own thinking, you begin to realize that reading someone else's mind is purely fiction. Why would you do it? There are two reasons: first, because your negativity has convinced you that you live in a hostile world, so you need every advantage to maintain control; and second, because if you anticipate the worst before it happens, you can feel prepared, and thus be in control.

The healthy alternative is to insist on the objective truth. Ask questions instead of guessing. As much as you may desire it, you can never know what someone else is thinking—not without asking. Recognize that mind reading is nothing more than a projection of your insecurity. Unless you're willing to ask what someone else is actually thinking, you must tell yourself, "I am not allowed to assume a negative!"

Have-Tos

"I have to finish today," "I have to succeed," "I have no choice; I must have that coat." Have-tos are traps most often employed by anxiety-prone individuals, and they represent the foundation of all compulsive behavior. Although a compulsive life is driven by anxiety, it quickly becomes a depressing way to live.

Have-tos are similar to tunnel vision, in that your perceptual field is narrowed down to whatever it is you feel you have to do. Whereas tunnel vision limits your perceptual choices, have-to thinking eliminates your choices altogether. You're convinced you have no choice and can be released from suffering only by getting to your goal.

Compulsive spending, cleaning, working, or even sex can all be expressions of have-to thinking that drags you around incessantly trying to sidestep anxiety. You tell yourself, "Once I achieve such-and-such, then I'll be okay." Unfortunately, have-tos are lies—one goal quickly evaporates as we are compulsively driven to the next. Have-tos greatly diminish, even eliminate, any joy or pleasure in life. Have-tos are hard work.

The healthy alternative is to understand that have-tos are feeble attempts to gain control and mastery over a dangerous world. Rather than recognizing and addressing the insecurity within, we externalize it and become convinced that we can become secure by doing this or accomplishing that. Security, however, doesn't flow from the outside in; it flows only from the inside out.

Black-and-White Thinking

"I'll never be happy," "Life will always be depressing," "I'll never feel safe." Black-and-white thinking is impulsive thinking. When you're anxious or depressed, you become impatient. Something is either good or bad, positive or negative, always or never—end of discussion. With black-and-white thinking, you don't have to live with ambiguity.

The problem is that life isn't black and white. By eliminating life's gray choices, you eliminate a whole array of possibilities. The insecure person is more concerned with feeling in control than with being accurate. Even if it's negative, at least the issue gets settled: "That's it, I'm a failure."

The healthy alternative is to learn to tolerate some ambiguity in your life, to recognize that an impulsive decision, if wrong, only creates more problems. By insisting on a more objective perception that life is rarely black or white, you can begin to recognize that your anxiety doesn't have to dictate your thinking. Stop treating thoughts as facts, and insist on being more truthful with yourself. Find out that most of your impulsiveness is just a habit. Once you stop your reflexive responding and take a deep breath, you may surprise yourself with the options that begin to float to the surface.

Name-Calling

"I'm stupid," "I'm such a wimp," "I'm too tall/short and skinny/fat." These are examples of name-calling. Name-calling is nothing more than a ploy. If you beat yourself up, you can give up. If you're a jerk, wimp, or loser, or you're dumb, then you've created an excuse for your shortcomings, and you might as well give up. Like black-and-white thinking, both anxiety and depression make you too eager to settle an argument because you're convinced you can't tolerate living with it.

As with black-and-white thinking, you need to recognize the impulsive habit involved in this behavior. The healthy alternative is to get tough and tell yourself that name-calling is not allowed. You're just not going to permit it! Name-calling is simply a ploy to avoid anxiety, so don't allow yourself to be duped. By further eroding your self-confidence, name-calling only makes your life more miserable. It's a lose-lose proposition. Stop beating yourself up; it doesn't pay.

Control-sensitive people can be very hard on themselves, especially when the quality of their lives erodes to such an extent that a flat tire or an unpaid bill can cause anguish, panic, or despair. As the strategies of control continue to fail and frustrate you, as you become more and more depleted by worry or depression, one inescapable truth begins to emerge: control is an illusion. Life cannot be controlled. The reality is that anxiety and depression are about as effective at controlling life as you are at defying gravity. Just as you'll never float through the air, your worrying and avoidance will ultimately solve nothing. The quest to control life is nothing more than an attempt to defy psychic gravity.

Self-Coaching Reflection
Control is only an illusion of safety.

All He Wanted Was to Feel Safe

At our first session at the rehab center, Henry told me he was going to rob a bank. The crazy thing about it was he didn't want the money; he wanted to get caught! Henry, you see, had been in prison most of his adult life, and now that he was on parole he was floundering between severe bouts of depression and panic. He couldn't cope with life outside the "joint." On the outside, he had to make decisions, normal everyday decisions that you and I take for granted: where, when, and what to eat; what to do every evening; and when to go to bed or when to wake up.

Somewhere in the thirty-three years he had served in a federal penitentiary, Henry had surrendered his right to control his own life. He had become institutionalized. Every aspect of his life was prescribed by prison rules. He didn't have to think about anything. He became the child, the prison his parent. In prison, Henry felt safe, controlled. Out of prison, with no personal resources, he felt exposed and out of control. When I met him, he had become obsessed with one thing: he wanted to go home.

One day, Henry just disappeared. After he didn't show up for our session, I checked his room. Gone. No one at the rehab center had any clue to Henry's whereabouts; at least, no one was about to say anything. Henry and I had had only a couple of sessions, barely enough time for us to get acquainted. I never heard from him again.

I'm convinced Henry's doing time right now. Somewhere in San Diego, a bank teller was probably traumatized by a scruffy-looking guy brandishing nothing more than a finger in his coat, demanding money. Why the robber walked slowly down the street after he left is probably still a mystery to the bank manager, but at least the felon was apprehended. Now, somewhere, in one of our federal prisons, Henry's finally at peace. He's starting each day at 6:15, going to breakfast, working in the laundry, stopping only for lunch, then again for supper, watching a little TV, and at 11:00 his lights are turned off for him. He doesn't have to think about anything. Henry falls asleep easily.

Don't be like Henry.

It's All Relative

Loss of control is a relative experience. For one teenager, a zit may be no big deal, while for another it could feel like the end of the world. Here are some common, everyday experiences where people report feeling a loss of control:

- Getting caught in traffic
- Forgetting someone's name
- Being late for or forgetting an appointment
- Speaking or performing in front of a group
- Getting sick
- Being unable to figure something out
- Being embarrassed or humiliated
- Having difficulty with confrontations
- Getting lost
- Not having enough money
- Failing a test
- Saying no
- Admitting a mistake

What about you? Are you one of control's victims, bullied about by anxious or depressed thoughts and fears? Like Henry, you may not realize to what extent control governs your life. Perhaps you feel a bit anxious now and then, occasionally depressed, tormented, or powerless, and you never realize that the culprit is a lack of self-trust expressed as a neurotic fear of losing control. Once you begin to understand the force behind your suffering, be it chronic or sporadic, you will realize that you have a choice. Rather than compulsively seeking control's protection and insulation, you'll be in a position where you can choose to reclaim a natural, gregarious vitality for living.

Your insecurity is nothing more than a long-standing habit. As with changing any habit, whether smoking or biting your nails, learning to live a secure life without anxiety and depression is first going to require that you break the habit of destructive, reflex thinking and replace it with mature, healthy, and—most important—objective, reality-based thinking. This is what your coaching and training will prepare you for. Keep reminding yourself that anxiety and depression aren't as ominous or mysterious as you once thought; they're just bad habits.

❖ ❖ ❖

TRAINING SUGGESTION

Logging Experiences Where You've Felt a Loss of Control

Shortly, you will be setting up a formal training log. For now, it's a good idea to get used to recording information that will become critical to your Self-Coaching efforts.

Begin by recording any experience you've had where you felt a loss of control. For now, look for any experience that you would describe as producing either anxiety or depression. If you're not sure, write it down anyway. There's no harm in guessing.

You might use the following example as a guide:

Loss of Control Experience	Reaction
9:40 A.M. Driving to work. Caught in turnpike traffic.	Intense anger, frustration, feeling fidgety and nervous, started pounding steering wheel.
3:00 P.M. Boss told me to redo my report.	Strong panic feeling—I screwed up! My boss won't tolerate this behavior for long. What will I do?
7:00 P.M. Sister-in-law called wanting to borrow money.	Wanted to say no, but couldn't. Felt bullied, out of control, and panicked. I really can't afford to give her the money!

❖ ❖ ❖

❖ ❖ ❖

TRAINING SUGGESTION

Thinking Traps

You may want to use the following template to record any thinking traps you've noticed. In a short while you'll begin to notice that you have definite preferences.

If you're comfortable sharing this with a spouse or other loved one, that person's perception of your typical traps can be invaluable. Ask—it's worth it!

Thinking Traps	Occurrences and Examples
Should statements	
What-iffing	
Tunnel vision	
Mind reading	
Have-tos	
Black-and-white thinking	
Name-calling	
Miscellaneous personal traps	

❖ ❖ ❖

7

Insecurity versus Self-Trust

I'd like to share with you an ancient tale, one that embraces the essence of my Self-Coaching philosophy.

There once was a monastery that imposed a very strict vow of silence. It was so strict that inhabitants were allowed to speak only two words every ten years. A novice monk, after spending his first ten years at the monastery, was asked by the head monk, "It's been ten years. What are your two words?" The novice monk replied, "Bed, hard."

Another ten years passed and once again the novice monk was asked for his two words. "Food, stinks," he replied with obvious frustration. After thirty years, the now elderly head monk once again asked for his two words. "I, quit," said the younger monk. "It doesn't surprise me," replied the old monk, "All you've done is complain these past thirty years!"

The novice monk in this story did the right thing; he spoke his truth. The only problem was that it took him thirty years to get to it! What about you? Have you been stuck, year after year, in endless spirals of doubts, negatives, and fears? Isn't it time for you to quit being anxious or chronically battling symptoms of depression? Isn't it time to say, "I quit! Enough is enough!" In order to do this you, like the monk in the story, are going to need only two words. Two words that in your case will unravel the mystery of why you suffer. Two words that will liberate you from the endless cycle of anxiety and depression.

The two words are *insecurity* and *control*. You learned about the first, control, in the previous chapter. Now we will focus on the second, insecurity.

In the chapters that follow, you'll find that a life contaminated by depression or anxiety will always be fueled by insecure thinking. The converse is equally true: the more secure you are—or become—the less your life will be damaged by the corrosive effects of worry, doubt, or fear. Because insecurity can often be subtle, even unconscious, take the following insecurity quiz to help you assess your insecurity quotient. Answer each question as being either mostly true or mostly false.

Insecurity Self-Quiz

T	F	I tend to be shy or uneasy with strangers.
T	F	I'd rather be at home than going out on an adventure.
T	F	I wish I were smarter.
T	F	I never have enough money.
T	F	I'm usually pessimistic.
T	F	I often wish I were better looking.
T	F	I don't think I'm as good as others.
T	F	If people knew the real me, they would think differently.
T	F	In relationships, I tend to cling.
T	F	I'm usually afraid to get too close to others.
T	F	I would be a lot happier if I didn't worry so much.
T	F	I have lots of fears.
T	F	I hide my feelings.
T	F	If someone's quiet, I might think they're angry with me.
T	F	I often wonder what people *really* think of me.

A score of 1 to 5 true answers indicates a tolerable degree of insecurity. You'll be using this book more for personality expansion rather than for repair. A score of 6 to 10 true answers indicates a moderate level of insecurity. Insecurity is probably undermining your capacity for effective living. You can expect this book to change significantly your view and experience of the world. If you scored 11 to 15 true answers, you may be suffering from substantial interference due to insecurity. Your self-worth has been eroded by insecurity, and it's clear you're going to need to restructure your thoughts and perceptions.

Insecurity + Control = A Toxic Mix

Maybe you've noticed yourself becoming a bit too perfectionistic, not wanting to make mistakes, or just trying too hard to avoid trouble. At other times, you may notice yourself worrying about life's what-ifs, trying hard to anticipate what life's going to throw at you. At still other times, you might catch yourself bullying your mate, such as by insisting on choosing your vacation spot. These are all expressions of how insecurity drives us.

All children, to a greater or lesser extent, will develop some insecurity, whether it's caused by loss, trauma, illness, or uncertainty. Some amount of insecurity is an inescapable by-product of living. If you think about the growing complexity of our world, the countless trial-and-error experiences you've had growing up, the traumas, the mishaps, and, of course, the reality that there are no perfect parents, doesn't it stand to reason that some insecurity is inevitable? From burglar alarms and karate schools to metal detectors, mace, and pepper sprays, our culture reflects this growing apprehension. We're becoming part of Generation I: Generation Insecurity.

A little insecurity isn't necessarily bad. The key word here is "little." It may be what prompted our earliest ancestors to band together in groups, defending against a hostile world, both real and imagined. In our lives, a little insecurity can also be put to good use. Anxiety about gaining a little weight or the health risks of smoking can certainly be used as motivation for positive change. But when insecurity goes beyond a little and becomes a lot, that's when you suffer. Instead of feeling concern over losing weight or quitting smoking, you become obsessed, depressed, or anxious about it. You may even panic as your everyday waking thoughts become filled with negativity and self-loathing.

First, before you can understand what's been undermining your life, you must recognize the degree to which you are insecure. The following progression reflects varying degrees of insecurity from normal to anxious to depressed. Which statement best reflects your thinking?

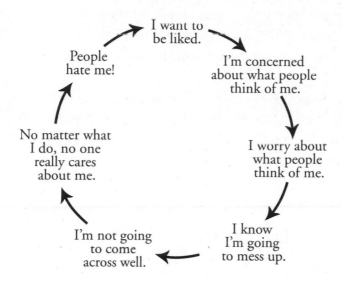

Self-Coaching Reflection
In life, there's no absolute security and safety,
so stop acting as though there is!

It All Begins with Insight

An insecure person (do keep in mind that this is a relative term) will insulate himself or herself by building walls higher and higher, always insisting, "Just a little bit more, then I'll surely be secure." Why do you think the lottery has become such a huge phenomenon? Millions of people walk into their local convenience store every morning, plop down a dollar or two, rattle off their sacred numbers, and walk out clutching that ticket, thinking, "Maybe today I'll hit the big one; then I'll never have to worry again."

If you think you can beat your insecurity from the outside in (such as by getting a better job, making more money, buying that fancy car, attracting that special person), you're dead wrong. It's also not uncommon for an insecure person to assume that the answer to their problem is only a question away. Someone, anyone (most often a therapist), may have the secret or the insight that will set them free—abracadabra! It's hard to convince people who distrust themselves to believe in themselves.

Sam, a forty-year-old computer programmer, couldn't stop asking for help. He was driving his wife crazy, as well as his friends, and even his kids. All he would say, over and over, was, "Am I getting better?" "What's wrong with me?" "Do I need to go to the hospital?" The more he asked, and the more he was reassured, the more compulsive he became. It was Sam's wife who initially called me, because she and her family couldn't take Sam's hounding any longer. Sam needed to break his cycle of looking outside of himself for answers. Once he did, with a little hard work, he found what he was looking for. It was there all the time. He just needed to build up his confidence to trust it.

Alcohol and Other Drugs

Alcohol and other drugs are particularly dangerous for the insecure individual. You don't have to look too far to understand why. What could be more appealing to an overthinking, insecure, worrisome person than not having to care about anything! Ah, the relief of being set free. Drugs, and especially alcohol, reduce anxiety by producing a cavalier, detached attitude, accentuated by a false sense of confidence, or false trust. With this attitude, being in control isn't nearly as important as getting high and staying high. If your life is riddled with anxiety and depression, you're a potential candidate for the devil's nectar, as an Alcoholics Anonymous (AA) friend of mine calls it.

I met Randy at an alcoholic rehabilitation center in San Diego, where I was doing one of my internships. He was an unemployed, twenty-eight-year-old electrician who had recently come to the shelter. Sober, Randy was terribly insecure, panicky, and fearful of life. Drunk, however, he saw things differently:

> When I drink I don't think about things. Nothing matters, only drinking. For a while I would hang with some friends, especially when we were doing drugs, but as I got more into booze, I just wanted to get high—alone. Everyone was a distraction. It wasn't social anymore. *All* that mattered was getting drunk. Nothing else. It didn't matter if I lied, stole, hurt, as long as I could get drunk. I know I did some terrible things, but when I was drinking, I didn't care about anything.
>
> Getting sober was another story. About six months ago, I tried to get sober, even went to a couple of AA meetings. But I had this attitude, I wasn't like that room full of drunks. I was different. I'd be able to control my drinking. Yeah, I was different! My father was on my back to go to work, I had bills, collection agencies calling . . . I couldn't take it. The worse things got, the more I wanted to drink. The last couple of months, I was managing to stay drunk all the time. A few weeks ago, I woke up here. I started drinking in Boston, and I wound up here! I have no idea how I got here. I have no idea what I've done along the way. For all I know, my picture could be hanging in the post office right now. I'm scared. Really scared.

Before turning to alcohol, Randy had been feeling anxious about being laid off. His self-esteem was so low that he avoided any socialization. At first, he found that marijuana took the edge off his anxiety, enough so that he began going out to clubs. His ritual was to get high on pot, go to a club, and drink all night. In the beginning, he was attracted to being able to discard his woes like a snake shedding its skin. He began to live for his evenings, sleeping all day and

85

partying all night. As Randy began to deplete his savings, he turned away from his marijuana habit and became mostly a shot-and-a-beer drinker.

For a short while, Randy thought he was on top of the world. He loved going out, partying, womanizing, playing pool, and meeting new people. He was feeling no pain, as long as he kept drinking alcohol and smoking marijuana. What he didn't count on was that the more he drank, the more the drink controlled him.

When it comes to life's insecurities, perhaps the very last place you'll find an answer is at the bottom of a whiskey bottle. Drugs such as alcohol are dangerous because they lull you away from your struggles, offering instead an anesthetized escape. Unfortunately, in order to stay in this surreal place of detachment, you have to stay high. As your life becomes more and more a shambles, the more you have to escape it. As every addict finds out, what appears to be an escape invariably becomes a prison.

The Insecurity Cycle

It helps to think of self-trust as a muscle. Use it and rely on it, and it becomes stronger. But when your insecurity convinces you that you *can't* handle life's challenges, your trust muscle begins to atrophy. The weaker your trust muscle, the more you rely on strategies such as worry, rumination, perfectionism, or avoidance to handle life. The lack of self-trust creates a vicious cycle of doubt, fear, and negativity, which invariably lead to anxiety and depression. There's only one answer: you must restore self-trust by breaking the insecurity cycle.

The insecurity cycle is sustained and fueled by what I call Reflexive Thinking. Reflexive Thinking is simply insecure thinking that, over time, has become automatic and reflexive. Take, for example, the C word: "can't." So many times in therapy I need to challenge someone who proclaims, "I *can't* stop worrying," or "I *can't* be happy." It's not a fact that you "can't," you just believe that you can't. It's a belief that has become so

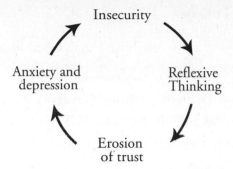

automatic that you've long since stopped challenging it. This is what I call a Reflexive Thought. (A more complete discussion of Reflexive Thinking will be given in the next chapter.) As long as Reflexive Thinking is steering your life, you're just a passenger along for the ride—a ride, as you've come to find out, filled with potholes, bumps, and occasional breakdowns.

As long as your Reflexive Thinking is left unchallenged, steering your life, you're looking for that "free lunch." Alcohol and other drugs are tempting because they require no effort, they offer immediate relief, and they create an illusion of invincibility. If you're drinking too much or using any illegal substance, you are contradicting your Self-Coaching goals. You must stop! If you can't, you need to get into a program (there's none better than AA) or at least consult with a mental-health professional.

If you really want to beat anxiety and depression, recognize the obvious: one foot going north while the other goes south can only waste your efforts. Self-Coaching will introduce you to Self-Talk, a powerful technique that is compatible with both a 12-step program and counseling. Self-Coaching can train you to choose and sustain one direction, one path—life.

Self-Coaching Reflection
No one else—only you—can do what's necessary
to heal you. The sooner you realize and accept this,
the more quickly you will progress.

Beware of Free Lunches

Before you decide that a free lunch isn't such a bad idea, let me tell you about a husband who thought he was side-stepping his insecurity:

Rod, a middle-aged man in his fifties, was about to leave his wife of twenty-five years because, in his words, "I've finally found happiness." He was a devoted father and husband who, until now, had never realized how unhappy he was. Because of insecurity, Rod was what most people described as "quiet" or "withdrawn." He seemed relatively content. Not even Rod knew that he was sitting on a powder keg of suppressed, restricted emotions. An overthinker, prone to worry and rumination, Rod's life was a listless routine of plodding along trying to stay one step ahead of the depression and emptiness that nipped at his heels.

All this changed the day Rod noticed Gail, a co-worker at the courthouse. According to Rod, "It was like the clouds parted and this ray of sunshine filled me, warming me, releasing me from a darkness." Rod went on to describe how, for the first time in his life, he felt liberated from worry and doubt. "It's like I was drunk; nothing bothered me when I was with Gail. I was happy, romantic . . . me, romantic! I couldn't believe this was me. I was totally open with my feelings. And I have to admit, it felt great!"

For Rod, this was nothing less than an intoxication, not from alcohol, but from infatuation. Infatuation is indeed a chemistry-altering experience. You literally do get high. And it was this intoxication that emboldened Rod to override his insecurity and chronic hesitations. He was in love with feeling secure, liberated, and free of the shackles of depression and self-doubt. Gail was a goddess who had set him free. Or so he thought.

As so often happens with infatuation, we become falsely convinced that the infatuation is real (rather than a state of projection) and will last forever. Rod found out the hard way that there are no free lunches when it comes to insecurity. He left his wife abruptly one weekend and moved into Gail's apartment. After a brief period of ecstasy, an uneasiness began to set in. Once an infatuation falls from the heavens and becomes bound to earthly reality, it can quickly lose its fascination. Gail wasn't the answer to Rod's insecurity, nor was his wife the problem.

With his growing uneasiness, Rod began to experience bouts of panic and a depression. One such episode was so profound that he wound up in a local hospital after Gail found him unconscious, with a bottle of tranquilizers still clutched in his hand. After leaving the hospital, Rod found that he had *no* feelings for Gail. Nothing! As abruptly as his infatuation began, it ended. Just being in the same apartment with her was impossible, "I would look at her and ask, 'What was I attracted to?' I couldn't figure it out." Disoriented and confused, Rod showed up at his home begging his wife to forgive him. She agreed to join him in counseling and that's when I got a call.

What we learned was that Rod's infatuation gave him what he had unconsciously been longing for all his life: a feeling of confidence, openness, and happiness. Unfortunately, what he experienced with Gail was only a facsimile of what he really needed. Rod was willing to understand—as was his wife—that his susceptibility to infatuation had more to do with his depressed, bottled-up feelings than it did with Gail. Rod just wanted to be happy. Because of his lifelong habit of insecurity, he just didn't know how to be happy. In a sense, he was easy prey for his infatuation, which catapulted him out of his flat, mundane life.

Now in a sober state, Rod came to recognize two things. No one would, or could, remove his insecurity, except him. And there was an unlived life waiting to happen, just the other side of his depression. He was all ears as I explained my Self-Coaching program. Rod now knew that enough was enough. For the first time in his life, he was ready to deal with the facts of his depression.

Do I Really Need to Change?

Ask yourself the following questions:

- Does doubt, fear, or negativity occupy a good part of my life?
- Does the need for control consume and frustrate my life?
- Have I noticed more anxiety, desperation, moodiness, or even depression creeping into my life?
- Has my have-to-be-in-charge attitude made me rigid?
- Are my relationships showing signs of deterioration, becoming strained and quarrelsome, if not hostile?
- What about my capacity for enjoyment? Has it diminished because my mind is always somewhere else, distracted by incessant "what-ifs"?
- Is my life being wasted, pooled up in a puddle of ruminations and frantic motion?
- Does my impatience make it difficult, if not impossible, to relax and have fun? Does it take having a couple of drinks for me to loosen up?
- Does everything always have to be done my way, or no way? Has delegating responsibility always been a problem?
- Do I find it hard to trust that I can handle life?

If any of the preceding sounds familiar, then you may have a control-sensitive personality. Don't panic; it's not a death sentence. It just means that Self-Coaching is going to become a valuable tool for you.

Self-Coaching Is the Solution

All your problems begin and end with insecurity. When your trust muscle atrophies and insecurity causes you to doubt your capacity to handle life, then you're doomed to compensate through a vicious cycle of control and Reflexive Thinking. The more you doubt, the more susceptible you are to trying to control life, rather than trust it. You do this in an attempt to handle what you perceive to be a treacherous world out there. Unfortunately, the more you concede to control and insecurity, the more likely you are to cause a depletion that inexorably leads to anxiety, panic, or depression.

What if I can show you that worrying more, trying to be more perfect, or insulating yourself from life isn't the answer to your struggles—it's the problem? And what if I can demonstrate that your deficiencies—your perceived inadequacies to handle life—are gross misperceptions born out of past wounds? Most important, what if I can help you recognize your genuine and spontaneous capacity for responding to life in a winning way?

Consider this: Let's say you're sitting out on the deck one balmy summer evening and a hungry mosquito decides to dine on your neck. What would happen? Without any debate, you'd raise your hand and smack it. Right? You wouldn't think about it; you'd just do it.

While out on one of my fossil digs in Wyoming, I came across an allosaurus tibia. Deeply engrossed in the tedious excavation, I hadn't noticed the three-inch scorpion crawling only inches from my face. Even though I had never come nose-to-claw with a scorpion in the wilds, I had an immediate recognition and split-second response. With my knife, I swiped away at the scorpion and sent it, along with a pound of sand, cascading down the cliff.

Growing up in the New York metropolitan area, I didn't have much experience with scorpions. Nonetheless, when it comes to taking care of business (and scorpions), we humans are formidable machines—unless, of course, insecurity and a demand for control have mucked up the works. Self-Coaching can teach you to "unmuck the works" with your unrehearsed natural talent to trust that you can handle life. A person driven by insecurity, rather than relying on his or her natural resources to handle life's challenges, instead leans exclusively on one resource: thinking. As formidable as your intellect may be, it represents only a tiny island in a vast ocean of ability. This ocean is your genuine capacity for automatic self-preservation and protection. The nice part is that you don't need to understand your ocean; just unleash it—and then trust it.

❖ ❖ ❖

TRAINING SUGGESTION

It's important to distinguish between a normal, healthy need for control and insecurity-driven desires. Writing down your expressions of control can really help you see the difference. If you get stuck coming up with examples, look at the quiz at the beginning of this chapter, along with those in chapters 1 and 6. They can help trigger a recognition for a particular struggle you might have had that day.

Use the following example as a guide, but keep in mind that success with this exercise will take some practice. Look especially for a certain desperate, compulsive, or rigid quality to help you spot insecurity-driven expressions (for example, a compulsive "I have to" versus a normal "I want to").

Expressions of Control	Normal	Insecurity-Driven
1. I'm always avoiding germs.	☐	☑
2. I like to please my husband.	☑	☐
3. I have to please my friends.	☐	☑
4. I can't stand it if one hair is out of place.	☐	☑
5. I'm a penny-pincher.	☐	☑

For the sake of clarity, let me show you how the preceeding expressions can switch polarities:

Expressions of Control	Normal	Insecurity-Driven
1. I don't want to catch her germs.	☑	☐
2. I have to please my husband all the time.	☐	☑
3. I enjoy pleasing my friends.	☑	☐
4. I like my hair to look nice.	☑	☐
5. I try to avoid wasting money.	☑	☐

❖ ❖ ❖

PART III

Self-Coaching: The Program and How to Do It

8

Self-Talk

When a coach sees her star pitcher begin to slump as batter after batter starts to get on base, what does she do? She calls a time-out and walks out to the mound. Once on the mound she has one job: to calm down her rattled ace. She uses whatever coaching strategies and tools are available to her.

With a high-strung, perfectionistic kind of kid, the coach might try reassurance with a bit of objectivity: "You know you're better than this. Your confidence is rattled—no problem. Just slow down and play your game. You're my star, right?" With a more obsessive type, the coach may choose a no-nonsense, tough-love approach, "You know what the problem is? You think too much! Stop thinking, and just throw strikes." Coaches need to know how to focus their athletes.

Like a pitcher who's in a slump and throwing nothing but meatballs, you, too, can quickly lose objectivity when your insecurity trips you up. "It's all too hard," you say. "I can't do it; but what am I going to do now? I'm such a loser." This is when you need a time-out, when you need to have a conference with your coach. But hold on a minute; because you're both the athlete and the coach, how can you possibly be objective when you're feeling out of control? You can, if you're using Self-Talk. *Self-Talk* is a technique that allows you to work with yourself, even when you're riddled by insecurity and self-doubt. With Self-Talk, you can actually coach yourself back to health, even when a part of you has quit and given up.

Self-Talk Basics

What's going through your mind right now? What thoughts are you aware of? Can you "hear" this inner talk? When you say, "I don't feel I'm ever going to get better," or "Why would he want me anyway; I'm such a loser," you're actually talking to yourself, not with your mouth, but with your mind. In order to be emotionally affected by your thoughts, two things have to happen: First, you—a part of you—must *listen* to what you're saying, and second, either you must accept what you hear as being the truth, or you must reject it.

A part of you talks, and a part of you listens. This may seem strange at first, but with some reflection, you can see how obvious it is. If I say to myself, "I can't lose weight; I'm just too weak," and then I find myself getting depressed, I've listened to and accepted this thought. I could just as well have chosen not to listen by insisting, "No problem, I'm going to work harder at my diet" or "Nonsense, I'm fine just the way I am." By understanding this simple concept that part of you talks and another part of you chooses either to listen or not to listen, you begin to understand the essence of Self-Talk.

Reflexive Thinking and Your Child-Reflex

If you were to monitor your "talking" you'd notice that most of your thoughts seem to be reactive to life circumstances, "Let's see, what will I do today?" or "I need to get more exercise; where did I leave my jogging shoes?" Other thoughts aren't so neutral. These are thoughts imbued with doubt, fear, and negativity. "I'll never make it through this day!" or "I know, I know, I need to stop worrying. I just can't do it." In order to release yourself from the struggle of anxiety or depression, you must first release yourself from reflexive, insecurity-driven thinking. Let's take a look at what I call Reflexive Thinking and see how this is done.

In life, reflexes can be helpful or destructive. Most helpful reflexes, such as tying your shoelace or dialing a familiar phone number, don't require any formal thinking; you just react automatically with very little formal cognition. This type of thinking might best be described as *autothinking.* Another type of reflex, which I refer to as Reflexive Thinking, is a kind of automatic responding that isn't at all efficient or helpful; in fact, it's downright destructive. It's a type of thinking that hammers you with doubts, fears, and negatives.

Reflexive Thinking, whose origins were established during your early developmental years, describes older, more childlike thinking habits that are insecurity-driven and destructive. This childlike component of Reflexive Thinking I refer to as your Child-Reflex.

All this talk about voices, different parts of you, and your Child-Reflex may leave you feeling a bit fragmented. First off, let me reassure you that it's normal and healthy to have different levels of conscious expression and awareness. Think of consciousness at any given moment as a view from a 35 mm camera. If you have a manual focus, you can turn the lens so that your dog, Fido, is in focus and the flowers in the background are all a blur. Turn the lens in the opposite direction and Fido becomes a blur and the flowers jump into crisp focus. With you, one moment your Child-Reflex may be in focus while your more mature side recedes into a blur. In contrast, Self-Coaching, specifically your work with Self-Talk, will teach you to stay focused on what's healthy and ignore what's unhealthy.

Imagine that someone followed you around when you were a young child and took videos of your every move. Watching these videos now, you might notice times when you became panicked about your mother leaving, or lay in your bed frightened over hearing your parents arguing in the next room. In another video, you might even notice yourself sulking and feeling sorry for yourself because you thought no one loved you. These images, captured on video, would show seminal moments of vulnerability that eventually shaped and molded the adult that you've become.

No matter how many times you watch the video, the child captured on that tape doesn't change—same fears, same panic, same doubts. Just as these images are permanently recorded on the videotape, they are also permanently recorded—imprinted—on your psyche. Along with this imprint of your Child are the misperceptions, distortions, and primitive thinking that eventually shaped your habit of insecurity.

Any child who grows up in a stressful environment will naturally, through a series of trial-and-error experiments, learn to incorporate an array of controlling strategies that offer some degree of insulation from insecurity. Where one child may rely on tantrums and hostility to coerce a malleable parent, another may seek to excel in all things in order to elicit a positive response from a distant or otherwise preoccupied parent. These child-strategies, over time, become imprinted on your psychic video, where they remain forever childlike and reflexive.

When your Child-Reflex is allowed to steer your thinking, you suffer. Why? Because your Child-Reflex has only one perception of the world, the primitive, distorted, out-of-date perception captured on that old video-tape. Self-Talk will teach you all about your Child-Reflex, but most important, it will teach you how to separate from the habit of adopting your Child's reflexive view of the world. It will teach you to turn off that video.

With practice, you'll begin to notice the childlike character of your troubled thoughts. Like your outer personality, your Child-Reflex has a distinctive personality that expresses itself in many different ways. Just as any personality is composed of many traits, the personality of your Child-Reflex is a mosaic of many different expressions. Sometimes you might hear yourself whining, "Nobody cares about my needs. I never get any help. Why do I have to work so hard?" Sometimes, you may hear a primitive tantrum, "No, I'm not going to give in!" or "Fine, I'll go to your mother's, but I'm not going to say a word!" At other times, you may hear a frightened, panicked child: "I can't go on, what's going to happen to me? Somebody help me, please." Just as the world sees your unique outer personality, you need to recognize your other unique personality—the inner personality expressed through your Child-Reflex.

Self-Coaching Healing Principle 1
Everyone has a legacy of insecurity that is expressed through
your Child-Reflex.

Let me introduce you to Jenna; her story will acquaint you with Self-Talk's basics. Jenna, an eighteen-year-old high school senior, came to therapy because of anxiety about her boyfriend:

Michael is a great guy. I don't know why I don't trust him. I make him call me every night. He thinks it's because I miss him; actually, it's because I want to know if he's at home. He's going away this summer for football camp at his college and I just know something awful is going to happen. He's never been unfaithful, and he says he loves me. I know it's stupid, but I feel he's going to cheat on me. It's crazy because I've got this great boyfriend who has never done one thing wrong and I just can't trust him. I'm not eating, I worry all the time, and lately I'm getting furious with him over the smallest things.

The insecure, distrusting part of Jenna's psyche that's talking is her Child-Reflex. Rather than fighting, or even challenging her Child's distortions, she accepts them without so much as a hesitation. Her Child-Reflex talks, and she listens—and then she gets anxious.

Self-Talk is a simple technique that will teach you three things:

1. How to separate negative, insecure thinking from normal, healthy thinking
2. How to stop insecurity-driven thinking and *choose* healthy thinking
3. How to build your trust-muscle

Building self-assurance and trust by choosing to replace the reflexive, paralyzing thoughts of insecurity with more objective rational thinking is just plain smart.

Self-Coaching Healing Principle 2
Healthy thinking is a choice.

You don't actually talk yourself out of negative thinking; well, not verbally. You talk by directing your thoughts: "I don't have to take this self-abuse any longer!" Most of the time, however, your thoughts are not directed; they're just part of a constant stream of semiconscious reflexive reverie: "I think I'll get a bite to eat . . . I'm so tired . . . I don't want to go to work tomorrow."

Take a second right now to hear your inner talk. You might be sitting, thinking, "I can't go on reading much longer; I've got to make that phone call." Your inner talk instigates and directs actions, precipitates reactions, and generates feelings. In the preceding example, telling yourself that you have to make that phone call might precipitate a slightly anxious feeling. You may feel a bit tense, unsettled, unable to concentrate as easily on your reading. This subtle pressure is a result of the thought/talk that innocently passed through your field of consciousness: "I've got to make that phone call." It was this thought that pulled you away from your tranquil reading. Instead of being in the moment, you were briefly living in an abstract future moment: thinking about getting up and making that phone call.

Self-Talk is directed talk. It's talk designed to wrench your thoughts away from insecurity and to insist on more appropriate thinking. With few exceptions, most other thinking is undirected. These are simply neutral meandering thoughts: "Hmm, that coffee smells so good." This, however, isn't the case with undirected thoughts driven by your Child-Reflex. I'm sure you know the experience of being gripped by a panic or a sour mood. You never directed—chose—this experience ("I think I'll let that comment upset me now . . ."); it just happened to you. Anxiety and depression are reactions to undirected thoughts that are driven by your Child-Reflex. These are thoughts that just seem to happen.

Living in the Moment versus Time Travel

Whether you're reading a book, enjoying a sunset, listening to music, or playing with your children, once you've abandoned the moment because you've become swallowed up in insecurity, you've lost an opportunity for relaxation and true connectedness with your world. You are either in the moment or you're not. Anxiety-prone people, for example, can usually be found living in dread anticipation of the future, rarely in the moment. Their inner (undirected) reflexive talk might sound something like, "What if I get sick? Then I'll lose my position. All my work will be ruined. I know I'm going to get sick." Depressive people, on the other hand, typically dwell in the melancholy of past defeats and rejections.

They, too, rarely live in the moment. Depressive inner talk might sound like, "If only I didn't say that. What's the use now? It's over, I'm doomed."

The irony is that the past and the future don't exist. They're nothing more than artifacts of our brain's ability to abstract; in a sense, when caught up in these abstractions we're time traveling (back to the past, forward into the future). We certainly are capable of mentally reexperiencing our past ("Why did I say that? She was so angry.") or launching ourselves into a projection of the future ("He'll never let me live this one down."). As seductive as time travel is, the only reality is the present.

Self-Coaching Reflection
Time-traveling is a habit of insecurity that pulls you away from here-and-now living.

If you're anxious or depressed, your life has been pulled away from here-and-now living, leaving you time traveling in a netherworld of worrisome regrets or anticipations. Your life has become congested with struggle only because you don't realize you can say no. Self-Coaching is going to change all that.

Self-Coaching Healing Principle 3
Thoughts precede feelings, anxieties, and depressions.

With the exception of simple reflexes, thoughts precede actions, reactions, and, most important, feelings. The thoughts that we do have are based on how we perceive our world. These perceptions are the conclusions we've drawn from our unique learned experiences. An abused or neglected child will arrive at very different conclusions about life from a child reared with love and respect. A relatively secure person, for example, may handle the silence of a therapy session calmly, thinking, "This is an unhurried chance for me to express my concerns." An anxious person, on the other hand, might react quite differently to the same silence: "What does he want from me? What is he expecting me to say? I hate this!" A depressed person, dealing with the same silence, might conclude, "I have nothing to say. I can't even do therapy right! I'm such a failure."

I Know I Worry Too Much, But . . .

Insecurity, self-doubt, and fear all create distortions of reality. Take a look at Linda's struggle. She shows just how easy it is to become confused by insecurity's distorted way of thinking so typical of a Child-Reflex. Linda is a twenty-four-year-old mother who, for years, had been struggling with panic and fear. Nonetheless, it wasn't until her daughter started school that she felt totally out of control and in need of help.

> With all that's going on in the world, I just can't stop being anxious about my daughter being in school. I'm sure they don't lock the doors at the rear of the school. Anyone can walk in. I know I'm the only mother who stands and watches until she's inside. During the day I find myself driving past the school. I know she's all right, but I just feel so nervous. I keep having these racing thoughts. "What if this . . . or what if that . . ." I know it's silly, but bad things can happen, right? How do I know they won't happen to my daughter? The only time I begin to calm down is when I see her coming out of the building after school.

Linda's thinking is somewhat extreme, but it does show how a little information combined with a lot of insecurity can begin to write a scary screenplay. Linda isn't any different from you and me. What's happened is that because of a lack of trust (self-trust and life-trust), she allowed her concerns and normal anxieties to piggyback one on top of the other, unimpeded. She developed a habit of tortuous, insecure thinking. Notice how all her thoughts are anticipations of future chaos (which happens to be as good a definition of anxiety as there is: *an anticipation of chaos*). As you can see, Linda clearly suffers from her distortions. If, like Linda, you begin to slide down the slippery slope of anxiety's seductive "what-iffing," then it won't be long before you'll feel like a dog chasing its tail. Anxious thoughts causing anxiety, causing more anxious thoughts, causing . . . you get the point.

Self-Coaching Healing Principle 4
Insecurity is a habit, and any habit can be broken.

Linda needed to understand that if you let insecurity dictate what's real, then you must pay a price. She paid with anxiety. Self-Talk helped Linda learn that her insecurity had a unique voice. In fact, it actually had a personality—in her case, a very worried, fearful, distrusting, primitive personality. This voice, different from her more rational, healthy voice, was her Child-Reflex. By using Self-Talk to first help her recognize who was talking to her (that is, healthy Linda or tortured, Child-Reflex Linda), she was ready to coach herself to fight off these distortions. She did this by replacing her Child's thinking with more rational, positive, directed thinking—Self-Talk. Linda chose to be healthy. Self-Talk insists on more appropriate interpretations: "I'm going to risk believing that my daughter is all right—no more 'what-ifs.' When I drop her off, I'm just not going to allow myself to dwell on such silliness." Linda found out, as you will, that once you take charge and direct your thinking using Self-Talk, anxiety and depression lose their power.

Self-Coaching Healing Principle 5
Healthy thinking is a choice.

It may be surprising to you that insecurity, fear, doubt, and distrust can actually have a voice and a personality. You're surprised because, over time, you've become identified with your destructive patterns. You see them not as contaminants to your persona, but *as* your persona. When you say, "I am depressed" or "I am anxious," you actually become your depression or your anxiety. On the other hand, if you were to say, "A *part of me* is depressed or anxious—a very destructive part," then you can approach your symptoms with the necessary detachment to liberate yourself from them.

You are not now and never were meant to be your anxiety or your depression. Anxiety and depression, although a normal expected part of life, should never dominate your life. If you are bullied by any of these destructive symptoms, realize that you are a victim of nothing more than misguided, insecurity-driven attempts to control life. Don't be misled by your symptoms. Habits are only habits; anxiety is only anxiety, and depression is only depression. They are not supernatural, unworldly, or beyond your ability to change; they are just bad habits.

Self-Coaching Healing Principle 6
A good coach is a good motivator.

Getting Started: A Tip from Super Mario

A few years back, my kids invited me to join them in playing one of their video games. I had observed them playing, making little Mario leap, jump, dodge, and scurry all over the screen. It seemed easy. With the controller in hand, I quickly found out otherwise. Don't forget that kids today have been brought up on video games. In my day, the only toys that moved were those you wound up. I was all thumbs.

The good-natured chiding from my kids only galvanized my resolve to develop this useless skill. Occasionally, after work, I'd slip into the basement for a few Nintendo minutes. At first I was frustrated. Just as when I've tried to write wrong-handed, I couldn't make Mario do what I wanted. It didn't matter how hard I tried. (This actually made things worse.) Then, after about a month, Mario began to do exactly what I wanted him to do! Somehow my brain, hands, and eyes all began to work together, and Mario became an extension of my will.

Your first attempts with Self-Talk may feel like "all thumbs" to you. Just as with my Nintendo experience, you will have to learn to do things over and over that feel unnatural at first. Keep reminding yourself that the frustration is only temporary. Accept from the start that Self-Talk takes practice—the more the better, and the sooner the better. Even if your technique is rough, go ahead and give it a shot. If you get confused or feel that you've made a mistake, you're allowed. Just keep trying and learning from your efforts. You've got absolutely nothing to lose, and so much to gain.

TRAINING SUGGESTION

Take any opportunity you have to practice differentiating between directed Self-Talk, undirected reflexive thoughts driven by insecurity, and neutral undirected thoughts. The following chart is an example of how to log these experiences. See whether you can come up with a few examples of each category from your day.

Undirected Neutral Thinking	Undirected (Reflexive) Insecure Thoughts	Directed Self-Talk
1. Guess it's time to call it a day; I'm tired.	1. It's too hard. I can't do it.	1. No, I'm not going to give up. I've worked too long and too hard.
2. What a beautiful sunset.	2. Why does he want to see me? What did I do? This is terrible.	2. There's nothing to be afraid of; it's just a simple cough.
3. What do I feel like eating? Guess I'm not that hungry.	3. My hair looks awful; I can't go to the dance. I want to die.	3. Enough is enough. It's time to get to work.

❖ ❖ ❖

9

The Three Easy Steps
of Self-Talk

The dictionary defines *insecurity* simply as a lack of confidence or assurance. Most people will tell you that it's an unsafe, doubting tension you feel from time to time. How would you describe insecurity? I would describe it as an anticipation of danger, vulnerability, or helplessness, coupled with a lack of self-trust. Insecurity has a voice (fortunately limited to three expressions: doubts, fears, and negatives) that expresses itself through what I generically call Reflexive Thinking. One specific form of Reflexive Thinking that leads to anxiety and depression is the Child-Reflex, which I discussed in chapter 8. It's your Child-Reflex that fills your head with doubt and fear, making it impossible for you to trust that you can handle life. Guess what—you've been duped. Your Child-Reflex may have some habit strength, but trust me, it's not that strong. There's only one reason you've been bullied for so long: this reflex has never been adequately challenged, until now. In just three simple steps, you're about to put an end to the erosion that has stripped you of self-trust and personal security.

Self-Talk Step 1: Separate Fact
from Fiction; Learn to Listen

Step 1 isn't complicated; it just takes practice. All you need to do is start by asking a simple question: Is what I'm reacting to a fact or a fiction? If you're like most people, the habits of insecurity that contaminate your life probably operate unnoticed on a reflexive level. And since most habits begin to feel natural over time, you're probably not aware of the effect they're having on your life. Let's say, for example, that you're sitting on the bus on your way to work. You look at your watch and realize you're going to be a few minutes late. You think, "What will my boss say? She's going to think I don't care. What if she thinks I'm taking advantage of her? What if . . . ?" As the trickle of doubts, fears, and negatives becomes a torrent of anxiety, you begin to feel a bit light-headed and nervous. "Was that a heart palpitation?"

That night you're riding home on the bus again, this time smiling. Your boss was an hour later than you today, you made a big sale, and you were told you might be in line for a promotion. You call your favorite restaurant and make reservations, thinking about that glass of wine you're going to celebrate with.

A week later, you're late for work again. Do you look back and remind yourself, "I went through this last week and I'm not going to put myself through the wringer again"? No, you don't! With a habit of insecurity, you don't learn from your successes. "Yes, nothing happened last week, but today's different—I *know* I'm going to get in trouble!"

So what can be done when insecurity holds us hostage? In order to stop being victimized by insecurity's doubts, fears, and negatives, you need to begin separating fact from fiction. Facts are verifiable and objective; fictions are not. And for the record, feelings are not facts. If your boss tells you he's unhappy with a memo you sent, this is a fact, and certainly cause for concern. Telling yourself, "I don't feel that my boss likes me" is a fiction. (We call this mind reading, and even though it may be true, unless verified, it remains a fiction.) If you allow yourself to treat fictions as though they are facts, you will suffer needlessly. How many times have you worried, fretted, or predicted doom and gloom only to find, as in the example of the late-running commuter, that factual reality is rarely consistent with what insecurity throws at you?

This simple scrutiny, "Is what I'm thinking a fact or a fiction?" awakens in you the realization that you have a choice. If you've been frustrated and unhappy, it's for no other reason than that you've been living a choiceless, reflexive life. Once you stop treating fictions as though they're facts and realize that you have a choice not to be anxious, fearful, doubt-ful, or negative, you'll begin to alter your entire outlook on life.

One surefire way to begin differentiating facts from the fictions in your life is to take it one step further by asking yourself, "Does what I'm hearing sound mature, rational, or reasonable? Or does it sound primitive, excessively emotional, childish, and insecure? Is this me, or is it my Child-Reflex controlling my thoughts?"

Self-Coaching Reflection
All Child-Reflex thoughts are fictions.

Take a look at Lauren, a twenty-five-year-old schoolteacher whose Child-Reflex was taking her for a ride:

> Last week I was watching TV, and my roommate walks up to me and drops this note in my lap and then goes into her room and slams the door. The note said she couldn't go on living with my sloppiness.
>
> I just sat there. I was fuming. My first reaction was to barge into her room and give her a piece of my mind. Okay, I'll admit it's true. I am a slob, but I wasn't aware that it was an issue for Sandy. She thinks she's so perfect. Well, we'll have to see about that. As far as I'm concerned she can start looking for a new roommate! From now on, she can start taking the bus to work—the taxi service has just ended. Do you believe it—a note? She couldn't even tell me face to face! Now we're not talking. I just turn away when she walks into the room. I refuse to be civil. Why should I be? I'll show her. She's going to pay for this. I don't care how uncomfortable it gets. If she doesn't like it, she can leave. You'd think she was Miss Perfect. The nerve! Guess what? I haven't done a dish since Sunday, my clothes are all over the apartment and the bathroom is absolutely gross—and I'm not changing!

Does Lauren sound mature, rational, or reasonable? Of course not. Lauren's thinking is highly emotional, childish, and spiteful.

It's classic Child-Reflex, and she's listening. Step 1 requires that she begin to evaluate her thoughts and reactions by separating facts from fictions. When Lauren first challenged herself with Step 1, she found herself defending her childish position as if it were factual, recalling all the terrible things Sandy had done in the past. Because Lauren was feeling so anxious, however, she rightly suspected that her Child-Reflex lurked behind her intense thinking. She finally admitted, "Yes, I'm acting childish. If I were more mature about it, I would have told her how much she hurt my feelings. Maybe we could have worked out a contract or something."

Self-Coaching Tip
Whenever you sense an increase in anxiety or depressive symptoms, suspect that your Child-Reflex is behind your distress.

Lauren is a good example of what I've found time after time. When pressed, most people can tell the difference between what is mature and what is ridiculous. Trust me, if nothing else, a Child-Reflex can be quite ridiculous.

If you get confused, as Lauren did, step back, let the dust settle on any emotionally charged incident, then just come back to your assessment again, and again if necessary. Don't be fooled by your Child-Reflex's attempt to fog the issue. In fact, you can expect it. Once you get the hang of it, you'll see it's not that hard to spot the influence of your Child-Reflex. After you've seen through your reflexive smoke screen a few times, you'll have no further trouble. In fact, you'll get so good at it, you'll be able to evaluate the quality of your thinking while you're thinking it. The rule is: if it's a Child-Reflex, it's a fiction.

Take a look at the following examples. See how good you are at spotting Child-Reflex thinking. Read each quotation. If you think it describes Child-Reflex thinking (fictions), circle yes. If it sounds like more mature, rational thinking (factual), circle no. You'll find the answers following the quiz.

1. "Fine, he doesn't want my opinion, then   Yes   No
   let's see how he likes my silent treatment."

2. "I'm never going to get ahead, I'm such a   Yes   No
   failure."

3. "Nothing ever goes right for me. Everyone is   Yes   No
   against me. Why me?"

4. "She hasn't called in weeks. That's not at all   Yes   No
   like her. I wonder if everything is all right.
   Maybe I should call."

5. "He didn't call yet. Something must be wrong.   Yes   No
   Maybe he had an accident. Maybe he's lying
   on the side of the road in a ditch."

Answers: Except for the fourth quotation, all of them are typical of the Child-Reflex (insecure, exaggerated, hysterical, and the like). If you're not sure about number four, just contrast it with number five. The fourth one is a rational question, whereas number five starts off not with an objective question, but with a negative, "Something must be wrong." This negative is followed up by more hysterical speculations.

Trying to come up with your Child-Reflex's personality can really help. Just as you can easily recognize others in your life by what they say and do, your Child-Reflex can become very predictable once you recognize its personality traits. Start out using the following list to help with your identification:

- What kind of Child-Reflex expressions do you encounter? Ask yourself: does your Child sound insecure, depressed, spoiled, panicked, fearful, sulky, or defiant?

- It helps to know the circumstances that typically bring about your Child-Reflex—for example, stress, confrontations, free-floating anxiety or depression without external conflict, anticipation of conflict or confrontation, fear of losing control, difficulty in maintaining control, and so on.

- Find out how, specifically, your Child-Reflex twists things around. What's its style: worry, anticipation of doom, excessive negativity, withdrawal, guilt, or hostility?

- Based on the personality of your Child-Reflex, see whether you can come up with a simple description or name that conveys your Reflex's childish essence (Scared Mary, Hostile Harry, Doomsday Dan, Whiny Wanda, Lonely Louise, and so on).

Long ago, I found that descriptions such as "the voice of insecurity" or "distorted thinking" are not effective in developing a working relationship with your insecurity. The more you flesh out and personalize your Child-Reflex, the more intimate you become, the more quickly you will be to recognize your Child's nefarious effect on your thinking.

Keep in mind that, like your outer personality, your Child-Reflex's personality expresses itself in many different ways. Your Child-Reflex, for example, may act panicked one moment, impulsive the next, and helpless or desperate the next. Just as any personality is composed of many traits, your Child-Reflex's personality is a mosaic of many different expressions. The following list gives you a hint of the many possible expressions you may encounter. See whether any sound familiar. (Note: Descriptions in italics are characterizations you will meet in upcoming chapters.)

Panicked Child: *Chicken Littles* believe that the sky is always falling; anxious, often with underlying depression (*Worrywarts, Turtles*)

Frightened Child: fearful; always worrying; the *what-iffers;* always anxious, with depression not far behind (*Worrywarts, Turtles*)

Manipulative Child: controlling and manipulative (*Martyrs, Chameleons, Politicians,* and *Diplomats*)

Bully Child: controlling through aggression and intimidation; black-and-white, opinionated thinkers; insensitive (*Hedgehogs*)

Hysterical Child: coming apart and waiting to be rescued; overly emotional; anxious and depressed (*Worrywarts, Control Freaks*)

Overwhelmed Child: a life-is-too-much, can't-go-on attitude; usually depressed and anxious (*Worrywarts, Turtles*)

Sulking Child: woe is me; "see what a pathetic wretch I am"; depressed (*Martyrs, Turtles, Worrywarts*)

Impulsive Child: black-and-white thinkers; impatient; need to be in control—right now; anxious (*Hedgehogs, Control Freaks*) and depressed (*Worrywarts, Turtles*)

Stubborn Child: my-way-or-the-highway attitude; prone to tantrums (*Politicians, Hedgehogs, Perfectionists—Stars, Control Freaks,* and *Fanatics*)

Helpless Child: overly dependent; clingers; looking to be rescued; anxious and depressed (*Worrywarts, Turtles*)

Hopeless Child: why bother, nothing-ever-works-for-me attitude; pessimistic; anxious (*Martyrs, Turtles*)

Separating fact from fiction is a crucial first step in your process of eliminating anxiety and depression from your life. So what do you do when you recognize a fiction? Simple: you stop listening to it! That's where step 2 comes in.

Self-Talk Step 2: Stop Reflexive Thinking

Self-Talk isn't simply "talking" yourself out of anxiety or depression; it's a matter of learning specifically *how* to talk to yourself. If, for example, a thought pops into my mind that I'd like a dish of ice cream and I know I'm watching my weight, I have a few choices. One would be to listen to my thought and go for the ice cream, in which case I'd be abandoning my resolve to lose weight and instead allowing myself to be driven by my impulse to have a dish of ice cream. Thus I'd let my thoughts sabotage my healthier desire to lose weight. A second choice would be to say, "I sure would like that ice cream, but I know I'm trying to lose weight. No, I'm not going to have any." In this case you said no to your thoughts.

Saying no to specific thoughts such as "No, I can't watch TV; I have to get those bills done now," or "No, I'm not going to have another drink; I have to drive," isn't unfamiliar. We say no all the time. Yet when it comes to more abstract struggles like worry, rumination, guilt, or anxiety, why are we surprised to find out that we can still say no? The main reason is the reflexive, habitual nature of insecurity that leaves us passive victims, accepting by default the perception that we are powerless to do anything to stop the flow of doubts, fears, and negatives. Sheeplike, we go through life allowing insecurity to bully us into depression and anxiety. Step 2 is all about applying the brakes to the runaway train of Reflexive Thinking.

Nest Building

My grandmother had a wonderful expression: you can't stop a bird from flying into your hair, but you don't have to help it build a nest!" You may not be able to stop that first, insecure thought from percolating into consciousness, but you don't have to build a nest by adding a second thought, and a third, and a fourth. These are the thoughts that you *can* eliminate. Because of the habit nature of Reflexive Thinking, you've probably long ago become an unsuspecting nest-builder, never realizing that you have a choice not to become part of the problem. Self-Talk can teach you that you don't have to become a casualty of destructive Reflexive Thinking.

Anxiety and Depression: Self-Generated Problems

Here's a metaphor that can change your life. When I was a kid I had a generator-powered headlight on my bicycle. The generator consisted of a small, knurled cylinder that rubbed against the tire. As you pedaled, the moving tire turned the knurled cylinder, which then generated the electricity to light the headlight bulb. When you stopped pedaling, the bulb would flicker off. Think of anxiety, depression, or panic as you would a bicycle headlight; it only lights up if you're pedaling (that is, using Reflexive Thinking). If you suffer, understand that anxiety and depression can't exist unless you generate them. There is no anxiety or depression, unless *you* produce it! Stop pedaling, stop the flow of Reflexive Thinking, and, just as a tire on a bicycle will gradually come to a stop and the headlight will lose power, anxiety and depression will dim, flicker, and die out. This is worth repeating. Just as it's impossible for a bicycle headlight to light up if you're not pedaling, there can be no anxiety and depression if you're not generating it. For this reason alone, Self-Coaching doesn't subscribe to the illness model of anxiety and depression. An illness is something that happens to you. A habit is something *you* generate. This simple distinction can change the course of your life.

Stopping the Runaway Train of Reflexive Thinking

Step 2 requires that you take your life back from the grip of insecurity. Typically this requires nothing more than a firm act of will—an emphatic decision not to contribute (generate) thoughts that sustain insecurity. This isn't complicated, but you might find it hard to believe that you can stop the runaway train of Reflexive Thinking. "I just can't stop worrying," is a typical lament. Since the Child-Reflex leaves you feeling victimized and powerless, you find yourself looking for any "secret" abracadabra solution that will rescue you from your struggles. Just take a walk down the self-help aisle of your local bookstore. You'll see book after book, all claiming to provide the answer, the secret, or the formula for happiness.

When looking for a solution to our anxiety or depression, we become lulled into thinking that the only reason we suffer is that we haven't found *it*, read about *it*, or been told what *it* is. The irony is that the last place most people look for "it" is within. Because of this, it's no wonder our perception of what we need has become distorted. It's not unusual that patients enter into therapy not wanting to change. They just want to become better neurotics! "I don't want to be less perfect; just show me how to be less anxious." We want our psychological cake and we want to eat it, too. If you want to be free of anxiety and depression, then you must embrace three truths:

1. You must challenge the myth that anyone can rescue you.
2. You must accept responsibility for change.
3. You must be convinced that you really have a choice.

Visuals Can Help

You've heard it said that a picture is worth a thousand words. When you're caught up in the chaotic moment of Reflexive Thinking, having a simple picture in your mind can be far more useful than a thousand words of analyzing and trying to understand. Starting right now, stop looking outside yourself to find easy answers, or worse, to be rescued. Don't listen to your Child-Reflex as it balks, "I can't do this!" Instead, recognize that it's time for *you* to stop the runaway train of insecurity. In a movie, if the hero wants to bring a train to a screeching halt, all he has to do is grab hold of the emergency-brake handle dangling from the ceiling, and pull. When your thoughts begin to run away, imagine a bright red handle, see it dangling right in front of you, and pull! Then, emphatically, from a place of strength and resolve, say, "Stop!"

Let's say you're feeling anxious and panicky about applying for a promotion. You tell yourself, "Maybe I'm not smart enough to handle any more responsibilities." There are two ways to respond. The first and more destructive response would be to allow your habit of insecurity to follow a runaway thought-train such as: "Who am I kidding, they're going to find out sooner or later that I'm a loser. What if I screw up and it goes in my record? What if . . . ?" and so on until you're awake half the night pacing. This is how we generate anxiety and/or depression.

The second option is to begin by separating fact from fiction and then stopping the thought-train of Reflexive Thinking by pulling the emergency brake. That first thought, for example, pops into your mind ("Maybe I'm not smart enough to handle any more responsibilities"), and you recognize this as part of your Child-Reflex. Since you've learned that all Child-Reflex thoughts are fictions, you immediately visualize the emergency brake and pull: "Stop! This is not a fact. I *know* I can learn. I don't have to listen to my Child."

Pulling the emergency brake represents one thing: a firm act of will. It's your refusing to go one more inch in the direction of self-destruction. Perhaps all this is vaguely familiar to you. I'm sure you've attempted to stop your runaway destructive thinking many times. You've probably thought about empowering yourself and saying no to insecurity, but just couldn't manage it. It's not a matter of thinking of pulling the emergency brake; it's a matter of just pulling it. It's the same reason the marketing people at Nike decided on the slogan "Just Do It!" rather than "Just think about doing it!" Take the tip from Nike: when it comes to saying no to destructive Reflexive Thinking, *Just do it!* This is one reason that I prefer "coaching" as a concept. I've found that if most people are given enough time, education, and encouragement, they can coach (rather than analyze) themselves to leap from impotence to empowerment. It's like throwing a switch; as you develop your trust muscle, there comes a point where you're willing to take the risk, to just do it—to stop being victimized by Reflexive Thinking.

❖ ❖ ❖

TRAINING SUGGESTION

Here's a way to practice building your trust muscle while stopping Reflexive Thinking. Throughout the day, look for examples where you may be procrastinating, postponing, or avoiding a task. For example, "I'll do it later (i.e., pay the bills, make that call, wash the dishes, floss, and so on); let me relax first." For the sake of muscle building, see these as opportunities. The only way for you to learn that you are not powerless is to prove it. Make yourself get up and do it!

For this experiment, you will not accept *any* excuses. You *must* make it happen. Start off with some easy physical challenges such as routine chores. As you gain some confidence, use this same technique to make yourself choose to stop Reflexive Thinking. Once you begin to recognize that *you*, not your Child-Reflex, are calling the shots, you'll be in a position to understand a bigger truth, that in all matters there is choice. You just have to get used to exerting your will.

❖ ❖ ❖

Changing Channels

Here's another visualization that I find equally as effective as pulling the emergency brake. I call it Changing Channels.

Changing channels is a handy technique to assist you in ignoring your Child-Reflex. Imagine that you're listening to the radio. The announcer is delivering an apocalyptic speech on the dangers of global warming.

You're sitting in your living room beginning to feel tense. As you continue listening, you find your mood becoming increasingly anxious. Finally, you can't take anymore, so you turn the dial and find another radio host talking about the expected balmy weather forecast for the weekend. You begin to relax.

Each radio announcer represents a variation of your own thinking—positive and uplifting, negative and depressing, or neutral. What you listen to on the radio is no different from what you listen to in your mind. Your conscious ego is capable of channeling your energy into a firm act of will, so using the techniques of Self-Talk, you simply change the channel and tune in to a more suitable broadcast. What you choose to listen to is what will influence you. Don't like what you're hearing? Change the channel. Once you get the hang of it, you'll see just how simple this can be.

Kerry, a forty-year-old receptionist, found that changing channels saved her life. I asked her to document her experiences for this book:

> I've been a control freak all my life. When I went to the doctor's for my cough last winter, I was shocked to find out that my blood pressure was high—really high. My doctor wanted me to start medication immediately. "No way!" I blurted out. If I had high blood pressure, I was going to handle it on my own. I've never had a problem with self-discipline. What was the problem? I read a few pamphlets the doctor gave me, and I was off. I started walking, losing a few pounds, cutting back on my salt, and checking my blood pressure at home. Unfortunately, my readings remained high. Nothing I did seemed to help. At one point my reading was 215/120! I began to panic. Nothing I was doing was working!
>
> My thoughts would race. "I'm going to die. What am I going to do? I don't want to be on medication for the rest of my life!" The more panicked I became, the more frantic my efforts, and the more my pressure remained high. I did some yoga, stopped smoking, increased from walking each morning to jogging . . . nothing

worked. I started to get more depressed. I was feeling really out of control. Thoughts of not being around to watch my daughter grow up, never retiring. . . . I couldn't sleep. I was irritable, snapping at everyone. I was getting headaches, but I wouldn't go back to the doctor because all he wanted me to do was get on medication.

That's when I started therapy. At first, I was elated with the concept that I could do something about my anxiety. Since stress was one of the things my pamphlet mentioned as a contributor to hypertension, therapy seemed like the next step. I found your technique of changing channels was exactly what I needed. At first, I wanted to see how many channels my radio had. It only had three: a panic channel; a distracted, neutral channel; and an "I've-got-to-do-something" control channel. After learning about control and Self-Talk, I recognized that I was limiting my thinking—and my channels. I added a fourth: the "fact-finding" channel.

The fact-finding channel required that I stop being so pigheaded and explore all options, not just the ones listed on channels one through three. I went to a hypertension specialist and had a consultation. I was shocked to find out that there were recent medications that had very little, if any, side effects. I had always assumed blood-pressure medication made you sleep all day and go to the bathroom all night. I told the doctor I would consider his recommendations.

Next morning, while out on my run, my panic channel came in loud and clear, "Don't give in, you can't be on medication the rest of your life." I knew this anxiety was coming from my Child-Reflex, and using Self-Talk, I decided not to listen—I changed the channels. I switched to the fact-finding channel. "Okay, so I don't want to take medication, but what's this pressure doing to my body? While I go on not deciding, I'm hurting myself. When I get back I'm going to research that medication." Okay, that was a success. I actually switched and listened to a more rational channel. But it was the accidental addition of a fifth channel that really surprised me.

Channel five, which I now call the "Mozart channel," was a channel of relaxation. I first realized it when, after deciding to research the medication, I felt a calmness. All of a sudden, I forgot about my panic. I actually finished my jog looking at the beautiful flowering trees! That was a first for me. I had been in my head so completely, I hadn't even noticed that spring had arrived!

Now, whenever I'm going crazy with insecurity or panic, I make myself switch to the Mozart channel. And when I tune in, I just sort of allow myself to come out of my head and observe what's around me. I've learned to pay more attention to colors, sounds, things that don't have to do with thinking.

I finally decided to try medication. I figured I would give it a month or so and then decide. I went on this ACE inhibitor medication. It was late afternoon. After dinner that evening, I took my pressure and almost fell out of my chair. After consistent readings of 200/110 and higher, I recorded a reading of 116/80! Could this be? Within hours?

I've been on that medication for over three months now. The panic channel rarely gets listened to any longer. The fact-finding channel has also gotten less play time. And I try to switch that control channel as quickly as possible. But the Mozart channel has become my favorite. I use it for lots of situations, not just panic. Sometimes, if I'm a bit down, feeling sorry for myself, or just acting out of sorts, I can switch channels and connect with my world.

Self-Coaching Reflection
Self-Coaching relies on Self-Talk to teach you how to change channels when what's going through your mind hurts you. Why put a stop to it? Because you have a choice, why not choose to feel good?

119

Feeding the Pigeons

Here's one last visual that seems to be a favorite of those I work with. I call it feeding the pigeons.

Imagine that one day you decide to go out to your patio to relax and read the paper. You notice a cute little pigeon milling about, pecking and minding its own business. Innocently, you toss it a few crumbs from a left-over sandwich you'd been eating. The next day you go out to your patio and within minutes your little pigeon buddy reappears with a companion. Enthusiastically, you throw out a few more crumbs. By the end of the week you're inundated with hundreds of pigeons leaving your once pristine patio a shambles of feathers, droppings, and a cacophony of cooing.

You call me up and ask, "What should I do?" I ask, "Have you been feeding the pigeons?" "Why yes," you answer innocently. Trying to control my exasperation, I respond, "Then *stop* feeding the pigeons!"

If you allow Reflexive Thinking to flock into your life with needless worry, fear, or negativity, then you're feeding the pigeons of insecurity. And if you insist on feeding your insecurity, than the distasteful truth is that you will suffer. From now on, keep the image of the pigeons in mind every time you find yourself spinning with Reflexive Thinking, then remind yourself, "*Stop* feeding the pigeons!"

I'm Feeling a Lot Smarter Now

With a little awareness, you can't help but notice just how ridiculous your Child-Reflex's twisted negativity, fear, or incessant need for control really is. Eventually, when you look back, you'll be amazed at just how gullible you were. Once you get used to rejecting Reflexive Thinking and switching those channels, you're only a step away from completely tuning out those twisted thoughts and recognizing your true source of strength: your mature and healthy ego.

Jay, a recently retired businessman, recounted the following:

> I still keep thinking something's wrong with me. Once in a while, I catch myself imagining terrible things and make an effort not to

listen. Yesterday was a good example. I was at my computer, and as I reached over to scratch my side, I was startled by a jolt of pain. My rib was very tender. I touched it again, confirming that something was really wrong. I began to tell myself that something was wrong. What if it's cancer? I was getting anxious, but somehow I realized I was taking a totally innocent soreness and making it into the worst possible scenario. I knew it was the work of my Child-Reflex, panicking, getting hysterical. I took my hand away from my sore rib, and I just told myself to stop being ridiculous. I refused to listen. I made myself repeat again and again: "Stop listening. It's just your ridiculous Child." It worked! I'm not sure how many times I had to fight off the Child, but it eventually worked. I completely forgot about my rib.

Later that evening when I was taking my shirt off, I remembered my sore rib. And you know what? I remembered that I had taken a yoga class at the gym the day before and was trying to do this impossible triangle pose. I probably stretched too much. I'm so glad I fought off that Child because I would have felt like such a fool had I gone to the doctor in a panic.

Jay is typical of many patients who need to find out that patience and perseverance pay off. The Child-Reflex is used to going unchallenged. Without realizing it, most people not only permit this reflex to take over, but also actually join in the hysterics. For example, had Jay not been aware of his Self-Talk training, he might have taken the thought of cancer and added a whole host of doom-and-gloom prognostications: "What else can it be; it must be cancer!" "I don't want to die!" The last thing your Child needs is your help.

Self-Talk Step 3: Letting Go

Now, using step 3, you're going to eliminate the deleterious effects of insecurity from your life by applying a little psychological jujitsu. Jujitsu is an ancient Japanese martial art stressing that force never meets force directly. Where steps 1 and 2 are more aggressive steps, thinking (separating fact from fiction) and doing (actively stopping Reflexive Thinking), step 3 is the opposite. And what is the opposite of thinking and doing? Letting go and doing nothing. Although it sounds like an oxymoron to "do something by doing nothing," my experience with a virus a few years ago can make sense of this seeming paradox.

A few years back my brother-in-law Ron and I had tickets for a New York Giants playoff game. Because of my lifelong friendship with Ron, which goes back to high school, where he was the fullback and I was the quarterback on our football team, going to Giants Stadium has become a kind of perennial ritual. Along with our gastronomic tailgate adventures, there's always time to wax rhapsodic about our own nostalgic football war stories.

Unfortunately, on the day of the big game I woke up with a throat that felt like I had swallowed broken glass. My body ached from head to toe; my eyes begged for more sleep. I felt terrible. I wanted to die. But because of the significance of our ritual, I managed to plod through the mechanics of showering, shaving, and donning my winter gear. Never once was I far from a constant, ruminative thought: "This is crazy; I need to go back to bed. I feel miserable!"

Judging from my dismal start, I was surprised—no, amazed—to find that it turned out to be a great day punctuated by great food, great company, and a last-minute winning touchdown by the Giants. Riding home from the stadium that night, I was startled to rediscover my "sick" feelings! The sore throat was back, the stuffy nose, the aches, the fatigue. But where had these symptoms gone all day? And this is my point. The symptoms didn't go anywhere; they were still there, but I had somehow managed to ignore them. Even through the haze of my virus that night, I recall being awed by the incredible power of the mind. You've probably had similar head-cold experiences in your life: if you pay attention to your symptoms, you suffer. If, on the other hand, you're able to ignore your symptoms, you wind up not suffering.

With the Reflexive Thoughts of anxiety and depression you may feel anxious, panicky, distraught, hopeless, defeated, worthless, or powerless. If you pay attention to these symptoms, focus on them, as you would with a head cold, your suffering will be magnified. But if you turn away from them, ignore them, let these thoughts go, you will be on your way to liberating yourself from a life of struggle. A virus is a physical illness, so ignoring your sore throat and stuffy head offers only subjective relief, not a cure. Anxiety and depression, on the other hand, are merely habits, and when systematically ignored, they begin to crumble. Remember: symptoms of anxiety and depression need *you*, your attention, to affect you. Without *you*, there can be no anxiety or depression.

In order to endure, anxiety and depression need you to be preoccupied with your symptoms. "Why am I so down all the time?" or "What if my anxiety comes back?" This preoccupation is what allows insecurity to turn your attention inward, congesting your mind with the doubts, fears, and negatives associated with Reflexive Thinking and thereby causing you to become the unwitting recipient of your own suffering. As mentioned previously, when it comes to habits, you're either feeding them or you're starving them. Step 3, letting go, is the quintessential form of starving anxiety and depression.

Recognizing how you're feeding your habits of anxiety and depression requires what I call practiced awareness. Alex was surprised to find out that his curiosity was a form of feeding:

> I can't understand it, I seem to go for days without any anxiety or panic, feeling totally normal, and then, as soon as I tell myself, "I've been doing really well lately. I wonder if these good feelings are going to last," wham! I start to get anxious. I haven't been feeding my anxiety, not that I'm aware of. It seems to come from nowhere."

By Alex's asking, "I wonder if these good feelings are going to last," he's turning his attention toward anxiety. He's becoming curious about whether he will continue to feel good. If he had adequate trust, he wouldn't have to be wondering about this; he would just assume it. I mention Alex's frustration because it illustrates that feeding isn't always as obvious as, "I know I have a mental illness," or "I'm nothing but a failure." Feeding insecurity can indeed be subtle, and that's why learning to let go is so important.

Self-Coaching Reflection
Remember insecurity's three tip-off words: doubt, fear, and negativity. When in doubt, ask, "Is what I'm feeling a doubt? A fear? A negative?" If so, then suspect that you're feeding.

Self-Coaching Heads-Up
In chapter 12 you're going to be introduced to a follow-through concept called Reactive Living. Reactive Living is such an important Self-Coaching component that at one point I thought of making it an additional Self-Talk step. After some careful deliberation, I've come to realize that it's more of a hyphenated step: letting go–living reactively. As much as letting go and living reactively go hand-in-hand, I recognized that Reactive Living requires a strong Self-Talk foundation *before* you can ensure that your efforts won't become contaminated by insecurity (which is why I choose to include it as a follow-through part of the program). I mention this now, because I want you to have a heads-up on the complete picture that *letting go and living reactively* comprise the quintessential formula, guaranteed to starve anxiety and depression.

❖ ❖ ❖

TRAINING SUGGESTION

Two Words That Can Save Your Psychological Life

When it comes to psychological struggle, it's not unusual for your well-intended Self-Coaching plans and efforts to be undermined by the emotional chaos of the moment. You might, for example, start out by telling yourself, "I have nothing to worry about; he said he isn't going to leave me," only to find out a few minutes later that you're spinning with anxiety and panic, "What if he does leave? How will I manage? I can't breathe." When struggling with intense emotions, remember a simple catchphrase that can make all the difference. From now on, when you begin to feel disoriented by insecurity, take charge, be assertive, and stay focused by telling yourself, "Stop and drop!" With two words, you *stop* the runaway train of Reflexive Thinking, then *drop* it. Let it go. Stop and drop.

❖ ❖ ❖

124

How to Survive a Panic Attack

A rip current is a powerful current of water that flows away from shore. An unsuspecting swimmer basking in the luxuriating surf one moment may be unexpectedly drawn out to sea the next. In the ocean, rip currents can be killers, accounting for over 80 percent of rescues performed by lifeguards. It helps to think of panic as a rip current, pulling you away from your shoreline of stability and security. And just like a rip current, your life can go from calm to chaos in an instant. If you suffer from panic attacks, step 3 will become your life preserver. Here's why.

If you're an unsuspecting swimmer caught in a rip current, the absolute worst thing you can do is fight it. The force of the current will defy all attempts, leaving you exhausted and fatigued. In order to survive a rip current, a swimmer needs to relax and conserve energy by floating along with the current until he or she is finally released. If a current of panic overtakes you, the worst thing you can do is to allow your thoughts to flail about, exhausting you while inadvertently feeding the panic. Instead, try to recognize that when you're panicking, this isn't the time to figure out what's going on or even to fight back. It's just a time to float along until the rip current of anxiety lets you go. Just as any rip current will eventually exhaust itself and release a swimmer, panic, especially if it's not fed by Reflexive Thinking, will dissipate, eventually letting you go. The more you fight it and contribute to your agitation and insecurity, the more you become victimized.

Self-Coaching will eventually build your capacity to eliminate the triggers that produce panic, but until that happens, keep in mind the simple wisdom that *less is more.* Most people, while in a panic will think, "Oh my God, what's happening to me? This is terrible! I can't handle this. I need help." When you give in to these thoughts, you're no different from the panicked, thrashing swimmer caught in a rip current. Don't be seduced by panicky feelings trying to convince you that you *have to* do something in order to survive (control) the situation. Next time you get swept up by a panic attack, try to picture a calm and knowledgeable swimmer, one who knows that floating rather than fighting makes more sense. Until you develop more trust and eliminate panic from your life, use Self-Talk's step 3 to ride out any rip current of panic you encounter.

Getting Creative

Self-Talk's first step is to distinguish between healthy thinking (facts) and Child-Reflex thinking (fictions). Then, with step 2, you decide to stop listening. Now, using step 3, you're ready for the "leap," letting go of Reflexive Thinking.

Whenever you allow your insecurity to contaminate your healthy ego, you can't avoid feeling disoriented. Self-Talk works because it helps you understand the separation that's necessary between you and your insecurity. Once you understand this separation, then it's just a matter of directing your thoughts until you begin to take your life back from Reflexive Thinking.

Are You Ready?

Self-Talk is a technique that requires practice, practice, and more practice—every chance you get. There's no need to be compulsive or rigid with your workouts, though. With a catch-as-catch-can attitude, your advances and insights will accumulate over time. Don't be greedy; be patient, and try to trust the program. I can almost guarantee you that your Child-Reflex will try to sabotage your efforts. Expect it. Remember, your insecurity trusts only its own neurotic attempts at controlling life, certainly not the prospect of change, and especially not the radical change I have in store for you.

If, because of depression, you feel overwhelmed and intimidated by your workouts, be patient. On the other hand, if anxiety leaves you panicked over whether you're progressing rapidly enough, be patient. In the chapters that follow, you'll learn many ways to motivate and sustain your daily workouts. For now, try to embrace every effort, no matter how small or how infrequent. Keep reminding yourself that it's impossible for the twisted thinking of insecurity to thrive in the cold, clear light of objective reality.

Think of your workouts as accumulating pieces of a jigsaw puzzle. Your job is the simple task of adding a piece here, a piece there—an insight, an observation, an intuition—always accumulating information about your Child-Reflex's distorted, insecure thinking. Encourage yourself to stay focused on the accumulation of pieces to your personal puzzle: learn the distorted thinking, feelings, and perceptions that precede your anxiety or depression. As with a jigsaw puzzle, although the picture may be hidden for quite a while, it may take only that next piece—then, there it is! The picture reveals itself. Similarly, the view of your objective, healthy reality will pop through the haze of distortions. Remember, no pressure, no time line. Just stick with the program, and your real truth will be revealed.

Although you will learn much valuable information in the chapters that follow, at this point, you're more than ready to begin experimenting with Self-Talk. Since most of what takes place in your mind can seem very logical, especially when you are caught up in intense emotion, it's often necessary to personalize your approach. Some people prefer tape-recording their results at the end of the day, using a tape recorder to have an actual dialog, switching voices to represent both their insecure voice and their healthy voice. Others prefer the no-frills method of discerning facts from fictions by keeping an ongoing, two-column list; one side for "facts that I need to be aware of" and the other for "fictions that trip me up." I had one patient who preferred sketching. Her caricatures were impressive, showing a child snarling, stamping her feet, and on one occasion, spitting. Be creative.

As important as are separating fact from fiction or stopping the runaway train of Reflexive Thinking, they are essentially preparatory steps that enable you to take that final leap contained in step 3, letting go. This is where you finally begin building a foundation of self-trust. And this is where you begin to become impervious to anxiety or depression.

Self-Coaching Reflection

You can always encourage yourself to let go of insecurity by reminding yourself, "It's just a habit!" Regardless of how you traditionally react to your Reflexive Thinking, from now on remember, "Anxiety, just a habit!" "Depression, just a habit!" "Doubt, just a habit!" "Negativity, . . . !" And if it's *just a habit*, then go ahead and take the shot, and let it go.

✢ ✢ ✢

TRAINING SUGGESTIONS

Alternate Nostril Breathing

Here's a technique I learned from my practice of yoga. It's a powerful way to step apart from any struggle, whether panic, anxiety, or depressive thinking. Alternate nostril breathing can help you break the pattern of a runaway Reflexive Thinking train.

Simply sit up straight, press the right nostril shut with the right thumb, and inhale for a count of three seconds through the open left nostril. Next, squeezing both nostrils shut with the thumb and index finger, hold the breath for three seconds, then release the thumb holding the right nostril and exhale through the right nostril for a count of six. Repeat the same process in reverse: inhale for three seconds through the right nostril, hold three seconds, exhale six seconds through the left nostril. Continue until you are relaxed and free from intrusive, reflexive thoughts.

The meditational effects of this technique are profound, but for our purposes of stopping and letting go of Reflexive Thinking, it's almost foolproof. Since it requires concentration, precise counting of breaths, switching nostrils at the proper moment, and most important of all, breathing evenly with no jerks or pauses, it's almost impossible to stay involved in Reflexive Thinking. A simple technique such as this can begin to teach you in a very direct, hands-on (pun intended) way that letting go and liberating yourself from insecurity's reflexive living is as simple as three-three-six. By finding out that you can willfully step apart from the deleterious effects of Reflexive Thinking, you will begin to understand the ultimate truth that anxiety and depression are choices.

✢ ✢ ✢

✤ ✤ ✤
TRAINING ASSIGNMENT

In chapter 11, you will be given specific instructions for setting up a training log. If you're feeling ambitious and want to get a head start, use the following chart on a daily basis. You can include these charts later in your log.

Start by recording as many anxious or depressed incidents as possible, filling in steps 1, 2, and 3. Once you get used to spotting your Child-Reflex and your Child's unique expressions, you will be able to recognize your Child immediately, without any aids.

Self-Talk Training Log

Describe any anxious or depressed incidents	Step 1 Were you able to determine whether your thoughts were facts or fictions?	Step 2 Were you able to stop listening to Reflexive Thinking?	Step 3 Were you able to let go of your reflexive thoughts and move on?
	☐ Yes ☐ No	☐ Yes ☐ No	☐ Yes ☐ No
	☐ Yes ☐ No	☐ Yes ☐ No	☐ Yes ☐ No
	☐ Yes ☐ No	☐ Yes ☐ No	☐ Yes ☐ No

✤ ✤ ✤

10

Self-Talk: Follow-Through

I learned about follow-through watching my son. Justin was a kicker and punter on the Princeton football team. After many a session with Justin and his coach, I kept hearing the same thing repeated after every kick: "Head down, follow through, let your leg swing through the ball." You'd think that once your foot contacted the ball, that would be enough to send it skyward. Nope. The results depend on the leg swinging through, beyond the ball, completing the motion. In sports, follow-through means finishing your motion. In Self-Coaching, once you succeed at directing your thinking away from your Child-Reflex, you need to follow through, not with continued motion, but with continued insight.

In order for you to successfully apply Follow-Through to your Self-Coaching efforts, you must first develop a working ease and familiarity with Self-Talk's three steps. Once you're comfortable using Self-Talk to challenge your Reflexive Thinking, you'll be in a position to use Follow-Through as a turbo-charged way of accelerating your progress. Using data from your personal history combined with an awareness of the emotional trends that have contaminated your life, you'll be in a pro-active position to eliminate psychological friction in your life.

Insecurity: A Time Traveler

In a previous chapter I mentioned that the tendency to become preoc-cupied with past or future thinking is what I call time travel. Now, I'd like you to think of your Child-Reflex, which is associated with insecurity, as a time traveler. The reflexive habits of insecurity that sustain and feed your anxiety and depression today are nothing more than vestiges of your past, established years ago, that have managed to travel with you into your present. As a child, when you faced vulnerability or helplessness, your motive was simple—survival. A child of an alcoholic parent, for example, may resort to becoming emotionally withdrawn, perfectionistic, or worrisome, trying desperately to avoid chaos. Within this context, attempts to ward off insecurity by trying to control life were adaptive, understandable, and appropriate.

When, however, the original motive (survival) is no longer an issue—the person is now grown up and the alcoholic parent is no longer alive—the question needs to be asked, Why am I still acting as if my drunk father is going to criticize me? The answer is simple: habit. Insecurity and your strategies to control it have traveled with you through time, becoming your reflexive habits of today. Every other aspect of you and your life may change, but your habit of insecurity, your Child-Reflex, remains stubbornly the same. You're no longer fighting the demons of your past; you're now fighting the ghosts of your demons.

Not only is your past repeated through Reflexive Thinking, but it is also reflected in the person you've become. Who you are in the moment reflects the sum total of all your experiences, good and bad, that have preceded you. Since the past winds up in the present, there's no need for you to have to rely on historical data in order to eliminate anxiety or depression from your life. Everything you need can be found in your Child-Reflex. You may not, for example, have any recollection that your parents were overly controlling as you grew up, but by scrutinizing your Child-Reflex's oppositional, negative behavior toward your spouse, you'll have everything you need to launch your Self-Talk efforts.

Since Self-Coaching can teach you to dismantle here-and-now reflexive habits of insecurity without the need for any in-depth, historical exploration, you'll come to realize that what matters is breaking these habits, not understanding them. But there is a *but*. This doesn't mean that your past, if accessible, isn't useful; quite the contrary. Self-Coaching is opportunistic. If, through an understanding of the past, you are more inclined to recognize the inappropriate ridiculousness of your Child-Reflex ("I'm forty years old and I'm still acting like my father's going to yell at me."), then historical data can be used as a valuable adjunct to your process of Self-Talk.

Self-Coaching Tip
Follow-Through isn't dependent on a complete analysis
and excavation of your past, only on whatever
information is available to you.

When looking for relevant historical connections, keep in mind that you're after quality, not quantity. Sure, some people have almost photographic recall of every detail of past events, while others have only vague, scant images from their childhoods. The key isn't analyzing every detail; instead, what you're looking for are more obvious connections to your past (you don't want to become too compulsive about pinning down every experience that may have wounded you in the past). An example would be a grown man who recognizes that the reaction he had as a child when hearing his alcoholic father open the front door is exactly the same fear-reaction he feels today when he's about to meet someone new. As helpful as Follow-Through can be, remember that it's not critical to your success. Whatever you come up with will be helpful. And don't make the mistake of believing that an interpretation of the past will set you free. It won't. In conjunction with Self-Talk, however, it can be used as a powerful incentive to convince you that listening to your Child-Reflex makes no here-and-now sense.

Child Motives

Let's say I've been feeling depressed and want to quit my job. After applying a bit of Self-Talk—separating fact from fiction, stopping the runaway train of Reflexive Thinking, and finally letting go—I opt for a little Follow-Through. I do this by gaining insight into my Child-Reflex's motives. If I can determine why my Child is so desperate, I can begin to fortify myself for my next skirmish by understanding what makes him tick, "My Child wants to quit because he can't handle the responsibility. Why? Because he's too scared of screwing up. My Child doesn't trust me!"

Why you're withdrawn, or why you worry all the time, are shadows of your past ("I'm sensitive to criticism because my mother was a control freak. Nothing I did was ever good enough." "Sure I'm insecure. When I was young, I was overweight. Everyone teased me, even my parents."). Somewhere in your trial-and-error development, you found that certain strategies of control worked and others didn't.

Laurel, a thirty-year-old secretary, recalled:

> My mother was a great one for using guilt. It would drive me crazy. I can remember sitting up all hours of the night crying, fretting . . . sometimes I wanted to die. I really wasn't a bad kid, but step out of line and immediately my mother would let me know how terrible I was. I was "driving her crazy." I tried to be a good girl, worked harder at school, did what I was told, but invariably, something would happen and I'd get nailed. I couldn't win.
>
> I remember one time, we were at the lake, and she asked me to go to the car and get her the suntan lotion. I must have grumbled, and with much ado, my mother gets up all in a huff and says, "Fine, I'll get it myself you ungrateful, spoiled brat!" I had to do something, I was starting to feel almost dizzy with anxiety. Something clicked, I can't describe it, but I just decided that I didn't care anymore. It was like an anger toward my mother, but more. Hard to explain. I didn't like her, I didn't need her, I began to pull away from her. At the ripe old age of ten years old, I began to become independent—fiercely independent!
>
> As the years went on, I developed a complete shell around me. I found that no one could hurt me if I didn't care. Unfortunately, my shell never stopped growing, and now I'm accused by my husband of being too detached and aloof. Even my friends criticize me, calling me the "ice princess."

Laurel's withdrawal worked for her and with practice became her lifestyle.

If one strategy of control works more than another to reduce anxiety, it's likely to be repeated. A child with a volatile parent may, for example, develop a habit of emotional rigidity. Learning to think before reacting could prove the difference between a night of calm or a night of chaos. Considering such early circumstances, a primitive strategy like emotional rigidity might become highly effective. Once you begin to develop a habit's muscle, it can become a permanent fixture in your psychic life. In the preceding example, Laurel's mother has been dead for more than ten years, yet Laurel's turtlelike strategy of control remains the same. Why? Habit—and once a habit is secure, it's usually ignored. We accept it as we do the nose on our face, or the color of our eyes—it becomes who we are.

❖ ❖ ❖

Self-Coaching healing principle 5. Insecurity is a habit,
and any habit can be broken.

❖ ❖ ❖

Trend Analysis

Before discussing other Follow-Through techniques, it's important to reemphasize a point made earlier, that as helpful as the insights from Follow-Through are, they're not indispensable to your overall Self-Coaching goals. The reason I emphasize this point is because in any self-exploration, when relying on memory and historical data, there's the possibility of distortion, faulty recall, or misperception. Complete reliance on historical data can sometimes be misleading and wind up frustrating your efforts.

I remember going through most of my adult life with a rather innocuous memory from when I was growing up. I remembered jumping down the flight of stairs in our upstairs apartment. I don't know why I remembered this; I just did. We moved out of the house when I was young, and many years later, just prior to the empty house being torn down, I revisited the old place. What I saw startled me. There were thirteen steps going up to the apartment. These were divided, ten straight up, turn right, up three more. Something else caught my eye. The ceiling running above the steps was about six and a half feet high. In order for anyone, much less a child, to jump these steps, the person would have had to jump, stop in midair, turn 90 degrees and proceed, and then, because of the low ceiling, accomplish this without any arc. As anyone who has ever tried to make a long jump knows, in order to cover any distance, you need to go up as well as forward to counter the effects of gravity. It would have been physically impossible for me, or anyone else, to jump those steps.

I suspect this memory came from what I would call a lucid dream, one where you're left with such a realistic, compelling imprint that you wind up incorporating it into your memory as an actual event. Had you met me before I revisited my old house, I would have told you of my historical leap, the one that never took place!

Since your past can unintentionally be worked over, changed, or even invented, I feel it's important for you to keep in mind that an analysis of the past should be viewed with a healthy skepticism and should not be seen as *the* royal road to solving your anxiety and depression. There's no doubt that making accurate historical connections can offer you a definite advantage in your ongoing skirmishes with your Child-Reflex, as long as you don't see it as a replacement for your Self-Talk training program.

What if you find that you can't make any historical connections? If this is the case, be satisfied with more casual observations of any familiar emotional or behavioral patterns that you do notice. This is what I call trend analysis, or simply observing the trends or patterns in your life without necessarily pinpointing specific memories connected to them. "I don't know where it comes from, but I've always been shy and withdrawn," or "Seems like I was born worrying. I don't ever remember a time in my life that I didn't worry."

Sometimes, however, even long-standing trends may not be obvious ("I think I have a fear of intimacy," or "I'm not sure, but I'd say I'm too perfectionistic"). If you don't know or aren't sure, by all means, feel free to guess. For now, don't worry about mistakes; it's the workout we're after, not the accuracy.

Trend analysis is a formidable component of Follow-Through, and since you don't need to find the historical source, it is usually accessible through simple reflection and observation.

✤ ✤ ✤

Self-coaching healing principle 6. Healthy thinking is a choice.

✤ ✤ ✤

Proactive Follow-Through

You may be getting the impression that Follow-Through is a passive process of connecting the past with the present. It's not. Proactive Follow-Through is an attempt, not just to interpret your reflexive behavior using historical data or trend analysis but to actively shift your point of view toward a healthier, less contaminated perspective.

Look at the following examples. The left-hand column lists passive, helpless, victim statements (Child-driven). Compare them with the statements on the right, which are proactive, constructive attempts to Follow Through:

Passive Victim Statements	Proactive Follow-Through
I feel guilty whenever I say no.	Why do I feel I'm not allowed to say no? I don't know, maybe because I had soap shoved in my mouth when I was a kid. I'm not sure, but I do know what the truth is—I *am allowed!* What's stopping me from giving myself permission?
I can't speak in front of people.	Why do I get anxious in front of people? Is it the vulnerability? Do I feel I have to be perfect? Just because my parents were never satisfied with me doesn't mean I can't learn to trust myself and not worry so much about messing up.

reVibe

221 Colborne St, Main
Floor
PORT STANLEY ON
N5L1C2
(226) 555-9221
www.revibeportstanley.com

Mar 2, 2022
12:49 PM

PURCHASE

Authorization 467764
Receipt x5F0
OSTHR5T x 789159744RT0001

INTERAC
AID A0 00 00 02 77 10 10

Custom Amount ÷ 1	$9.00
($9.00 each)	
Custom Amount	$10.00
Custom Amount	$45.00
Sub total	$64.00
PST	$5.12
GST	$3.20
Total	$72.32
Interac 9308 (Contactless)	$72.32

APPROVED

reVibe

221 Colborne St, Main
Floor
PORT STANLEY, ON
N5L1C2
(226) 559-9221
www.revibeportstanley.com

Mar 2, 2022
12:49 PM

PURCHASE

Authorization 461764
Receipt xSFo
GST/HST # 789357944RT0001

INTERAC
AID A0 00 00 02 77 10 10

Custom Amount × 3 ($3.00 each)	$9.00
Custom Amount	$10.00
Custom Amount	$45.00
Subtotal	$64.00
PST	$5.12
GST	$3.20
Total	$72.32
Interac 9308 (Contactless)	$72.32

APPROVED

Passive Victim Statements	Proactive Follow-Through
I'm so depressed about getting old.	Why do I feel it's so terrible to get old? Is it losing my sexual attractiveness, my looks, or my health? Maybe it's just feeling less in control of my life. I've always been able to charm people, but now I probably don't anymore. What I need is a deeper sense of security and self-worth—one that goes beyond the superficial, the physical.

Whenever you become a victim of exaggerated, mountain-out-of-molehill views like the preceding passive statements, you feel as though you're sinking. When you're clobbered with panic and anxiety, you're going down like a lead weight. You start feeling powerless and helpless, unable to do anything about it. Proactive Follow-Through statements, in contrast, start with the premise that a loss of control isn't fixed in stone; it's a problem that can be solved.

When Thoughts Become Ridiculous

Just asking why is the key that eventually unlocks the mystery of your irrational lifestyle. You'd be amazed at knowing how many control-sensitive people just plod through each day, blindly accepting their self-imposed fate, their perceived lot in life, never thinking to ask why. When you do Follow Through and ask, "Why am I doing this?" on one level, you're recognizing that you have a choice. Once you understand you have a choice, you can proactively ask, "Why am I *choosing* to do this?" You won't be a victim of control any longer—the truth shall set you free. Victims, by definition, have no choice. When you eventually understand the "why" of your control, you will begin to understand the motive of your insecurity. With this insight, you'll have the added advantage of seeing just how primitive your Reflexive Thinking can be.

If you're not convinced, and want to see just how ridiculous Reflexive Thinking can be, let me introduce you to Jane and her attack of the frizzies.

Self-Coaching Reflection
Asking "why" is the first step in realizing
you have a choice.

Jane, an energetic young lawyer, called me early one morning in a panic over having a "bad hair day." (I kid you not!) "I have the most important meeting of my life in three hours," she said. "You should see my hair . . . I look like a cleaning lady! I just can't go to that meeting; there's no way. This is terrible . . . I can't let anyone see me this way. What am I going to do?"

I've been awakened by many things in my professional career, but never by a bad-hair emergency. Even if you wanted to be generous, could you possibly, on any rational level, consider this a crisis? But Jane was convinced she was having a 911 day. "I don't believe it," she said. "I'm going to blow my chance because of this damn hair. I just can't go in today . . . I mean I *can't* go in! They'll be forced to give the case to Larry."

You and I, removed from Jane's panic, can certainly see that her bad-hair day was only a molehill. To her, though, it was a mountain of a problem. Sure, everyone likes to look good, and most of us get frustrated when we don't, but would you blow a once-in-a-lifetime opportunity over the frizzies? I hope not.

How about you? When was the last time you blew something out of proportion?

A History Lesson

In Jane's case, by exploring some historical recollections along with a bit of trend analysis, we were able to shed some Follow-Through light on her obviously excessive reaction. It will help if you first understand what she describes as her professional image and where it came from. For this type of historical exploration, you don't need a Ph.D. or years of therapy, just a little common sense.

Jane's parents were selfish, uncaring people whose parenting skills were neglectful at best, appalling at worst. For example, Jane's mother frequently forgot to make Jane any supper. "Oh, I'm sorry," she would say. "Mommy ate earlier and I just forgot about your dinner. I was going to get to it." Because of this neglectful environment, Jane began to experience a trend of intense and nagging feelings of inferiority that plagued her throughout her life. This inferiority wasn't buried; Jane was very conscious of it. She just accepted it as a part of life.

Growing up, her only solace came from school. With her Shirley Temple cute looks and her relentless study habits, she quickly earned a place in the hearts of her teachers. All that mattered at school was winning attention and admiration. School was truly her salvation. School gave her what she couldn't get at home: a sense of worth and pride. As long as she managed to control her image, no one had to know what she knew deep inside—how *really* worthless she was. Jane was a straight-A student who managed to graduate at the top of every class, from elementary school all the way through law school. At the law firm where she was currently employed, her popularity and stellar performance were quickly noticed, and she was given more high-profile clients to work with. She gave 110 percent effort all the time, and she took obvious pride in calling herself a workaholic.

Regardless of her bright prospects, emotionally, Jane never progressed far from her childhood inferiority. Trend analysis revealed that she saw herself as a sham. When she was growing up, she believed her parents. She was convinced—even years after she had moved away—that anyone who really knew her, like her parents, would certainly realize how worthless she was. At all costs, she had to prevent this secret from getting out.

No wonder Jane developed such a strong need for control. She worked hard at controlling what people knew, what they felt, what they thought, and what they saw when they looked at her. She felt all this was necessary because of her secret: her worthlessness.

Jane's call to me that morning was about losing control over her precious appearance. Without her image, she felt naked. Because everything in her life was held together precariously by thin threads of control, once she began to feel exposed, an old and all too familiar emotional avalanche began to bury her. Her fantasy was that her associates, seeing her this way, would start thinking differently of her. They wouldn't want to associate with her and eventually would wind up rejecting her—just like her parents had.

Sound extreme? Of course it does, but if you combine Jane's history of insecurity with her years of patterning, you can understand how and why such extremes exist. Jane's reaction is a vivid illustration of how mountains begin their lives as molehills, or in her case, bad-hair hills. Jane's history also reveals an important point about the general nature of control: it's driven by insecurity.

Insecurity is the bedrock on which control rests. Jane's insecurity clearly had nothing to do with her ability to perform. She'd been a star all her life. Her insecurity was an extension of her underlying life-long trend of feeling worthless. Her performance was simply a veneer masking her well-kept secret.

Separating Fact from Personal Fiction

In therapy, Jane's tenacity and seasoned work ethic proved to be an indispensable asset in dismantling her insecurity. Using Self-Talk, Follow-Through, and various Self-Coaching techniques discussed in this book, Jane quickly began separating facts from personal fictions. Her new, less contaminated, more realistic self-image provided a comfort and security that had always eluded her. She learned a simple truth, one that would eventually set her free. She learned that she was okay. Actually, she learned that she had always been okay; she just hadn't known it.

Jane also came to understand that her trend of turning molehills to mountains made her particularly vulnerable to anxiety because of her perceived worthlessness. As a child, she obviously wasn't equipped to challenge these insecure feelings; what child is? The best she could do was try to avoid her pain by learning to control her circumstances.

As her burgeoning sense of security grew, Jane had one final challenge. Knowing that she was okay wasn't enough. That wasn't the hard part. She needed to *feel* that she was okay. In order to do this, Jane had to take an emotional leap of faith into unknown territory. Self-Coaching paved the way, eliminating her confusion. Her choice became simple: Should she be ruled by twisted, sloppy thoughts or by the truth? Jane chose truth. Sure, she had to go against all her neurotic thoughts and risk believing—*really* believing—that she was okay, but once she did, the need for control began to evaporate.

Seeing and understanding your "truth" (that is, an objective view of who you are) is half the battle; the other half has to do with trusting what you see, accepting it, and living it. Because you've been hurt for so long by Reflexive Thinking, expect some confusion differentiating between real truth and neurotic truth. One helpful rule is to be skeptical of any "truth" that seems too negative (such as, "I'm just a drunk and a cheat. I don't care about anyone else except myself. I don't care who I hurt. Life sucks.").

Given the right circumstances, emotional security, and some proactive, straight thinking, people invariably find that their truth—their real truth—is positive and compatible with others. It's insecurity's twisted stranglehold that produces false, negative and hostile untruths. For now,

141

just trust that as you continue to straighten out distorted, Reflexive Thinking, your truth will reveal itself to you. Like a mountaintop hidden by clouds, it patiently awaits your discovery. Here are two things to be aware of:

1. Self-Talk and Follow-Through, by eliminating Child-Reflex thinking, will bring you to a realization of your truth.

2. Recognizing your truth is only 50 percent of the battle; the other 50 percent is embracing it.

Like Jane, you can learn to let go of excessive control and start to trust your innate capacity for handling life. You do this through your basic training. If you want to run a marathon, you have to build a foundation, or base, consisting of long weekly mileage. Without an adequate base, you will not only jeopardize your goals but also risk injury. Psychological Self-Coaching, like marathon training, requires a base; that's what Self-Talk and Follow-Through teach you. It's this base of mental clarity on which everything else is built. Once you've established your base, you're ready to rumble.

Getting Hooked

A simple and useful extension of trend analysis: try to find your *hooks*. A hook is any trend that you typically get snagged on. In Jane's story, Jane's hook was her bad-hair day. Whenever your insecurity gets hooked, it's hard to maintain any objective perspective. Once you lose perspective, a vicious cycle begins as shown on page 143.

Here are some typical hooks. Do any of these sound familiar to you?

- Do you get a knot in your stomach when the traffic light turns red? What about being caught in a traffic jam?

- Do you have a hard time accepting criticism? If someone does criticize you, do you get defensive?

- Whenever you lose, does it seem like the end of the world?

- Does it take you forever to finish a task you find distasteful?

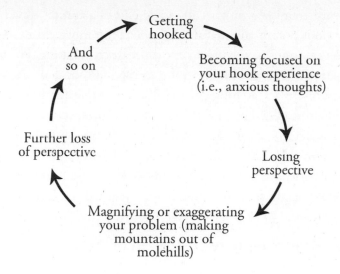

- Do you fear being on bridges, in tunnels, in open places, or in elevators?
- Does confronting someone cause you anxiety?
- Do you find asking for help to be a real problem?
- When you get sick, is your distress magnified?
- Do you have a hard time whenever anyone is angry with you?

Any of the preceding molehills can become a hook for insecurity and can quickly become major problems (in other words, mountains).

One Last Tip: How to Catch Clues

I hope that you're becoming convinced just how vital Self-Talk and Follow-Through are. By eliminating Child-Reflex thoughts, you simultaneously begin to dismantle a history of knee-jerk insecurity, allowing a more natural flow of energy and vitality to enter your life. Without the depleting effects of Reflexive Thinking (remember, doubts, fears, and negatives alter not only your emotions but also your chemistry), you also begin to restore your natural chemical balance, ensuring that anxiety and depression will never rule your life again. At this point, as you begin to initiate your training, you're at the wide end of a funnel—every piece of information is potentially useful. In time, as you move closer to your specific insecurity traps, you will become more discriminating. For now, however, maximize your gains by learning to catch any and all clues that may present themselves. Catching clues requires a simple attitude shift. Rather than feeling threatened by insecurity, shift your perspective by seeing struggle—any struggle—as an opportunity to advance your training. As a general rule, remind yourself that anything that makes you feel anxious or depressed must have been preceded by Reflexive Thinking. Ask yourself, "Now, what exactly was I thinking before I started to get so down?"

Why Do Some Symptoms Just Seem to Happen?

Sometimes anxious or depressed feelings seem to come out of the blue, leaving you convinced "I wasn't doing anything wrong; it just happened!" This is partially true. You may not have been actively feeding your insecurity when you got clobbered, but if you want to understand your meltdown, you need to know that Reflexive Thinking is cumulative. Think of a balance scale. When a good portion of your day is spent reflexively worrying, ruminating, doubting, or stressing, you're accumulating debris that begins to tilt the scale. You reach a critical point and the scale tips. Then *wham*—seemingly out of nowhere you find yourself in the grip of anxiety or depressive symptoms.

Just as the effects of Reflexive Thinking are destructively cumulative, the effects of Self-Coaching are positively cumulative. Every attempt at building trust and dismantling insecurity is an additive process that eventually will begin to tip the scales in your favor. What are you waiting for?

Self-Coaching Healing Principle 7
Thoughts precede feelings,
anxieties, and depressions.

At first, you'll be amazed how often your Child-Reflex calls the shots of your life. Sam's story demonstrates how a negative experience can become a positive opportunity for catching some clues.

Sam always dreaded his morning bus commute to Manhattan, particularly when crossing the George Washington Bridge, where he would experience extreme panic and disorientation. His anxiety was so severe that on Sunday nights he would begin pacing and panicking just thinking of the work week starting up again and his bus ride in the morning. He began to consider leaving his very lucrative job for one in New Jersey, just to avoid the commute. That's when he called me.

Using Self-Talk, we began to reorient not only Sam's thinking, but also his approach to his thinking. Rather than looking at the bridge as a negative to be dreaded, Sam began to see it as an opportunity to learn, as a teacher that could offer him clues to his Child-Reflex's twisted world of excessive fear and panic. Once he became curious, things quickly began to shift.

Sam went off to work each day determined to "catch" a few clues. It became almost a game for him. His curiosity began to challenge his anxiety. As soon as he became aware of any anxiety, Sam would rewind his thinking and hunt for twisted, Child-Reflex thoughts. No longer was he a passive victim of his anxiety. Now he was becoming proactive and eager for the bridge to yield his secrets. Sam was delighted to find out that once he welcomed the bridge as a challenge, as an opportunity to grow as a person, his anxiety quickly diminished.

The truth was that Sam's bridge phobia was nothing more than his Child-Reflex's distorted perception that he wasn't safe (that is, in control). From this hysterical notion, his Child began to pile on images of cables breaking and falling into the Hudson River far below. Sam's Child was just looking for a hook to hang his insecurity on.

Like Sam, don't be afraid to confront the challenges of your life. After being victimized by the passivity of your struggles, you'll find that a simple proactive shift in perspective can make all the difference. When catching clues, as with all aspects of Follow-Through, I offer one last bit of advice: *look, but don't dwell.* If you can't readily backtrack your thoughts and expose the trends/hooks of your Child Reflex or make any historical connections, move on. You'll be able to catch the little buggers next time, or the next. The last thing you want to do is become frustrated, causing more anxiety.

❖ ❖ ❖
TRAINING SUGGESTION

Each day, be on the lookout for any conflict, struggle, or experience of psychological friction. (Remember that conflict and struggle are opportunities to catch clues and build psychological muscle.) Use a chart similar to the following one to record your responses. (These data will be an important part of your training log, which you will learn to set up in the next chapter.)

Exercise 1: Child-Reflex Expressions of Control

Look for any thoughts that contaminate your life. Example: "I'm obsessed with my looks." _____

_____

_____

Exercise 2: Relevant Historical Connections

Look for any relevant historical connections that shed light on your current struggles. Example: "I was tormented and teased as a child because I was overweight." _____

_____

_____

Exercise 3: Trend/Hook Analysis

If you experience exaggerated, "mountain-out-of-molehill" reactions, look for your hooks (such as traffic jams, things that make you defensive, fears). It's a good idea to become familiar with this list and not let your Child-Reflex surprise you. The same holds true for patterns (trends) of behavior (for example, defensiveness, perfectionism, shyness). Example: "My trend is never to feel okay," or "Whenever I see someone with a nice body, I immediately get hooked with depression." _____

_____

_____

_____

Exercise 4: Proactive versus Passive Follow-Through

Look for any passivity in your Self-Coaching approach. Remember, passive thinking is often victim thinking. Any thinking that leaves you feeling powerless, hopeless, or doubtful is usually in need of a proactive shift. Example: "Enough with all this superficiality and insecurity! From now on I'm going to count the number of times I look in the mirror each day." _____

_____

_____

Exercise 5: Catching Clues

Shift your perspective. Recognize that in every struggle there's an opportunity for learning. Example: Instead of sitting on the beach trying to hide, I'm going to be daring and venture out into the water. I intend to listen very carefully to the ridiculousness of my Child. I suspect I might get an earful." _____

_____

_____

_____

❖ ❖ ❖

11

Motivation

Congratulations. With this chapter, you're completing the first two phases of your Self-Coaching program. You now have a basic understanding of your anxiety and depression, along with Self-Coaching's most powerful weapon, Self-Talk. In order to *guarantee* your success, however, your training program needs to add one last Follow-Through component: motivation. Yes, you heard me right; I did say you can guarantee your success, providing you have the right attitude.

Attitude Adjustment: Throwing the Switch

In the previous chapter, you read about changing passive, self-defeating thinking into proactive, positive thinking. In this chapter, you'll learn more specifically how to accomplish this shift. It's all about finding and owning that right attitude. What's the right attitude? Very simply, it's one that demands success.

What exactly is the difference between attitude and motivation? *Attitude* is a mental orientation, an emotional position, such as "Hey, I'm a good person." Attitudes shape who and what we are. If your attitude supports anxiety or depression, then you suffer. If, instead, your attitude supports healthy, constructive ambition, then expect to start feeling better. *Motivation*, on the other hand, is simply the ability and energy required to sustain an attitude. If attitude is the fire, then motivation is what fans it.

Adjusting your attitude isn't necessarily difficult. It's a matter of shifting your mental position. Sometimes this can be as easy as throwing a toggle switch. When this happens, all that was negative and frustrating gets replaced with the fire and determination to succeed. Think of times in your life when you threw that switch, times when you got fed up and decided not to take it anymore. If you can't think of specifics in your life, take a look at the list on the left and compare it with the attitude adjustments on the right.

Insecure, One-Sided Attitudes	Adjusted Attitudes
I can't do this! It's too hard. I just can't go on. Why bother?	Okay, now get a grip. The truth, the real truth, is that I can go on! Sure I'm tired, but I refuse to go on living this way. Today I'm going to be tough!
How do I know I can handle life?	I've managed to survive all these years, haven't I? Guess that proves something. It's time to risk believing what I know to be true. I can do it!
What if no one likes me?	Of course I'm going to be liked. I'm going to go to that party to socialize, be cheerful, and have a terrific time. It won't kill me.
I can't. I'm too scared!	There's nothing wrong with being scared; but the truth is I *can* do it! My Child-Reflex wants me to believe I can't, so I can avoid the pain. It's only impossible for my Child-Reflex, not for me.
There's no hope.	I'm fed up with feeling powerless. I'm really tired of feeling crummy all the time. I deserve better.

George Carlin is credited with saying, "If you try to fail and succeed, which have you done?" It's your Child-Reflex that's trying to get you to fail. For your Child-Reflex, failing is its success. Don't you allow it. Find your rebuttal, and begin living it.

It's All about Hypnosis

What you say to yourself and what you believe is a fundamental cornerstone of Self-Coaching. With anxiety and depression, you've inadvertently allowed insecurity's doubts, fears, and negatives to talk you into a life of struggle. It's a form of self-hypnosis. What do you think happens when someone gets hypnotized? Once you take away the mystique of hypnosis, it's simply a matter of getting the patient to accept and then believe the hypnotist's suggestions. In a sense, a hypnotist needs to be a salesperson, convincing you to believe the hypnotic suggestion.

I did a lot of hypnosis years ago. I found that the more I set the stage with lighting, voice amplification, timing, and delivery, the better the results: "You're going deeper, deeper into a complete state of relaxation . . . listening only to my voice . . . deeper . . . letting go of all thoughts, just listening to my suggestions." Patients looking for that magical quick fix were usually eager to be hypnotized, and the more I played into their expectations, the better the results. Whether it was quitting cigarette smoking, losing weight, or dealing with a fear of flying, hypnosis worked, and it seemed to work well. What prompted me to abandon my practice of hypnosis was the realization that although hypnosis was a great trigger that could initiate change, it unfortunately couldn't sustain it.

A hypnotist has a distinct advantage in that you, as a potential subject, project a sense of power and control onto the hypnotist. This hypnotic power really does exist, but it's not coming from the hypnotist; it comes from the patient! It's the power of the mind. Your job is to find a way to stop the negative, hypnotic effects of Reflexive Thinking and replace it by toggling over to a more adaptive belief. In life, if you believe (in a sense, hypnotize yourself) that you can move mountains, somehow the mountains will be uprooted. The power's there, if you'll only embrace it and begin to recognize that autosuggestion works. Go for it!

Positive Attitude + Motivation + Self-Coaching = Success

An attitude reflecting hope, desire, self-belief, and trust is the first step, but without adequate motivation, you'll find it hard, if not impossible, to sustain. Think of motivation as the mobilization of energy required to sustain your attitude and move you toward a healthy, productive life. The big question is this: How do you mobilize your positive energy? You start by becoming your own coach. First, two essentials:

1. You can't teach motivation; you can only instill it.

2. A good coach is a good motivator.

If your goal is to beat anxiety or depression, keep in mind that techniques and training aren't enough. Techniques and training, unless coupled with the right motivation, can sputter and run out of gas long before you reach the summit, in which case you'll shrug your shoulders and conclude that you wasted your time. In *The Divine Comedy*, Dante is guided through the bowels of hell by his guide, Virgil. Virgil, representing human reason and understanding, has been sent to lead Dante from error. In Self-Coaching, your Virgil, your guide to better understanding, is your training program. As Dante found out, however, understanding can get you only so far. Something else is necessary for the final ascent out of the depths. In Dante's case, it was another guide, Beatrice, a symbol of divine hope and love. Your program will falter without your own Beatrice—that is, your attitude of hope and conviction. Virgil and Beatrice, understanding and hope, insight plus motivation—you need both. Self-Talk teaches insight; you provide the motivation.

Pep Talks

Okay, let's get ready for a pep talk. Pep talks are another form of toggling your attitudes. The only difference is that with a pep talk, you're not just concerned with adjusting your attitude, you're also concerned with igniting motivation. Compared to a pep talk, a toggled attitude adjustment is more of an intellectual challenge, attempting to direct your thinking toward a healthier position. Pep talks, in contrast, are more spirited, emotional confrontations. You may remember an old TV commercial of a guy who violently slaps on some aftershave, then tells us, "I needed that." Pep talks are the attention-getting slap you need to awaken and mobilize your energy.

When successful, a good pep talk will leave you with a can-do attitude, by standing nose-to-nose with your Child-Reflex and challenging it with an adjusted attitude fueled with high-octane motivation. Don't, however, minimize what you're up against. Expect your reflex to challenge you with an array of distorted, constricted attitudes. Here are some examples of the narrow, constricted attitudes you may expect to encounter:

- "Yes, but" statements
- "I can't" statements
- "I should" statements
- "I have to" statements
- "What if?" questions
- Put-down statements, such as "I'm not smart (strong, tall, pretty, handsome, rich, educated, or successful) enough"
- Whining statements, such as "It's too hard (too much, too confusing, too long, or too complicated)"

Let's challenge each of the foregoing statements.

Constricted Attitude Statements	Pep Talk
"Yes, but . . ."	"No, not 'yes but'—*yes* period! There's no 'but' about it. I can be strong enough—I will be strong enough. I don't have to undermine every positive I have. No more 'buts'! From now on, I risk saying 'yes' without doubting."
"I can't . . ."	"Who's saying I can't? Maybe my Child-Reflex, but not me! I can succeed if I'm

	willing to risk believing in me. And, yes, I'm willing to take that shot—right now!"
"I should . . ."	"I don't have to be compulsive. If my Child-Reflex doesn't like it, too bad! I can live with that. I *will* live with it."
"I have to . . ."	"Baloney! I don't have to do anything I don't want to. All I have to do is be strong enough to accept this—and I am!"
"What if . . . ?"	"I don't have to anticipate life; I just have to be strong enough to live it. I trust that I can handle what life throws at me—and I can handle it without living in constant fear all the time. Just watch me!"
"I'm just not smart enough . . ."	"I'm smart enough to know that my Child-Reflex is trying to find an excuse. I don't need to be different, I need to *think* differently—positively! I'm smart enough."
"It's too hard . . ."	"It's hard, but I can handle it. I can handle whatever my Child-Reflex throws at me. I can handle it because I refuse not to! I choose to succeed, and I will handle whatever it takes."

A pep talk is an opportunity to get tough. It's the only time when you want to use black-and-white thinking. You have no room for wishy-washy attitudes here. You're all business, and your job is to get the team up and ready for the challenges ahead. It may help you to play the role of a coach, rather than just to think of yourself as one person. Step out of your Child-Reflex script and into your Knute Rockne script. As a coach, you know that your team needs you to be completely positive and encouraging—no room for doubts or hesitations. When giving yourself a pep talk, it's important to take as much time as necessary to settle into your coaching role. Once you are centered, then let the sparks fly.

Slaying Inertia with Pep Talks

The reason you need to be motivated in the first place is inertia. *Inertia* is your natural tendency to resist change. Even if you're anxious or depressed, your Child-Reflex wants to protect the status quo: it's better to work with the devil you know than the one you don't know. In order to get beyond your reflexive negativity and inertia, you have to expect it. Expect it, then kick butt! Remember, you'll need to be encouraging. Do this with regular pep talks. Keep the following in mind:

- Some inertia is inevitable—doubts are normal.
- Motivational clichés are helpful. Find one that works for you, and use it.
- Visualize yourself as a "coach," prancing around the locker room getting yourself pumped up.

As your own coach and motivator, it's all up to you. When you're caught up in the throes of anxiety and depression, obviously the going can be tough. That's when you need a pep talk the most. No matter how overwhelmed or beat up you feel, just hang on, wait for a break, and then take your next shot. It's the accumulated efforts of Self-Coaching that eventually topple the Reflexive Thinking stranglehold on your psyche. Every opportunity to resist or fight the Child is one more step toward building the strength and muscle necessary to liberate yourself.

It's Time

I wish I could be as clever as the people at Nike and offer you a "Just Do It" slogan for you to carry with you, but your motivation won't come from me. Nor will it come from a simple slogan. As important as positive thinking, positive affirmations, or even pep talks can be, they represent only 50 percent of the solution; the other 50 percent is positively believing (that is, letting go of Reflexive Thinking's doubts, fears, and negatives). Once you take the leap of faith that trusts you can, then you will. You'll find your best slogans and pep talks, along with all your motivation, in your own heart. It's the believing part that's up to you.

Granted, that leap of faith toward self-trust may feel risky, but trust me, it's really not risky; it only *feels* that way. You've lived long enough with pain and suffering; now it's time for action, time to demand the quality of life you deserve.

Your Child-Reflex has no power to run your life; it can't exist unless you keep it alive by feeding it. Only you possess that power. Reflexive Thinking is able to do what it does because you have inadvertently allowed it. Now you know better. Now you have no more excuses.

I hope my program serves you well. I've used it for years with my patients and with myself. From personal experience, I can tell you that the answers you seek aren't complicated. Actually, they're rather simple. See your goal for what it is—breaking the habits of Reflexive Thinking, nothing more than that.

Putting It All Together: The Training Log

When I self-coach for a marathon, I find a training log to be indispensable. For example, notes reflecting distance, time, weather, physical condition, heart rate, and even mood prove to be essential for analyzing and understanding what's going on with my training. A couple of years ago, I was struggling to understand a disturbingly steady decline in my overall performance and stamina. I turned to my training log and reviewed the previous month's entries. I didn't have to look far. I found that after each Wednesday's hill workout, my times and performance dipped for at least two or three days. By the time my performance began to stabilize, it was time for the next hill workout. The conclusion was obvious, I wasn't recovering sufficiently from these strenuous workouts! I started taking the day off following a hill workout, and guess what? My performance not only rebounded, but it quickly improved.

The last—and often the most important—part of Follow-Through is keeping an ongoing training log. Whether you are planning on running a marathon or charting your Self-Talk progress, a training log is an indispensable tool for gaining insight. Sometimes your log will offer startling revelations, and at other times it will show a more subtle chipping away at your Child-Reflex's defenses. Not only will your log give you an overview of your program and your efforts, but it will also act as an ongoing source of feedback. Your log will help you make some very sensitive, day-to-day adjustments in your training. At the very least, these efforts will give you a sense of connection between your life and your struggles.

When it comes to motivation, your training log can really be an asset. What better place is there to challenge destructive attitudes? Look especially for your Child-Reflex's characteristic patterns of self-defeating attitudes, phrases, or words. Your job as coach and self-motivator is to represent the opposite (healthy) point of view; even if you don't completely buy it at first. Think of it as an exercise for eventually developing your winning attitude. When your Child-Reflex says no, you need to say yes. When it says black, you need to say white. Write down your responses. Reflect on them. When you come up with a positive affirmation—such as "I can say yes!"—repeat it often. Don't ever underestimate the value of repeated positive affirmations. Remember that little train? "I think I can, I think I can."

Although I will suggest a format using the training suggestions and workouts from previous chapters, your log can be as formal or as casual as you like. If your log becomes a chore, beware. This usually means that you're not getting enough out of it. Perhaps you need to put more into it. Don't be rushed. Writing in your log is a vital synthesis of the day's events and should be seen as an integral part of your program. It's important to look back through your log often. It's this comparison of daily efforts that gives you a genuine understanding of both your progress and your areas of resistance.

The training log format I suggest includes the following three key elements:

1. A section on your Self-Talk efforts

2. An ongoing review of your Follow-Through

3. Any significant incidents, insights, or daily observations

4. A section for pertinent exercises reproduced from this book.

Anyone who has ever kept a diary can attest to the fact that revealing and sometimes startling insights are not uncommon. Writing uses a different part of the brain from thinking, especially if you try not to think too much and just let your words flow. You'll be amazed, for example, how quickly your log will expose the nuances of your Child-Reflex, or how insights into your insecurity just seem to appear. The objective feedback you get from your log will also act as a catalyst for maintaining your motivation. That's why you don't want to skimp on this part of your training program.

Incidentally, because your training log will become a valuable record of your efforts, make sure you purchase a suitable binder, journal, or notebook that reflects its important function. Take a look at the sample "Training Log Format" I've included in the appendix. You can copy this format exactly or modify it to suit your unique style. You don't need to spend hours filling in every sheet each day. Instead, select the particular worksheets that meet your need for that day. Let's say that today, for example, you were working very hard at "being in the moment." You may have spent a good portion of your training attempting to be more involved with your kids and less involved with your Child-Reflex's demands. In this case, you would want to be sure to include and fill out the worksheet entitled "Learning to Get Out of Your Head."

I suggest that you print out a number of sheets of each workout, put them into a three-ring binder, and use one every time you have an update. Your log should never be about quantity, always quality. Be as thorough as you want, but if you are pinched for time, be selective and choose to record only the most important observations for that day. If, on the other hand, you find yourself getting compulsive, this is a reason to back off and relax. Challenge any compulsive, rigid, or perfectionistic tendencies. The last thing you want is for your training log to become a tool of your Child-Reflex.

You can begin your log today. The sooner you begin accumulating data, the better.

✣ ✣ ✣

TRAINING SUGGESTIONS

Pep Talk

It's really important that you get familiar and comfortable with pep talks. Throughout the day, look for any opportunity to visualize yourself as your own coach delivering your stirring half-time speech. Be black and white, be tough, and—most important—be inspirational. Look for that can-do attitude and promote it. You're going to be surprised at how effective pep talks can be.

Find Your Coaching Style

You might model your coaching style after a strong, inspirational person from your past (a coach, a teacher, a priest, or a rabbi) a historical figure such as Knute Rockne, Eleanor Roosevelt, General George Patton, Mother Teresa, or Dr. Martin Luther King Jr., or just conjure up a fictional coach. Just choose someone who gets you hopping.

PART IV

Self-Coaching: Working with Specific Personality Types

12

Self-Coaching
for Worrywarts

I was in grammar school the first time I saw a copy of *MAD* magazine at the newstand. There on the cover was this gap-toothed, freckle-faced, tousle-haired caricature of a boy with a wily grin that mesmerized me. There was something in that devil-may-care face that reflected an attitude of being totally unaffected by life's troubles. Whatever it was, it left an immediate and lasting impression on me. (Here I am referring to it almost fifty years later!)

The very thought of someone that removed, that oblivious, that liberated, made me smile. Alfred E. Neuman, the boy on that cover, knew something I couldn't even fathom. This was confirmed by his slogan, "What, me worry?" For the longest time, my slogan had been, "What, me not worry?" Unlike Alfred, I was often referred to by the very unglamorous title of Worrywart.

If you've ever thought of yourself as a Worrywart, then you're no stranger to worry. Worrying, as you know, is what your Child-Reflex does best. If you consider yourself a worrier, you're also no stranger to the phrase "what if." "*What if* I need a root canal?" "*What if* she asks where I've been?" "*What if* I get caught?" "*What if* I don't do well?" What-iffing is a Worrywart's first line of defense against things going awry (in other words, losing control). Such things as getting sick, making a mistake, messing up, being caught off guard, and feeling humiliated or embarrassed are just a few of the many things Worrywarts worry about.

161

Self-Coaching Reflection
Mountain-out-of-molehill thinking distorts and
exaggerates your loss of control. Worrying is a
neurotic attempt to get it back.

What's Wrong with Worrying?

What's wrong with a little innocent worry once in a while? For most people, nothing, but for a Worrywart, worry is anything but innocent—or "once in a while." Worry, especially chronic worry (which is the cornerstone of anxiety and depression), exacts a psychological price that is often exorbitant. Physically, our bodies may translate the stress and tension of worrying into headaches, stomach distress, hives, insomnia, reduced immune-system response, or even heart attacks—not to mention anxiety and depression. Whether we're warding off a common cold or being susceptible to cancer, there's no doubt our bodies abhor worry.

Emotionally, worrying is no bargain either, leaving us feeling off balance, insecure, and often quite frantic. We become glass-half-empty pessimists, wringing our hands as we try to anticipate what might go wrong and how we're going to handle it. Worrywarts worry because their world has become riddled with doubt and distrust. If you can't believe in life, you're doomed to fear it. If nothing else, worry gives you a sense that at least you're doing something to brace against life's curveballs. I guess you could say that spitting in the wind is *doing* something.

Why We Worry

Unfortunately, Worrywarts feel there's little or no choice but to worry. For them, worry is the only way to survive having things go wrong. Heaven help them if they get a bit complacent, lazy, or too relaxed—*wham!* Life will deliver them a blow from which they may not recover. If you're a worrier, you're probably convinced that if you just worry enough, you may be able to figure out (control) all those what-ifs and then stop worrying. In a sense, you worry so you won't have to keep worrying.

Sometimes, worry is a form of damage control: because you're expecting the worst, you try to minimize the pain, and sometimes worry is just panic translated into thoughts. If, for example, you can't believe you'll survive that important meeting in the morning, you might find that the anticipation of losing your job, being disgraced, and never, ever having another opportunity throws you into a Chicken Little mentality. When the sky begins to fall, don't count on getting much sleep.

Self-Coaching Reflection
Worrying is the anticipation of chaos.

Recall from earlier chapters that all forms of control—not just worrying—are attempts to counteract what you feel insecure about. Because you have so little trust in your capacity to handle life—to be spontaneously successful—you begin *what-iffing* in a twisted attempt to figure out what can go wrong before it happens. You become seduced by the notion that if you can figure out what's in store for you (time traveling), then you can feel less vulnerable, or if not less vulnerable, then at least braced and ready. It would be like knowing the questions that are going to be asked on a test. Even Chicken Little's panic was an attempt to do something, anything, rather than let the sky keep falling.

Self-Coaching Reflection
We try to control what we feel insecure about.

Worry versus Concern

Don't get me wrong—I have nothing against planning. After all, who wouldn't agree that it makes good sense to prepare for a presentation, to check the fluids in your car before a long trip, or to dress appropriately for bad weather? Anticipation of life doesn't make you a Worrywart. It's when your anticipation focuses on those things that might go wrong—the doubts, fears, and negatives—that good common sense is exchanged for the not-so-good sense of the Worrywart.

Whenever I give a talk, I can count on someone asking, "Isn't worry a normal part of life? I can't imagine what would happen if I didn't have *any* worries. You've got to admit, sometimes worry can be a good thing." My response is always the same, "No, worry is *never* a good thing!" The reason I respond so adamantly has to do with understanding the difference between worry and concern.

Being concerned has to do with circumstances and facts. Let's say you hear that sleet is expected for the morning commute. It's good common sense to be concerned and to anticipate the extra drive time and get on the road a half hour earlier. No problem here. Given the same scenario, the Worrywart may also hit the road a half hour earlier, demonstrating the same good common sense. Then, unfortunately, since worry is driven by Reflexive Thinking, it's not fact or circumstance that determines the Worrywart's thoughts, it's insecurity. "What if I get stuck in traffic? What if I have an accident?" What-ifs are not facts; they're mental fictions generated by insecurity. And that's why worry is never a good thing.

Self-Coaching Reflection
Being concerned is healthy because it is fact based.
Worrying is destructive because it is fiction based.

Because *what-iffing* is based more on reflexive projections of insecurity, worrying has very little to do with actual problems (facts) or their solutions. A Worrywart suffers from chronic, often intense, insecurity. In the preceding example, it's not the difficulty with the morning commute that initiates the what-iffing, it's the worrier's insecure presumption: "Nothing ever goes right for me. I can survive only if I prepare for the worst."

Understanding Panic

Sometimes, worriers are inclined to add an element of hysteria to their worry. This can result in the devastating cocktail called a panic attack. Panic attacks are triggered by a faulty perception that you're losing control and can't handle some aspect of life. Accompanying this perception are typically intense and gripping emotional and/or physical symptoms.

Emergency rooms are no strangers to these attacks. When, after a battery of tests, frantic would-be heart attack victims are told to go home ("There's nothing wrong with your heart; it's only anxiety. You're having a panic attack"), they're devastated, unable to believe that the heart palpitations, light-headedness, disorientation, and sense of doom were "all in their mind."

Given extraordinary circumstances, panic attacks aren't that unusual. Someone yelling "Fire" in a crowded movie theater might create a chain reaction of panic in much of the audience. Panic in a traumatic situation is normal, and quite contagious. If you're a Worrywart, living your life primed and ready for panic, well, let's just hope no one is between you and that exit door. The biggest problems Worrywarts face aren't fires or traumas, however; they're things such as elevators, bridges, open spaces, flying, driving, speaking in public, taking tests, and of course, all the imagined possibilities of chaos that exist in the world—all those what-ifs.

You may not realize it, but worrying isn't a free lunch. Every time you indulge a worry-thought, you're not only eroding your confidence and trust, you're also increasing your general level of insecurity. And it's this accumulation of insecurity that can reach a tipping point, launching you into a panic attack. For this reason, sometimes a panic attack may seem to come out of nowhere. "My heart just started feeling funny, then I felt light-headed. Everything was going just fine; I was relaxed and having a good time. What's going on?" Although panic (as well as anxiety and depression) may at times seem independent of what's currently going on in the moment, don't let this perception fool you: somewhere recently, you've been feeding your insecurity.

If you find this to be the case for you and you're not able to put your finger on a specific Reflexive Thought that triggered your panic, begin to focus more aggressively on your overall Self-Talk efforts. By recognizing that worry fuels all your struggles, you can effectively use Self-Talk to minimize the needless buildup of insecurity. And if your insecurity is never permitted to reach critical mass, you can eliminate panic from your life. It's that simple. By rolling up your sleeves and patiently challenging Reflexive Thinking wherever and whenever you can, one thought at a time, you'll finally be giving your trust muscle that long-needed shot of confidence.

Self-Coaching Tip
When symptoms, especially panic, don't seem to be connected directly to any preceding Reflexive Thought, look to the past twenty-four hours and see if you've been feeding your insecurity with worry.

Remember the classic children's tale of Chicken Little? In the story, when an acorn hits Chicken Little on the head, he, in true Worrywart fashion, becomes convinced the sky is falling. Running hysterically through the streets, he begins to infect the likes of Henny Penny, Ducky Lucky, and Cocky Locky with his panic. As Chicken Little and his band of Worrywarts find out, it's their panic that provides Foxy Loxy with a meal ticket. The moral of the story for you: when panic takes over, you can be devoured by it.

There Is a Better Way

In any given confrontation, if you remain relatively calm, not only will you think more clearly, but you'll also become more instinctual about protecting yourself. Rather than confining your reactions to your Child-Reflex's hand-wringing thoughts, doesn't it make more sense to trust your psyche's instinctive, intuitive ability to do what's necessary? It sure does. Remind yourself that anticipation and worry are not facts: "If she says that, then I'll say such and such. . . ." Just as the concept of time travel is a favorite theme of science-fiction writers, so too is psychological time traveling (that is, leaving the factual present for the nonfactual future) a favorite theme of all Worrywarts. When you're willing to risk staying in your present, trusting that your instincts and intuitions will handle your unfolding world, then you'll be opening up your full potential to live without the fear that makes you worry about what may—or may not—be coming around the corner.

The Ultimate Goal: Becoming Reactive to Life

If you're a worrier, you may agree that a more spontaneous, less scripted life sounds more desirable than the congested, fretful world you live in. You may agree, but you won't trust it. You're wedded to the belief that you can make it through life only if you've braced and rehearsed for it. According to the twisted thinking of your Child-Reflex, this can happen only if you worry. Let's say I were to initiate a rather preposterous experiment where, without any provocation, I threw a pillow at every Worrywart who entered my office. It wouldn't surprise me if there were a few who would be convinced they should somehow have been able to anticipate that I might do that: "Why did I let that happen?"

Worrywarts believe (or at least act as if they believe) that life is a kind of mathematical code that what-iffing can break, if they work hard and long enough. When something surprises them, they shake their heads and say, "I should have known that was coming." Worrywarts leave no room for messing up—it's too dangerous: "What if he throws a pillow during the next session?" Unfortunately, worrying generates anxiety, tension, apprehension, and depression—proven antagonists to clear and effective thinking.

The simple truth is that if you choose to handle yourself in a rigid, narrowly defined, or rehearsed way, you become less effective, one more victim of control. A better choice is to work on your Self-Talk steps, learning eventually to "let go, let life." You do this by becoming more reactive to life: when pillows and other life challenges are thrown at you, you trust in your instinctual, intuitive capacity for survival, knowing you'll react appropriately.

At first, being reactive to life may sound impossible, but the truth is you do it all the time in nonthreatening situations. Think about a conversation you've had with someone you're totally comfortable with—a spouse, a parent, a sibling, or a friend. Your "comfortable other" said something and you responded. The conversation flowed spontaneously, back and forth in this manner, right? You weren't thinking, rehearsing, or worrying what you were going to say, you were just reacting and responding to the ongoing dialogue, in the moment, allowing the conversation to just happen. This is being reactive! When you step out of your worried, anticipatory, controlling mind (which happened in your "comfortable other" conversation because you were feeling secure) and allow your instinctual, intuitive reactivity to occur, good things happen. Being reactive to life lets you step out of the logjam of worry-thinking and allow life to flow more naturally and effectively.

Before leaving this concept of being reactive to life, I need to offer a caution. A young man came up to me after a talk I gave recently, challenging what I had said. "I think you're wrong. I was reactive the other day and wound up being totally embarrassed." I asked him to explain, which he did. "I was trying to return a Christmas gift when the salesgirl informed me 'I'm sorry sir, you can't return this here.' I saw red. I remember thinking, They're trying to screw me! I knew it, I'm not going to let them do this to me!" Yes, this guy was being reactive, but, unfortunately, he was being reactive to reflexive, insecure thinking ("They're trying to screw me!"). The real reason he couldn't return the gift, as he later found out, was because it was purchased at another department store.

Unless you use your Self-Talk to establish a foundation of self-trust and awareness, you, like our embarrassed fellow, may find your reactions contaminated by Reflexive Thinking, not facts. I offer this caution only to ensure that you see living reactively as an additional part of your Follow-Through efforts, not as a replacement for the Self-Talk training that must precede it.

Self-Coaching Caution
Living reactively is part of your Follow-Through training, not a replacement for Self-Talk.

Soapbox Derby Lessons

Once you establish a foundation of self-trust, living reactively needs to become your goal as you release the braking effects caused by worrisome doubts, fears, and negatives. I remember one such "braking" experience I had one summer when I was about nine years old. Using old discarded lumber and some rusty baby carriage wheels, I managed to build my first soapbox cart (every boy growing up in the fifties dreamed of one day participating in the soapbox derby held each year in Akron, Ohio). My soapbox wasn't much to look at, but it was functional, sporting a state-of-the-art friction brake, a rudimentary steering device, and a bright red enamel finish compliments of a serendipitous discovery I had recently made in our garage.

I took the cart to the longest, steepest hill in town. Sitting poised at the top of the hill, eagerly anticipating my maiden voyage, my mind began to wander. What if I crash? What if I can't steer? In spite of my worry, I nonetheless began my descent. Unfortunately, I kept grabbing the brake. At the bottom of the hill I was fuming. I had ruined what could have been a great ride. Soapbox in tow, determined to override my fear and risk trusting my little cart, I doggedly climbed back up that long hill, vowing with every laborious step not to use the brake on my next run. I'll never forget that next ride! I probably hit thirty miles an hour as I flew down that hill, wind whipping at my hair, feeling nothing but this incredible exhilaration, excitement, and satisfaction. This was what my cart was meant to do.

How about you? Is worry limiting your exhilaration and excitement for life? If you want to give it a go and release the braking effect of Reflexive Thinking, then next time you go to a party, don't anticipate, just show up and react. Meeting someone new? Don't rehearse, just trust and react. Worried about how you'll handle tomorrow? Why not wake up and just put one foot in front of the other and find out how it unfolds? This is reactive living. This is courageous living. And this is what you were meant to do.

Letting Go—Living Reactively

I've found in my practice that simply telling someone to let go and not focus on the doubts, fears, and negatives associated with anxiety or depression is often met with confusion, "I just don't seem to be able to get it. The more I try to let go, the more I find myself thinking about letting go and getting frustrated." The simple remedy for this confusion is learning to become reactive to life. Here's a simple visual that illustrates this important point.

Imagine that you're driving your car, windows rolled down, feeling the beautiful warm breeze, listening to your favorite CD. All of a sudden a squirrel runs out in front of your car. What do you do? Instinctively, you hit the brake while jerking the steering wheel enough to avoid the little critter. This happens without any formal thinking; you just react.

When it comes to driving a car, you don't drive around anticipating, "What if a squirrel runs out in front of my car? Should I hit the brake first or should I . . . ?" You don't do this because you trust your ability to react, in the moment, to the road's changing circumstances. Living with insecurity and worry is no different than anticipating life's squirrels (that is, the doubts, the fears, and the negatives). Next time you find yourself anticipating, worrying, or ruminating, remind yourself: stop looking for squirrels! Trust your instincts to handle and react appropriately to what crosses your path in life. Release yourself from the congestion of anticipatory worry and then turn up the music.

❖ ❖ ❖

TRAINING SUGGESTION

In order to facilitate your Self-Talk efforts, it's essential that you become familiar with how and why you worry. Because worry is the cornerstone of both anxiety and depression, you'll need to work hard at isolating this damaging habit. Use the following chart as a template for listing and redirecting your worries.

Worry Thought	Child-Reflex Elaborations (Fictions)	Directed Self-Talk (Facts)
I don't want my daughter to go on that class trip.	I know something will happen to her. What if she gets lost? No one will watch her the way I do.	I'm not going to let my Child-Reflex ruin this for my daughter. If I'm that uncomfortable, I'll call the school and discuss my concerns.
I don't want to get sick.	I haven't been sick for months. I know I'm due! My worst fear is throwing up. Now I've done it. You know what they say about jinxing yourself. Now for sure I'm going to wind up with a stomach flu!	No one likes to get sick—especially me. It does me absolutely no good to ruminate about such "what-ifs." I refuse to allow myself to think that by worrying, I can control my fate.

13

Self-Coaching for Hedgehogs

Before being influenced by our discussion on Hedgehogs, take the following self-quiz to assess any tendencies you may have. Answer each question as being either mostly true or mostly false.

T	F	My feelings often leap from dislike to hatred.
T	F	If people get too close, they will hurt you.
T	F	I often feel threatened.
T	F	I usually have to get even.
T	F	I often feel attacked.
T	F	I feel safest when I'm left alone.
T	F	I have trouble trusting people.
T	F	I'm too negative.
T	F	I'm too suspicious.
T	F	My relationships are often filled with resentment.
T	F	I'm often jealous.
T	F	I often feel rejected.
T	F	I often harbor anger that gnaws at me long after an infraction takes place.
T	F	I'm too competitive.

If you scored between 11 and 14 true, you possess strong Hedgehog tendencies and need to recognize the importance of not letting these particular habits persist without some Self-Coaching intervention. A score between 8 and 10 true suggests moderate Hedgehog tendencies. Be aware of the warnings in this chapter, and don't allow any progression toward Hedgehog hostility to develop. A score of 4 to 7 true indicates you have few significant Hedgehog tendencies. You may, however, be prone to occasional Hedgehog defenses when dealing with stress. A score of 3 or fewer indicates no significant Hedgehog tendencies.

Don't Tread on Me

Have you ever found yourself snarling at someone in the express check-out line because the person's cart had too many items? How about on the road? Do you blast your horn at another driver who's poking along when you're in a hurry? If someone hurts your feelings, do you retaliate? What about if someone criticizes you—does that person become your enemy? Is your motto "I don't get mad, I get even"? If any of this describes what you do, or what you want to do, you may have a pattern of Reflexive Thinking I call Hedgehog tendencies.

Have you ever seen a hedgehog? It would be hard to find a more adorable creature. A tranquil hedgehog held in the palm of your hand offers a wonderful experience of silky-soft comfort and cuteness. In contrast, however, when riled up and defensive (which doesn't take much for these wary little fellows), they roll up into a ball, forcing countless porcupinelike spines to project out in all directions. In this configuration, hedgehogs become unappealing to all the world.

A hedgehog protects itself by repelling danger. A control-sensitive person may use this same defense when feeling insecure and out of control. A normally amiable person may suddenly recoil with hedgehoglike spines of hostility. Hostility has a predictable effect on people: it repels and discourages them. Keeping people at arm's length is a Hedgehog way of controlling, by creating either physical or emotional distance. Hostility has many forms. It can be passive, aggressive, abusive, obnoxious, resistant, or just plain cantankerous. The result is usually the same: "No one's going to take advantage of me!"

A Hedgehog defense is of particular importance because of the profound effect it can have on your personality, as well as on those around you. While most people would agree that Worrywart tendencies are rather obvious and clearly quite stressful, Hedgehog tendencies are generally more insidious and less likely to be seen as a personal problem for the sufferer; it's always the other guy who's at fault. Since anger and hostility tend to push others away, Hedgehogs have a feeling of invulnerability perpetuated by a who-needs-'em attitude. Hedgehog defenses tend to be long-standing, relatively unnoticed, and better tolerated (for the Hedgehog, not those around him or her) than those of some of the other personality types. Although better tolerated, these tendencies are not necessarily without consequence. Because of the corrosive, defensive, negative outlook on life, Hedgehogs are particularly prone to depression and mood disturbances.

Clenched teeth, a strained voice, and a confrontational attitude may be a more traditional image of hostility, but there is another form, equally as unpleasant, but much less in-your-face. This is passive hostility. It's a favorite defense of children and of adults who act like children. Ask passive-hostile Hedgehogs a question, and you may find them pretending they can't hear a word you're saying, leaving you frustrated, angry, and powerless. Humor in the hands of a passive Hedgehog can often leave you feeling quite uneasy: "Do you think I really care that you didn't invite me to the wedding? Sure, I understand you had to limit your guest list. I was just joking when I asked if you could set a table outside the reception hall for your not-so-close friends." When it comes to Hedgehog humor, very little is ever said in jest. And if you've ever wondered about a friend who doesn't return your calls, it may be that your friend's a bit of a Hedgehog who's passively teaching you a lesson (letting you suffer) for canceling dinner plans last week. Whether hostility is obvious or passive, either way it still hurts.

Part-Time Hedgehogs

Many fledgling Hedgehogs are only part-timers. Because their confrontations are few and far between, part-time Hedgehogs have the ability to keep their spines covered up most of the time. This can be a problem, especially when it masks the burgeoning adoption of a Hedgehog way of life.

If Sam and I hadn't been working on the nature of his Child-Reflex only the week before, he might never have noticed his tendency toward Hedgehog hostility, or if he did notice, he might have quickly swept it under a rug of denial.

Sam, a thirty-six-year-old accountant, had been coming to therapy feeling mildly depressed and "aimless." Sam and his family had flown to Disney World for a long weekend. Upon arrival at the rental-car booth, he was told that the van he had requested wasn't available. Seeing the frustration on his wife's face and the impatience of his kids, something snapped in Sam's normally mild-mannered approach:

> The girl was telling me she was sorry about the mix-up and how she couldn't do anything about it. I was annoyed, but not upset. Then I hear my wife grumbling. She was obviously tired and frustrated. For some reason, hearing her complain made me feel threatened. I can't explain it, not clearly. I kind of felt I had to be more of a man. My family needed me! That's when it started. All of a sudden I was feeling hostile: Who the hell does this woman think she is? No one treats me this way!
>
> At first, my anger was controlled: "This is unacceptable," I said. "I don't want to hear any excuses, I want that van." The girl smirked, giving me an I-don't-need-this attitude. She was definitely challenging me! That's when I went into the red zone. In a much louder voice, almost shouting, I went on: "I want to speak to the manager. Call your manager. Just because you don't know what you're doing doesn't mean I have to tolerate it!" As my anger grew, my thinking became more muddled. I was saying things that were totally ridiculous, like, "You think I'm a fool, well you're the fool. . . . I'm going to sue . . . you just wait until I call my lawyer!"
>
> When I saw my wife's embarrassed look and my kids cringing in disbelief, my tirade ended as quickly as it started. It was like I got hit

over the head with a two-by-four. I became immediately quiet, and upset. I don't even know what the girl was saying at that point. I only wanted to get out of there. It was terrible, I was so embarrassed.

I was only trying to be strong and not let anyone take advantage of me. I wound up feeling awful. What the hell is wrong with me? I've always thought of myself as a nice guy. Yet I can turn into this monster. That girl didn't deserve what I said to her. Once I lost it, there was nothing I could do. I was totally exposed, embarrassed, humiliated. I felt like crawling under a rock!

Sam's outburst was 100 percent, grade-A Hedgehog. The sales-girl's attitude of indifference was the last straw. Sam's manhood was put on the line, along with his status as father and husband. He felt he had no choice; he had to put that woman in her place. His thinking proclaimed, "No one is going to get away with cheating my family!" What was most upsetting to Sam was the eventual loss of control he felt.

The truth is that Sam did have a choice. He could easily have protected his family without becoming hostile. Unfortunately, Hedgehogs have little trust. They believe that people will take advantage of you unless you go on the offensive. This is an impor-tant distinction. Where most people might get a bit defensive when feeling challenged, a Hedgehog will bypass defensive and go right for the jugular (with, of course, the exception of the passive-hostile Hedgehog, who prefers a more indirect, disguised approach). A healthy person might handle an attack with an assertive response by taking care of whatever business is necessary, while a Hedgehog handles a challenge (real or perceived) with aggression. For Sam, what could have been simply a matter of asserting his frustration ("I'd like to speak with a manager") ended up as his worst night-mare. Rather than establishing control over the situation, he wound up embarrassed and exposed to all the world.

In the past, similar experiences had left Sam crushed and depressed for a while, but that was it. He learned nothing because he was convinced that his hostility was necessary to protect himself. Unfortunately, Sam's confrontations were beginning to generate more anxiety and stress, so his perception was that life was becoming more chaotic. He was also worried about the progression of his negativity, which, for a Hedgehog, is a critical first step: admitting that hostility is *your* problem. Sam was primed and ready for a little Self-Talk.

Here is a condensed version of Sam's Self-Talk work.

Self-Talk Step 1 Review. Separate Fact from Fiction; Learn to Listen

Practice hearing your thoughts. Ask yourself, "Does what I'm hearing sound mature, rational, or reasonable, or does it sound primitive, excessively emotional, childish, and insecure? Is it me, or is it my Child-Reflex talking?" If it's my Child-Reflex, then it has to be a fiction.

Keeping in mind step 1, separating fact from fiction, Sam and I reviewed his narrative. The earliest hint of Child-Reflex thinking was when Sam felt threatened about not being more of a man. He could recognize the primitive, insecure flavor of his reaction, especially by the time he arrived at the specific thought *"Who the hell does this woman think she is?"* By reviewing his reactions, Sam had no trouble recognizing the presence of a Child-Reflex who was about to have a tantrum. The flash point for his tantrum was his perception, "She was definitely challenging me!" There could be many interpretations for the salesperson's response: frustration, irritation, impatience, a stomachache, or simply a long day on her feet. What Sam was doing was mind reading. He interpreted what he was seeing as nothing less than a challenge to his manhood. (Incidentally,

Sam's Follow-Through work revealed that this trend was related to his father, a burly steelworker, who was totally intolerant of any weakness or frailty in his son. Sam can still hear his father's admonition, "Be a man!")

Self-Talk Step 2 Review. Stop Reflexive Thinking
When you realize that your Child-Reflex is speaking, decide not to listen. Then make yourself stop listening!

Sam had not only listened to his Child-Reflex; he had allowed himself to become his Child. Ideally, what he needed to do in that heated moment of conflict was to stop listening (Self-Talk step 2) to the reflexive, confused avalanche of his Child's panic, and demand a more factual, adult response. In order to get to a place where he could effectively override his ranting, raving Child-Reflex, some Self-Talk training would be necessary. It's unrealistic to think that Sam, or you, can dismiss the Child-Reflex without a Self-Talk foundation of understanding and practice. Had Sam had some Self-Coaching training prior to his Disney meltdown, he might have responded, "This isn't life or death!" Then, after a deep breath, "I will not let my Child confuse me! I'm not going to let this ruin my vacation [step 3, letting go]. I do love Florida."

Self-Talk Step 3 Review. Letting Go
After you stop letting your Child-Reflex steer your thoughts, do something about it. Take a leap of faith and let go of Reflexive Thinking.

Sam also found that by personalizing his Child-Reflex, he was in a much better position to anticipate his Hedgehog reactions. He did this by calling his child Travis. It was from one of Sam's favorite movies, *Taxi Driver*, with Robert DeNiro. The character, Travis Bickle, was a tortured, paranoid, self-appointed vigilante—a perfect match for Sam's Insecure Child. Travis's famous line was "Are you talking to me?" Whenever Sam caught himself sounding like Travis, he would immediately recall the sick, demented character from the movie and have no further trouble distinguishing Travis's voice from his own healthy, factual, and more mature voice.

Sam began to understand that his hostility was based not on actual threats (facts), but on perceived threats (fictions)—served up on a platter by his Child-Reflex. Understanding this simple truth allowed him to begin directing his thinking toward more reasonable ways to handle conflict. Step 2, stop listening to Reflexive Thinking, proved to be pivotal for Sam as he began to see other options. Referring back to the example with the salesperson, Sam had the following insight:

> I wish I could go back and handle that situation with the car rental differently. I would have insisted on not taking things so personally. When you think about it, it was so ridiculous. Travis [Sam's Child-Reflex] convinced me that my manhood was at stake. I just let him manipulate me. From now on, I call the shots, not Travis! The only reason I went crazy was because I let myself get convinced I was being attacked.
>
> I'm starting to get the picture, finally. I had an opportunity this morning at the mall. I was about to pull into this parking spot, and out of nowhere, this guy coming from the other direction pulls into my spot. Travis was ready to jump out of the car, but I pushed him aside, took a deep breath, told myself that I'm not going to permit myself to act foolish, and drove off. Sure, I could have just blown my horn or said something nasty, but I know me, and I know that whenever I get into it with someone, I pay a price. A big price! It took a minute or so before I was able to let go, but I got there, and when I did, I felt pretty darn good. It wasn't much, but it sure convinced me that I have a choice. What's funny is that I don't feel any less of a man. Guess you might say I'm finally breaking that old habit.

Full-Time Hedgehogs

Unlike Sam, who was able to interrupt the progression of his Hedgehog evolution by using Self-Talk, some people allow their hostility and negativity to go on too long. Whereas a part-timer such as Sam may have some capacity for amiability, full-time Hedgehogs, even when feeling in control, tend to be chronically nasty. Take one look at Sally, and you'll quickly understand why Hedgehogs need to halt the progression.

Sally is a third-grade teacher who had had many reprimands from her principal for repeated negligence, such as coming to school late, leaving her class unattended, and so on. Sally came to therapy enraged: "I work with morons," she told me. "At the last faculty meeting, I gave them a piece of my mind. There are a lot of teachers who aren't very professional. Why should they single me out? I named names! I don't care who gets in trouble. I don't care who likes me. I shut my door when I go in, I do my thing, and I leave at 3:30." Sally was controlling the situation with her anger, and her hostility got her exactly what she wanted—everyone avoided her.

Hedgehogs live in a world divided into two kinds of people—those who threaten and those who are potential threats. It's a bunker mentality, where the enemy can be anyone—a neighbor, a boss, even a spouse. From their dark bunkers, Hedgehogs peer out at life through small window slits. With such limited perspective, traps such as tunnel vision, black-and-white thinking, or mind reading are common.

Sally, our black-and-white thinking, tunnel-visioned example, relied on her hostility to isolate her from her accusers. If you're generous—very generous—you might say it was self-defense. Sally felt she needed to defend herself against the assault of her colleagues, but the real problem wasn't coming from her coworkers; it came from within. She was unable to recognize her own irresponsible, childish behavior. Sally needed to come out of her bunker and see the bigger and more objective picture. She needed not only to straighten out her thinking, but to straighten out her perceptions and tuck in those sharp spines.

Ask yourself, has your view of life become too narrow? Are you beginning to see more negatives than positives, more threats than friendly gestures, more enemies than friends? Are confrontations becoming routine for you? Are you beginning to live your life in a bunker, overly protected and leery of attack? Most important, is hostility becoming a part of your steady diet? If so, it's time to get serious about this altogether avoidable habit.

Don't be seduced by hostility's quick-fix way of controlling a situation. Eventually, all this repelling leads to tension, irritability, sleep disturbances, social and marital conflict, negativity, and, because of the intense defensiveness of this reaction, depression. Like it or not, hostility turns you into a bully. What begins as a simple attempt to escape anxiety hardens over time into a resistant personality pattern wrought with anxiety and depression.

Hedgehog Traps

In chapter 6 you learned about various insecurity traps to avoid (should statements, what-iffing, and so on). Hedgehogs show a particular vulnerability toward certain traps: jealousy; bigotry, racism, and prejudice; competition and threats, fears, and intimidation. These traps, or hooks, can snag an unsuspecting Hedgehog with considerable force. They are linked by a common tendency to see people as the enemy.

1. Jealousy

Jealousy is a curse in any relationship, and Hedgehogs, because of their anticipation of rejection, are particularly susceptible to it. Because Hedgehogs usually expect the worst, they live in a state of constant imbalance—a state of disequilibrium that quickly becomes intolerable. In their attempt to control, Hedgehogs then become hawkish in their jealousy. Bottom line: Jealousy is just another word for oppressive control.

2. Bigotry, Racism, and Prejudice

Bigotry, racism, and all forms of prejudice are particularly troublesome Hedgehog problems. These problems are distinctive because they involve anonymous people or groups, not individuals with whom you have had conflict. These anonymous people or groups have the dubious honor of having your insecurity projected outward and attached to them. Living with projected hatred and hostility is an attempt to distance yourself from those who you feel will hurt you. In reality, it's an attempt to distance yourself from the insecurity within yourself that you feel will hurt you.

3. Competition

Even though Hedgehogs seem to thrive on competition, they really hate it. When challenged in any real or imagined way, they feel trapped, because all challenges are experienced as a threat to their control. Whether it's competing with a friend at tennis or with a coworker for the boss's praise, Hedgehogs can quickly lose perspective, becoming extremely tunnel-visioned and intense.

4. Threats, Fears, and Intimidation

Just as competition can ignite a knee-jerk hostile response, threats, fears, and intimidations are equally toxic to a Hedgehog. These intentionally aggressive experiences demand quick, compensatory reactions.

Am I a Hedgehog, or Am I Just Angry?

How can we tell when our hostile feelings are appropriate? Clearly, there are times when anger is an appropriate reaction. When someone hurts, insults, humiliates, or embarrasses us, it's only natural to feel anger. When anger is coupled with insecurity, when it's more about control than legitimate self-defense, then a hurt, insult, humiliation, or embarrassment takes on a whole new meaning. Now anger festers. Long after the affront, we are still stewing in the juices of our hostility. Festering emotions are one reliable tip-off that Hedgehog insecurity is involved.

I'm reminded of a story about two Zen Buddhist monks walking along a stream. Coming upon a young lady in distress, the older monk inquires about her problem. The young woman needs to cross the swiftly moving stream, but confesses that she is frightened to make the attempt. The older monk takes the young lady in his arms and carries her across, letting her down on the far bank. Later that afternoon, the two monks, having been walking in silence since the incident, stop to rest. The younger monk can't contain his anger any longer and blurts out: "I can't believe you picked up that young woman, allowing yourself such physical contact." The older monk replies, "I carried the woman only for a moment; you've been carrying her all afternoon in your mind." The young monk was angry, not at the old monk, but at his own suppressed desire to touch the woman. The old monk's actions were hitting too close to home, and it was too much for him.

If ever you encounter a situation where anger doesn't dissipate rapidly but instead seems to get under your skin, beware. As with the young monk, there's usually more to it. Rather than suspecting the other person's shortcomings, suspect that your own insecure personality is leaving you feeling out of control.

Self-Coaching Tip
As mentioned in the previous chapter, learning to live reactively is a goal of Self-Coaching. If, however, you're prone to Hedgehog hostility, keep in mind that impulsive, reflexive reacting is a problem for you. For this reason, it's necessary to be particularly aware of the need to use reactive living *only* as part of your Follow-Through, ensuring that it is preceded by an adequate foundation of Self-Talk.

Self-Coaching Reflection
Anger that festers is driven by insecurity.

TRAINING SUGGESTION

Tape-record your reactions to any specific situation that has caused disruption, difficulty, anxiety, or depression in your life. Doing so can really give you the flavor of your Child-Reflex. When trying to express or write down your thoughts, you're often not tuned in to the nuances of tone, feeling, and spirit that reflect the essence of your Child. This is particularly true for any Hedgehog recollection. Hearing the hostility and negativity of your Child can really be an eye opener.

Although it's not necessary to make recordings every day, I do recommend it for any significant Child-Reflex encounters. Once you begin to really hear what your Child sounds like, you won't need to rely on your tape recordings.

❖ ❖ ❖

14

Self-Coaching
for Turtles

Take a look at the following self-quiz to determine whether your natural Turtle tendencies (that is, occasional respites from stress) are moving in a direction of unnatural avoidance and control. Answer each question as being either mostly true or mostly false.

T	F	I prefer to avoid confrontation.
T	F	I prefer being alone.
T	F	I don't have many interests or hobbies.
T	F	I watch too much TV.
T	F	I prefer working alone.
T	F	Relationships are mostly problems.
T	F	I hate phones.
T	F	I don't have many friends.
T	F	I hate social commitments.
T	F	I struggle at parties.
T	F	I'm usually late.
T	F	I am more comfortable with things rather than people.
T	F	You can never be too safe.
T	F	I don't take criticism well.

If you scored between 11 and 14 true, you have definite Turtle tendencies and need to recognize the importance of not letting these particular habits persist without some Self-Coaching intervention. A score of 8 to 10 true suggests a moderate tendency toward Turtle living. Be aware of the warnings in this chapter and don't allow any progression toward Turtle escapism to develop. A score of 4 to 7 true indicates few significant Turtle tendencies. You may, however, be prone to occasional Turtle defenses when dealing with stress. A score of 3 or fewer indicates no significant Turtle tendencies.

Me, a Turtle?

When you think of a Turtle, what comes to mind? Its shell, right? When life gets too rough for Turtles, they just pull inside their old shells and wait for better times. Humans don't have shells, but sometimes they act as though they do. Anxiety and depression can encourage Turtle behavior. For the overly anxious person, pulling into a shell of avoidance may provide an effective vacation from chronic or intense stress, and for the beleaguered, depressed person, crawling into a shell can provide a sanctuary that makes the intolerable tolerable.

All Turtle experiences have one thing in common: they allow you to retreat from some aspect of life where you feel a loss of control. Once in your shell, you feel protected and secure, in control. Arguably, one of the most famous—albeit bizarre—Turtles in history was the brilliant billionaire inventor and shrewd businessman Howard Hughes. In order to ensure his complete isolation, especially in his final years, Hughes descended into a Turtle shell of paranoia and drug addiction. From his black-curtained luxury hotel rooms, the emaciated and deranged Hughes slipped further and further into a self-created Turtle world of fanatical control. One of Hughes's aides, for example, was reportedly summoned on Easter Sunday morning to chase a fly that infiltrated Hughes's sanctuary. With all the money in the world, Howard Hughes found he couldn't buy what he wanted most—absolute control.

No one, not even a billionaire, can build a perfect shell. There will always be a fly buzzing around somewhere. Clearly, not all Turtle behavior is as obvious or eccentric as Howard Hughes's. In fact, most Turtle behavior is no different from normal, everyday behavior. I know this sounds confusing, but it really isn't. All you have to know is that Turtle behavior is defined not by *what* you're doing, but by *why* you're doing it. Take, for example, watching TV, listening to music, or just reading a good book:

- If the reason *why* you're engaging in these behaviors is to relax and unwind, then you aren't behaving like a Turtle.

- If the reason *why* you're engaging in these behaviors is to control some aspect of life by providing a haven, an escape, or an insulation, then you are acting like a Turtle.

Turtle behavior is simply any behavior that allows you to retreat from, rather than deal with, life. Who doesn't need to kick back and retreat from stress once in a while? Clearly, by this definition, a little Turtle behavior can be perfectly normal, and at times a necessary part of living. We all act like Turtles sometimes. Hey, it's why we have vacations, right? Like most things in life, Turtle behavior in moderation won't harm you. Nor is it true that a little Turtle behavior now and then will make you a Turtle. Like all the traps of insecurity mentioned earlier (what-iffing, mountain-out-of-molehill thinking, black-and-white thinking, Hedgehog defense), Turtle behavior becomes problematic only when used as an ongoing strategy (not an occasional respite) to control life.

When used occasionally to recharge your psychic batteries, Turtle behavior can actually be beneficial. Unfortunately, an innocent tendency to "kick back" and regroup, especially when combined with insecure thinking, can progress into a serious habit of avoiding life's demands. Be clear on this point, however: it's not life's demands or circumstances that cause excessive Turtle reacting; it's your habit of Reflexive Thinking that creates a fiction, insisting that you can't handle these challenges. This fiction, once embraced, leaves you diving headlong into your insulated shell of avoidance.

Because life's demands can at best only be postponed, never eliminated, Turtle behavior is a habit that inevitably generates considerable anxiety and depression. Once anxiety and depression get thrown into the mix, Turtles may mistakenly think the only way out is not out, but further in—into their shells. When this happens, they've reached the point where insecure Turtle thinking has concluded that life is too difficult, too hard, and too impossible. "I just need to be left alone."

Self-Coaching Reflection
Life can be avoided but never escaped.

When we're overwhelmed, the sanctuary provided by a shell becomes more and more inviting. Why wouldn't it? It's a seductive place of quiet, peace, safety, and relative control—but don't be fooled. (Self-Coaching healing principle 4: Control is an illusion, not an answer.) For humans, a Turtle shell is an illusion of safety created by avoidance. No matter how thick your shell or how secure you feel tucked away inside one, at some point you must poke your head back out and deal with life. Of course, none of this is a problem if your shell experiences are used sparingly to provide a bit of relief from a specific stressor, such as a bad day at work or a fight with your spouse. Here, once you've licked your wounds, you're up and out of your shell in no time. It's only when occasional relief turns into frequent escape that poking your head out causes significant anxiety or depression, and sometimes both.

Aside from contributing anxiety and depression to your life, Turtle behavior also has a tendency to become addictive. For example, you might notice that one day you're staying in your shell a little longer than necessary, avoiding a bit of responsibility, copping out, or just "forgetting" about an engagement. The more you become acclimated to your shell, the easier and more attractive it becomes to stay there.

Blame it on insecure, Reflexive Thinking. Insecure thoughts are the reason you have a shell, the reason you get addicted to staying inside your shell, and most important, the reason you suffer. Procrastination is one common example of the type of insecure Turtle thinking that can leave you feeling overwhelmed and pressured. "I heard you, damn it! I said I'd do it later." Once you begin to sidestep a demand, pressure begins to build. When a Turtle says, "Yeah, yeah, I'll do it tomorrow," it's the Turtle's Child-Reflex hoping against hope that given enough time, the demand will just go away.

Your Child-Reflex prefers procrastination because it's safe. Because the Child already feels overwhelmed and vulnerable, it seems to make sense to avoid any more responsibility and further depletion. Unfortunately, however, procrastination, rather than decreasing pressure, actually increases it (because life can only be avoided, not escaped). You eventually wind up damned if you do and damned if you don't. Like plants in a hothouse, depression and anxiety thrive in this atmosphere heated up by ambivalence.

If you're already depressed, any and all Turtle behavior becomes magnified. Depression can make you feel there's no choice but retreat. Because you feel you can't deal with life anyway, going into a shell doesn't sound like such a bad deal. In fact, it may sound very appealing. Like most deals that sound too good to be true, however, this one is, too. Turtle living may begin as a haven, but it always winds up a prison.

Self-Coached Turtles

If you suspect you have Turtle problems, then it's time for some Self-Coaching. Using what you've learned thus far, you'll need encouragement to poke your head out of your shell and challenge the insecure, Reflexive Thinking that leaves you feeling overwhelmed. Self-Talk will allow you to pull away from your Child-Reflex's panic and to risk believing the truth. The truth insists that there's no reason you can't begin to handle life outside your shell. The truth says that if you want real protection, you're not going to find it locked up in a prison of a shell. The truth affirms that power, real power, is the legitimate capacity to trust your own resources to handle life. The truth allows you to see that avoiding life is never a satisfactory answer, only a sidestep.

Use the case studies presented in this chapter to get a feel for applying your own Self-Coaching techniques. Although these are examples in which I coach patients, recognize that my interventions represent what you'll be doing with your Self-Coached program. It's not that hard. With a little practice and repetition, the techniques will become predictable.

Is It Heaven or Is It Hell?

Lest you begin to ascribe Turtle symptoms exclusively to oddball billionaire types or weirdos, let me introduce you to Tom. Although his behavior is clearly excessive, it has elements most of us can relate to, especially the tendency toward avoidance. Tom, a thirty-three-year-old single automobile mechanic, was an avid movie buff. Piece by piece, he began to construct an expensive home theater system. It started with a forty-inch TV, followed by a DVD player, then a surround-sound speaker system, and finally the pièce de résistance, his $2,000 shiatsu-massage leather recliner, about which Tom couldn't say enough. "It was actually designed by NASA to provide a zero-gravity position during lift off!" Tom was truly at one with his entertainment center—and that's precisely what turned out to be the problem.

That was a year ago. When I first met Tom, guess what was bothering him? For starters, he had gained forty pounds, was staying up all night watching TV, was having a hard time at work because he was so tired, and was feeling mildly depressed and anxious. "Once I get in that chair, that's it for the night. Things got really bad when I bought one of those satellite dishes: five hundred channels. Now I just can't turn the damn thing off. I don't get to bed before two or three in the morning! I never go out. Look at me, I'm a slob. I'm not taking care of myself, not paying bills. All I do is come home and plop in my recliner. What scares me most is I just can't seem to change my behavior."

A big problem for Tom was that every time he tried to break his nighttime ritual, he became more anxious. Once his efforts were sabotaged by anxiety, he just wanted to sink further and further into his surround-sound equipped shell. A decent blockbuster movie was all it took to melt away his discomfort. Then, at least for the duration of the movie, there was no struggle, only his zero-gravity state-of-the-art media environment.

Unfortunately, the further he sank, the further out of control his life became. He had to stay constantly entertained to avoid feeling anxious. When on the job and away from his addictive lifestyle, Tom felt miserable. Life was passing him by, and he was—very literally—a spectator. His anxiety was shifting quickly to depression, especially when he considered the lack of intimacy in his life. It was this growing dissatisfaction, powerlessness, and fear that led him to me.

Tom entered therapy with some insight. He knew, for example, that just because you retreat into a shell doesn't mean life will wait for you to come out. Jobs, bills, social responsibilities, and physical and psychological demands such as diet, exercise, and relationships were all suffering. Whenever your capacity for handling life's responsibilities erodes, problems that were once easily sidestepped become highly exaggerated and overwhelming. An addictive cycle begins:

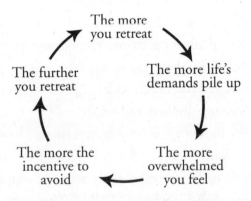

Intellectually Tom knew what he had to do. Instead, however, he listened to his Child-Reflex, which convinced him he was too weak, too tired, and too powerless to change his behavior. Interestingly, when his Child's struggle became intense, Tom usually wound up heading for the kitchen for cookies and milk, just as he did twenty-five years earlier, when his mother upset him by making him finish his homework. (Some habits have very long tails.) Night after night, Tom found himself no match for his Child-Reflex, as he allowed himself to sink further and deeper into his world of avoidance. And the more he sank, the more depressed he became. Poor Tom; his hi-tech sanctuary was supposed to bring years of bliss. As they say, be careful what you wish for!

Shell-Shocked

Using Self-Coaching, Tom and I began to look at his Child-perpetrated, insecure thinking. He had become convinced that he, unlike a normal person, was too weak to handle life. Actually, at this point he was right. Once depressed, Tom began to feel emotionally and physically drained. The further he went into his shell, the more inactive he became, and the more fatigued he felt. He recognized that his lack of exercise, weight gain, loss of sleep, and depressed mood were all contributing to his mental and physical malaise. From inside his dark shell, however, doing anything about his predicament was just too much to ask. "It's too hard!" No wonder Tom reported feeling drained and tired.

Initially, Tom thought the only reason he was having problems was because he had become addicted to his TV and had let too many things pile up. This was a fairly accurate snapshot of Tom's dilemma. Using Self-Coaching's Follow-Through, however, we were able to establish that it was his entire lifestyle—long before his TV addiction—that instigated the construction of his elaborate shell.

As far back as he could remember, Tom had never had any luck dating. This, more than any other factor, was an enormous stressor that played heavily on Tom's mind. The months leading up to his TV purchase were filled with insecure and panicky ruminations about never finding a wife and spending the rest of his life alone. He had begun to drink, not excessively, but nightly. He knew he needed to do something about his anxiety and depression but didn't know what. It was during this tailspin period that Tom happened to walk past a surround-sound home entertainment center set up at a local electronics store. His decision was made on the spot.

Tom was a loner from as far back as he remembered: "When I was in school, I stayed to myself. I wasn't a joiner. Maybe I was shy, or maybe I was just insecure." Tom's Follow-Through efforts were finally allowing him to nail down the "why" aspect of his behavior. He now recognized that his media addiction was both a compensation for and a distraction from the life he wasn't living. This left him with a lose-lose choice: poke his head out into a world of frustration and rejection, or stay in his shell getting more and more depressed. The answer we came to was simple and straightforward. Poke your head back out into the world, but instead of living with distorted, insecure, Child-Reflex thinking, replace it with effective Self-Talk.

Tom never enjoyed being a Turtle. He always wanted to be part of the world. He just never felt it was meant to be. His recliner and his home theater were really just extensions of a shell that had been thickening for years. His self-image had suffered as he unwittingly, over the years, accepted a pattern of insecure, self-defeating thinking.

Even as we progressed, Tom would continue to fall prey to his Child's toxic perceptions: "I'm thirty-three years old; I've had only a few relationships, and they weren't serious. Any woman's going to think I'm a freak. It's such an embarrassment. Eighteen-year-old kids in high school are more experienced than I am!" Tom just couldn't bear to face being exposed for what he felt were his inadequacies. He originally entered therapy to break his habit of excessive TV watching, but instead, he was introduced to a pathetic, insecure, Child-Turtle, trying hard to avoid life by never taking responsibility for it.

Tom had grown sloppy with his thinking, especially his acceptance of self-condemnation. He had to get disciplined with his Self-Talk workouts. We agreed on a zero-tolerance approach to his Child-Reflex. Tom began to fight back. He began to appreciate how his indulgent, avoidant lifestyle was directed by his Child's incessant doubts and fears. He had no trouble hearing his Child-Reflex and decided he was ready to stop listening. Rather than trying to limit the amount of TV time and struggle with his ambivalent, whining Child, Tom found it easier not to argue; he just turned the TV off. Of course, this made him anxious, but he was willing to accept this discomfort rather than to be ruled by Reflexive Thinking.

Tom wound up responding with one of the most constructive decisions of his life. Recognizing that breaking his habit caused anxiety and provoked addictive desires, he decided to join a local gym and get physical about his resolve. He began to come home from work, and instead of turning on the TV and fighting with his Child-Reflex thoughts, he would head right over to the gym. He would make himself stay at the gym until he felt better about himself. This usually didn't take long.

Self-Coaching Reflection
If your Child-Reflex/insecurity senses weakness, the
Child will take over. If your Child-Reflex/insecurity senses
strength and resolve, the Child will back off.

Within months, Tom began to regain not only a life but also his strength and his physical shape to boot. His newly found confidence was an asset in maintaining his Self-Talk program. He had absolutely no tolerance for a self-defeating Child-Reflex. Thoughts that once Ping-Ponged around in his head were stopped dead in their tracks. In the past where he would listen to these thoughts and even contribute a few doubts of his own, now, as soon as he determined it was his Child trying to get his ear, he automatically chose the opposite path—the path of directing his thinking toward responsibility and engagement. He challenged himself to sustain eye contact with women, then he progressed to talking, and eventually he began flirting. What his Child-Reflex had always seen as impossible became possible as Tom abandoned his shell once and for all.

Self-Coaching the Right Attitude

Tom wound up meeting someone at the gym, and guess what? Not only did she never notice his lack of experience, but to her, Tom was absolutely perfect! He didn't need experience to be loved; he just had to be courageous enough to be himself.

By undermining your confidence, your Child-Reflex always prevents you from learning how effective your natural, spontaneous personality can be. Like Tom, in order to get beyond your Child's stranglehold, you have to be willing to risk finding out the truth. There's no other way. You might feel it's reckless to leap off that cliff of self-doubt and timidity into the unknown, but this couldn't be further from the truth. You'll find that the cliff that you thought was so impossible, so dangerous, isn't much of a cliff at all. In fact, it's only an illusion. Your Child-Reflex created the illusion, and you, over time, sheepishly accepted it.

Just as Tom did, you will reach a point where you'll need to turn off the TV and take the action necessary for that leap of faith. You need to be reckless enough to risk believing in yourself. Granted, it may be a bit intimidating or even frightening to consider abandoning your trusty shell, but keep in mind that risking self-trust is really not risky at all, or reckless. It only feels this way because you're used to your shell of control living.

Why not make the decision now? Decide to be reckless enough to be okay. If it's a turtle shell you're worried about missing, think again. The only reason you cling to your shell is because you don't allow yourself to believe in a life outside of it. Know anyone who wants to buy a forty-inch TV?

Shells Come in All Shapes and Sizes

What about you? Are you building shells right now? In order for any behavior to be considered your Turtle shell, it must show an attempt to avoid some aspect of life in order to feel more in control. As a general rule, any excessive behavior should be questioned as a possible deflection or avoidance of life. Here are a few common examples of what shells are made of:

- Watching TV, listening to music, reading
- Emotional withdrawal
- Social isolation
- Shyness
- Internet overuse
- Compulsive eating
- Use of alcohol and other drugs
- Gambling
- Compulsive running or bodybuilding
- Excessive or compulsive pursuit of a hobby
- Overworking
- Hypochondria (illness-focused withdrawal)

Heads and Tails

Just as heads and tails represent opposite sides of the same coin, so too do Hedgehog and Turtle behaviors represent opposite sides of the same goal—control. As different as Turtle and Hedgehog behavior may seem, they're joined by a need to control. That's why it's possible to be a Hedgehog sometimes and a Turtle at other times. At work, for example, a husband's Turtle attitude may prevail as he avoids conflict, hides in his office, and desperately tries not to make waves. When a Turtle husband comes home, however, where he feels safe, he may become a Hedgehog around his wife and kids, snarling, attacking, and attempting to keep them and their needs at arm's length. "Get away from me. I've had a rough day!"

Not all defensive behavior is predictable. External circumstances may precipitate a surprise noxious response. Depending on these circumstances, one minute you may repel, and at the next retreat. If nothing else, control-sensitive people are consummate opportunists. Control is all that matters. I'm reminded of the agnostic's prayer: "Dear God, if there's a God, hear my prayer." This prayer was clearly penned by a control-sensitive person—cover your bases, don't take any chances, and if there's a God, please let me feel I'm in control.

Your unique personality will steer you more toward certain strategies of defense rather than others. Based on your strengths and weaknesses, through a process of trial and error, you have come to learn what works for you and what doesn't. What works for you will be practiced over and over again by your Child-Reflex. Do keep in mind, what works *for* the Child works *against* you.

❖ ❖ ❖

TRAINING SUGGESTION

Take a look at the common Turtle tendencies listed on the left of the chart on page 198. Next to each tendency, you will see a scale ranging from 1 (never) to 5 (often). Grade yourself regarding any Turtle behavior that you've noticed in yourself within the past three months.

If you've listed any Turtle tendencies, include this self-assessment in your training log. As you progress with your Self-Coaching program, you'll want to retake this quiz periodically (I suggest once a month) to assess the effect the program is having on these tendencies. Scoring is simply a matter of totaling all your responses and then comparing this number with the previous months' tallies.

Turtle Tendencies	Never		Occasionally		Often
Watching TV, listening to music, reading	1	2	3	4	5
Emotional withdrawal	1	2	3	4	5
Social isolation	1	2	3	4	5
Shyness	1	2	3	4	5
Internet overuse	1	2	3	4	5
Compulsive eating	1	2	3	4	5
Use of alcohol and other drugs	1	2	3	4	5
Gambling	1	2	3	4	5
Compulsive running or bodybuilding	1	2	3	4	5
Excessive or compulsive pursuit of a hobby	1	2	3	4	5
Overworking	1	2	3	4	5
Hypochondria (illness-focused withdrawal)	1	2	3	4	5
Miscellaneous withdrawal	1	2	3	4	5

15

Self-Coaching for Chameleons

Most people are familiar with chameleons—perhaps not with the actual pocket-sized, arboreal lizard whose tongue can snap a bug from a distance of one and a half times the length of its body, but at least with the chameleon's distinctive ability to change the color of its skin. Calling someone a chameleon is usually derogatory and suggests that the person changes his or her personality according to circumstances. Chameleons, aside from their trademark defense of camouflage, are also secretive, solitary, territorial, and bad-tempered—an interesting but not very appealing list of attributes, especially when found in humans. Although human Chameleons may share some of these traits, one in particular stands out: the ability to manipulate how they are perceived. In lizards, this is called protective coloration; in humans, it's called being a fake, a phony, or a fraud.

In the wild, protective coloration is often found among the most helpless creatures, those who have little or no other means of defense. (Protective coloration can also benefit predators such as a tigers or cheetahs, but I'm referring to animals that use it strictly for defense.) Although not as glamorous a defense as claws, wings, teeth, or poison, it's nevertheless extremely effective. (Just try to spot a snowshoe hare lying in the snow fifty feet in front of you.) Human Chameleons don't change color, but they can be shifty and deceptive, and like their lizard counterparts, they can be extremely effective at manipulating a situation. Chameleons come in two basic varieties, which I call the Politician and the Diplomat. Each attempts to control by adjusting either the context of a situation (how you see her or him) or the content (what the person tells you). Nothing is sacred to the Chameleon, except being in control.

By now, you probably recognize that controlling life is an illusion. Chameleon solutions are no more effective at offering control and stability to your life than any of the other control strategies mentioned thus far. Also, like all the other expressions of control mentioned in this book, the opposite always remains true: rather than lessening your debilitating symptoms, these strategies only feed your Child-Reflex, which is the source of your chronic anxiety and depression.

Chameleon traits can be difficult to detect because they are protected by a veneer of rationalization and denial. Most Chameleons have become so knee-jerk in their deliveries that only under unusual circumstances will they begin to see, much less question, their own behavior. As with any controlling strategy, the more extreme its defensive expression, the more resistant it becomes to treatment. Also, because Chameleons are so effective at manipulation, they aren't looking to change a good thing—hey, if it works, why fix it? Over time, however, this shallow, empty, and superficial way of life begins to generate depression or anxiety. Psychological struggle gets your attention, and humbles you. Even the most hard-boiled Chameleon begins to question his or her way of life when distressing symptoms start to trip him or her up. This is the point where Self-Coaching can really help.

Self-Coaching Reflection
Security can come only from your moral center,
never your Child-Reflex.

The Politician

The highest ambition for a Politician is converting you to her or his point of view and getting your vote. A psychological Politician is no different. They're usually debaters who are much more comfortable with thoughts rather than feelings, and they are never, ever wrong about anything. For them, it's all a matter of perspective—theirs.

I don't know about you, but when I listen to an elected official, I usually wind up fatigued trying to figure out the truth lying somewhere under all the self-serving platitudes. Where, oh where, is the truth? Perhaps the single most archetypal political comment ever made was during President Bill Clinton's videotaped grand jury testimony. When asked (regarding a previous statement about a sexual relationship with Monica Lewinsky), "Is that correct?" Mr. Clinton responded, "It depends on what the meaning of the word 'is' is." This one statement, in my mind, will forever define the essence and soul of all politicians, even the Chameleon kind. There is no center. Truth, guilt, morality, and reality are all relative. It's a matter of interpretation. I'm not trying to take anything away from President Clinton. Far from it; I feel he is what he has trained to be all his life: a consummate politician. We expect as much from our political figures and our political system, but we are usually less adept at recognizing or dealing with Politicians (the Chameleon kind) in our everyday lives.

You Just Don't Understand Me!

George is thirty-seven years old and single, an insurance salesman who happens to be a Politician. He was part of a counseling group I ran a few years back. No matter what the group threw at him, he, being a Politician, would skillfully deflect it and wind up sidestepping any and all responsibility. Needless to say, things got a bit testy one night when the group demanded some accountability for George's constant lateness (he showed up at least fifteen minutes late for every session). George responded:

> I can understand why you guys are upset with me for coming in late
> . . . has it really been every week? I don't think that's particularly
> accurate, but if you say so, I'm willing to accept it. I'm not trying to
> make excuses, but take tonight, for example. I was at work late and
> had to call a few clients. As much as I value this group and each of
> you, I still have a moral obligation to my clients. I really did the best
> I could to hurry my calls. I could have spent another hour with

those calls, but you guys are too important. I cut my calls short and got here as quickly as I could. I even risked getting a speeding ticket, which I would have gladly accepted, rather than having to be one minute later than I was.

The group, tired of the same old, same old, wasn't happy with George's nondenial denial. Sensing this tension, George throttled up to a higher gear:

And I bet each one of you has already eaten supper, right? I could have stopped for a burger, but I didn't. Guess I'm trying to tell you how hard I'm trying. I'm really doing the best I can. Maybe you can put yourselves in my shoes. I'm sure if you did, you'd quickly realize I'm putting as much into this group as you. Actually, considering how much I sacrifice to get here, I'm probably guilty of being too involved with this group. I really think it would be great if you guys would cut me a little slack.

The group reluctantly accepted George's political mea culpa for the time being. After a while, however, it wore thin. He continued to show up late, and he always had a reason, always had an excuse. Even when George was eventually backed into a corner by the group's unwillingness to accept any more excuses, he didn't flinch. He stuck to his guns and just kept letting the group know what a wonderful, albeit misunderstood, guy he was ("it depends on what the meaning of the word 'is' is").

The following are three tip-offs if you suspect Politician tendencies:

1. Politicians can't take responsibility for any mistake (nor can you ever criticize a Politician). There's always a rationale, a "yes, but." You will rarely ever hear a Politician simply declare, "You're right, I'm sorry." (If you want to see this tendency in action, just tune in to any political press conference on TV. You'll get the picture.) Politicians have to be believed in order to feel in control.

2. Politicians have a compulsive need to convince you that their point of view is correct. "How can you say that wasn't a great movie? Let me tell you why you're wrong. . . ." Always being correct is a form of control.

3. Politicians aren't necessarily liars: think of them more as great debaters who know how to be creative with the truth. "There's absolutely nothing wrong with me stopping for a drink after work. It's better for me to unwind first before coming home and taking out my frustrations on you and the kids." Since Politicians are adept at finding that one grain of truth to support their arguments, they are totally convinced of their righteous position.

Self-Coaching Reflection

A very interesting aspect of chameleons (the lizard kind)
is that their eyes are covered by the same kind of skin
that covers their bodies. There's one tiny pinpoint hole
in this membrane from which the little critter sees.
Politicians are like lizards; they are unable to see
beyond their pinhole of Reflexive Thinking.

Politician Self-Quiz

Because Politicians are usually unaware of their political defenses, a self-quiz may help you detect whether your Reflexive Thinking is political. Mark each statement as being mostly true or mostly false. If you're not sure, leave the statement blank.

T   F   I have to be right.

T   F   If I am criticized, I can usually turn things around.

T   F   Thinking is a much more valuable trait than feeling.

T   F   I have to be liked, admired, or appreciated.

T   F   In an argument, I'm not likely to give in.

T   F   Even if I don't believe in what I'm arguing, I still have to win.

T   F   I don't take criticism well.

T   F   When threatened, I become shrewd and calculating.

T   F   Feelings often get in the way.

T   F   I have a hard time admitting I've done anything wrong.

T   F   I can always justify my actions.

T   F   I would rather convince than defeat an opponent.

T   F   I often see people as adversaries.

T   F   You can never be too safe.

T   F   I'm generally quite persuasive.

T   F   I don't let people affect me.

T   F   I would rather win than be right.

If you scored between 13 and 17 true, you possess strong Politician tendencies; between 8 and 12 true, you have mild tendencies; between 4 and 7 true, you have weak tendencies; with a score lower than 4 true, you have few or no Politician tendencies.

The Diplomat (the Yes Person)

The second category of Chameleon is the Diplomat, also known as the Yes person. Whereas the Politician wants to convert you, the Diplomat wants to appease you. Before you feel flattered, keep in mind that your appeasement has little to do with your well-being or happiness; it's all about the Diplomat's control. When you're pleased with a Diplomat, you're not going to be a threat. If you're not a threat, the situation is controlled. "That's right, Officer, I was going over the speed limit. I'm really sorry to have troubled you. Your job is difficult enough without having to chase after someone as careless as me."

The worst-case scenario for Diplomats is having someone get angry with them. When people are angry, who knows what they'll do? It's this uncertainty that leaves Diplomats feeling insecure and out of control. Diplomats can get pretty paranoid about offending someone.

Looking for Peace

Take a look at Rudy's reaction to a coworker who tried to flirt with his girlfriend, Mary:

> Ever since I called him and told him to stay away from Mary, I've been going crazy. I was so panicky last night, I asked my mother for one of her tranquilizers. I just keep asking, "Why? Why? Why?" I don't know what came over me. I should have ignored him. That's what Mary wanted. Why didn't I listen to her? I just seemed to snap. I remember yelling at him; I'm not even sure what I said. He never reacted to me; he just had this smirk on his face . . . what was that all about?
>
> It was so out of character for me, so stupid. There's nothing I can do now. How do I know I haven't provoked him into something? I always thought he was a little strange. Who knows, maybe he's the type that could be waiting for me with a baseball bat, or maybe he'll try to hurt me some other way. I don't know, maybe call my boss and start a rumor, threaten my girlfriend, trash my car. Who knows what he's capable of? I don't see how I can ever put my guard down. It could be months before he decides to take action. When will I feel safe again?

Poor Rudy was not used to risking his feelings. From the magnitude of his paranoid reaction, you can understand why. Look at the fallout. Rudy's experience (yelling at this cad) was out of character for him. It was, in fact, undiplomatic. He was used to controlling a situation and minimizing consequences by not making waves—not even ripples. "Give 'em what they want, and they'll leave you alone" has been a motto that served him well. Rudy's anxiety suggested a solution (unfortunately it was his Child-Reflex's solution):

> I'm tempted to talk to him, you know, let him know that I'm cool with the situation. I'll offer to shake hands. Ask him to understand why I got so upset. I'm beginning to feel better already.

Rudy was feeling better because he just found a way (his Child's way) of restoring control. It has nothing to do with what Rudy believes or wants. It has to do with trying to mollify his antagonist with a diplomatic solution—not very satisfying, but safe. It's true that being a Diplomat can eliminate all but the most difficult of conundrums, but at what price?

Throughout this book you've been shown how control is always a shortsighted attempt to feel secure. Rudy can go on for a long time pleasing everyone, walking on eggshells and trying to avoid conflict, but the real question is, can someone like Rudy ever find true peace in a world that requires complete acquiescence? Peace maybe, but no solace.

Saying Yes When We Mean No

Diplomats are Yes people who have a hard time saying no to anything or anyone. It doesn't matter that this strategy burdens their lives with added responsibility and demands; they just can't say no. Well, that's not entirely true. If their refusal isn't their fault ("I'd love to help you out, but I have to go on an interview and won't be in town") then it's okay. In this case, the Diplomat feels blameless and therefore insulated from your anger.

Matt, a fifty-three-year-old social worker, was having a hard time saying no. Everyone loved Matt. And why shouldn't they—he was a pleaser. Ask him to do anything, and chances are he'll do it with a smile. Don't let that smile fool you, though. Inside, he was a cauldron of conflict and anxiety:

I told my boss that I'd fly with him to Chicago the end of next week to work out the specifics on a deal we'd been working on. Last night, my buddy calls screaming with excitement that he just got a couple of tickets for the World Series, and he's counting on me to go. The tickets are for the fifth game of the series, which is when I'm supposed to be in Chicago! What's wrong with me? I'm on the phone, I know I have to refuse the tickets, I know I have no choice, and what do I say? I told him it was fantastic and that I couldn't wait. I'm insane! I just couldn't say no. You know what's even crazier? Not only wasn't I saying no, but I found myself trying to get my buddy all pumped up about the game. I'm either crazy or stupid!

The tickets are for the fifth game of the series. If the Yankees sweep, I'll be okay. Then I'm off the hook and can fly out first thing in the morning and meet my boss. If the Yankees don't sweep, I'm dead. I really don't know what I'll do.

Fortunately for Matt, the Yankees did sweep the series, and he was off the hook. Did he learn anything? Yes, he did. One thing he realized was that his World Series dilemma wasn't unusual. Looking back, there was a whole history of similar predicaments. Some of these were resolved naturally (like the Yankees' sweep), others by worming his way out (feigning sickness or injury), and still others remained unresolved, leaving a trail of scars and hard feelings.

Matt was particularly vulnerable to invitations. Over the years, there were many things he did that he absolutely hated. Matt's essentially a beer, hot dog, and ball-game kind of guy, yet over the years, he's allowed himself to be coerced into attending the opera, the ballet, and a guided tour through the Metropolitan Museum of Art. Lately, Matt's noticed that his sleep is generally interrupted and that he has become more moody over the past year. When Matt and I started talking, he was flirting with a Turtle solution to his problems. He was, quite literally, trying to hide from everyone.

Luckily, Matt and I began to talk before he had a chance to create a formidable shell around himself. He was still ready and desperate to learn how to say no. We began with Self-Talk. He had no problem seeing how his Child-Reflex (aptly called Wimpy) would begin to panic whenever someone made a request of him. "You're right; I feel just like a child who's afraid to say the wrong thing because I'll get in trouble." Matt had to assimilate the notion that just because his Child-Reflex couldn't say no, that didn't mean *he* couldn't. Although it was terrifying for Matt to consider not being a Diplomat any longer, the notion of being able to do what he wanted appealed to him.

We did some role playing where I would pretend to ask Matt to join me at different functions. Rather than having him listen to his Child-Reflex, I wanted him to get used to hearing his healthier, more mature self. Matt enjoyed this exercise. In this no-risk environment, he found that saying no wasn't so strange or—once he got the hang of it—difficult. He couldn't help smiling as he would tell me, "No, I'm sorry, Doc, I can't join you this weekend." He was smiling because he loved how it felt—saying what he wanted to say. Just trying on this more honest persona had a liberating, energizing effect on him. He left our session almost hoping for an opportunity.

It didn't take long. The very evening after our session, Matt was sitting with his wife when his sister called to invite him and his wife to their niece's piano recital on Saturday. This wasn't an easy challenge, but Matt was primed, practiced, and ready to try.

As it turned out, he had been looking forward to playing golf on Saturday with an old friend and really didn't want to spend it in a hot, stuffy auditorium looking at his watch. Matt stifled his Child-Reflex, which was prompting him to blurt out, "Sure, Sis, we'll be there." Instead, he swallowed, told Wimpy to back off, took a deep breath, and made himself say, "I'm sorry, Sis, I've already made plans that I can't break." The next part was just as hard for Matt. Now he had to fight an intolerable Child urge to take back his refusal with something like, "Well, maybe I can break my plans, I'll let you know." He steeled himself, managed to stick to his guns, said no to Wimpy's panic, and made himself sit through a difficult moment of silence. His sister, a little shocked at this refusal (after all, no one in recent memory could give you an instance where Matt had said no to anything), said she understood and hung up.

TRAINING SUGGESTION

Diplomats need practice saying no. If you're a Yes Person, it's imperative for you to get a little practice. Start off by looking at yourself in a mirror, then watch and hear yourself saying no: "No, I'm not going to do that." Just getting used to allowing "no" to roll off your lips is an important first step (along with your Self-Talk) in breaking the reflexive habit of appeasing everyone.

Matt had mixed emotions. He was elated that he was going to do what he wanted on Saturday and that he didn't have to sit through any of that music, but he was also feeling panicky. In our next session, when we talked about the panic, Matt realized that he wasn't used to feeling out of control. Refusing his sister had left him feeling vulnerable to her anger and resentment. By being the Diplomat, he had escaped ever feeling this vulnerability. It took some straight thinking and Self-Talking for Matt to recognize that his vulnerability was only a habit—a habit with no here-and-now business, other than to screw up his life.

As Matt continued his "saying no" practice, he still needed to do something about his anxiety. It was hard for him to trust that he really could be a more secure person. At first, saying no was bittersweet. He liked being liberated but was still getting hammered with anxiety about being vulnerable. There was no objective basis for Matt's insecurity. His anxiety and panic were echoes of a long-past skirmish with his parents, echoes that continued to reverberate throughout his life.

Early on in our sessions, one thing that kept tripping Matt up was that he was paying too much attention to his discomfort. Rather than dealing with his Child-Reflex more directly and forcibly, he was becoming worried about his worry, "I don't know, I'm not sure this is working. I've been feeling shaky inside. I think I'm getting worse. I shouldn't be feeling shaky; I should be feeling better. What's wrong with me? Why am I worrying so much about all this?"

I told Matt to treat his symptoms as he would any cold symptom—a stuffy nose, a sore throat, a headache—uncomfortable, yes, but nothing to worry about. "When you have a cold, the less you focus on your symptoms, the better you feel. Sometimes you even forget you're sick. It's the same with anxiety. The more you focus on your symptoms, the more nervous you get. Accept your symptoms as you would a runny nose. Forget about them, and focus on working with your Child-Reflex. That's the only important thing. Your symptoms aren't important; dismantling your Reflexive Thinking is."

Matt's progress was steady and uneventful. He worked hard and finally overpowered Wimpy. Once he liberated himself from his habit of insecurity and found that he didn't have to please everyone, Matt found that taking care of himself and living a more honest life was actually quite easy, and very natural. He also found that saying no and being more up-front with the world didn't make him a bad person. He could actually be himself and still be worthwhile. Diplomats don't understand this simple truth. They are forever hiding what they see as their unacceptable desires.

❖ ❖ ❖
TRAINING SUGGESTION

Chameleon tendencies are difficult to detect because they are protected by a veneer of rationalization and denial. Reread the sections on the Politician and the Diplomat, being as objective as possible. If you think you may have Chameleon tendencies, it really helps to solicit the opinion of others. A spouse, a friend, or a relative can be helpful with this assessment. Sometimes, specific behaviors patterns or habits, such as saying yes when we mean no, can point to a Chameleon tendency.

Chameleon tendencies are difficult to rate objectively. Do your best to (1) isolate specific Chameleon tendencies, (2) subjectively decide how often these tendencies occur (use the following scale), and (3) periodically reassess these tendencies to chart your Self-Coaching progress.

Chameleon Frequency Scale

Never				Sometimes					Often
1	2	3	4	5	6	7	8	9	10

❖ ❖ ❖

16

Self-Coaching
for Perfectionists

Let's start out by assessing your level of perfectionism. Answer each question as being either mostly true or mostly false.

T   F   Whatever I do, it has to be done just so, or I can't put it down.

T   F   I have no tolerance for getting ill.

T   F   I have an image to maintain.

T   F   I get anxious when things go wrong.

T   F   I'm usually right.

T   F   Details are a very important part of life.

T   F   I've been called a control freak.

T   F   I hate when things are out of place.

T   F   If you want to get a job done right, you have to do it yourself.

T   F   I have trouble being on time.

T   F   I have to win.

T   F   I have a hard time letting someone else drive my car.

T   F   I tend to overdo everything.

T   F   I'm never caught off guard.

T	F	I have no tolerance for mistakes (mine or other people's).
T	F	I fuss too much when I'm getting ready.
T	F	I've been accused of being too neat (or fanatical, or obsessive).
T	F	I've been told I'm too rigid.
T	F	Whenever I get involved in something, it has to be 100 percent.
T	F	I'm more intellectual than emotional.

If you scored from 16 to 20 true, you have definite perfectionistic tendencies and need to recognize the importance of not letting this particular style of defense persist without some Self-Coaching intervention. A score of 11 to 15 true suggests a moderate tendency toward perfectionism. Be aware of the warnings in this chapter, and don't allow any more rigid, compulsive behavior to develop. A score of 6 to 10 true suggests few significant perfectionistic tendencies. You may, however, be prone to occasional perfectionistic defenses when dealing with stress. A score of 5 or fewer indicates no significant perfectionistic tendencies. In your case, continue maintaining your natural tendencies to handle, rather than control, life's demands.

Anything but Average

There are three kinds of Perfectionists: the Star, the Fanatic, and the Control Freak, but they all have one thing in common; they all believe that if you're willing to work hard enough, you can eliminate (control) your vulnerability in life. The logic is simple: if you and what you're doing are perfect and no one can find fault, then no one can hurt you. As long as all your ducks are lined up neatly in a row, you feel completely in control.

Perfectionism isn't a personality trait for the lazy or less motivated; it's a full-time job that takes full-time commitment. Whereas Hedgehogs are defined by their hostility, Turtles by their retreating, and Chameleons by their manipulation, Perfectionists are defined by their excessively high standards and unflagging effort. Whether it be cleaning a closet, taking a test, or influencing someone else's opinion, Perfectionists have no choice: they have to perform flawlessly, each and every time.

Perfectionists are also snobs—control snobs. It may be okay for other people to come in second, to flub an exam, or to ignore stains on their blouses, but not for a Perfectionist. There is no flexibility—they must be first, the best, and without blemish. Perfectionists venerate their compulsive way of life, seeing it as a higher calling. They are elitists who see mediocrity as a curse. If you want to see Perfectionists cringe, just call them "average." The A-word automatically gives rise to anxious or depressed feelings, followed by fanatical efforts to reverse this abhorrent stigma. "Me, average? Never!" For the Perfectionist, winning isn't everything, it's the only thing. It's a life of compulsive effort, driven by black-and-white tunnel thinking.

Perfectionists know only one happiness. They believe that living flawlessly is the only way to ensure control and mastery over life. There is a grain of truth to this perception, but there is a big downside, too. Once you believe that flawless, perfect living will steer you away from vulnerability and insecurity, you wind up with no choice—you either live flawlessly, or you suffer. It's no different from any other dependency or addiction (alcohol or other drugs, gambling, spending money, overeating, and so on). When you rely on externals to make you feel better, you unwittingly create a *have-to* mentality. Just like drug addiction, perfectionism will leave you with tunnel vision, insisting that all your ducks not only have to line up in a row, but also to stand at attention.

To all the world, Perfectionists often do appear perfect. Their homes are immaculate, their cars are freshly waxed, they tend to dress impeccably, never run out of gas, and are winners and leaders, especially those who are Stars. Whatever they do, they never skimp on energy or effort. For the Perfectionist, "Ain't no mountain high enough!" They often appear as superhuman beings. And why not? They usually accomplish more in a day than most people do in a week. They make the rest of us seem lazy and ineffective in comparison. Don't be deceived by the Perfectionist's flurry of accomplishments, however. Take a closer look.

Perfectly Miserable

The key to understanding the dark side of perfectionism is the realization that perfectionism isn't really striving for perfection. It's actually the avoidance of imperfection, and herein lies the problem—for many, the curse. A hair out of place, a spelling error on a report, or spots on the silverware can all generate intense anxiety. This is a terribly stressful way to live, always being on call, maintaining control, and never being allowed to mess up. Living with the intensity of perfectionistic demands means living with anxiety and pressure.

If you are a Perfectionist, you have an apprehensive way of life that eventually depletes and depresses you. Unfortunately, as with all control strategies, the more anxious and depressed you feel, the more likely you are to intensify rather than moderate your controlling efforts. The cycle of control, as you've seen expressed in previous defensive strategies, becomes an upward spiral.

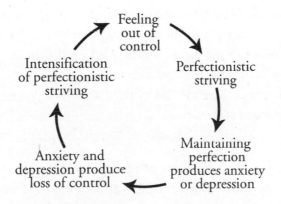

When caught in a control cycle, Perfectionists who seek therapy don't want to be liberated from their Child-Reflex's perfectionistic ways. Far from it—they really want to become better and more perfect neurotics. They're only looking to give their defenses a lube and oil, not to abandon them. Perfectionists have a particularly hard time believing—and risking—that perfection isn't the answer. In fact, in therapy, they often want to be perfect patients. They bring notes, write down their dreams, ask for homework, and hate to leave at the end of the hour. The Perfectionist, especially the Star, wants to become your favorite patient and secretly wants you to give up the rest of your practice so you can appreciate just how wonderful they and their problems can be.

Self-Coaching Reflection
Perfectionism isn't a desire for perfection.
It's a desire to avoid imperfection.

Philosophically speaking, why would striving for such a noble and exalted goal as perfection be such a problem? Simple answer: Nature abhors perfection, at least as the Perfectionist defines it. Although Perfectionists like to believe they're pursuing a lofty, aesthetic ideal, in reality, they're only looking for a tool with one mundane application—control. No doubt it's this exalted illusion of complete and perfect control that gets so many people hooked. You know how wonderful you feel when you manage to get that room cleaned up just so, or serve that perfect dinner, or make that positive impression. You're on top of the world, feeling fulfilled and satisfied. It's normal to enjoy success and to relish having things work out.

Self-Coaching Reflection
Bettering yourself, improving, learning, moving forward—
all can be seen as constructive and worthwhile ambitions.
It's okay to move toward an ideal of perfecting yourself,
as long as you see this as an ideal and not a reality that
you can possess. When you insist on being perfect, that's
when you move from a constructive desire to improve
your life to a destructive desire to control it.

216

If you're prone to perfectionism, you're not surprised by your success. You're a firm believer that you make your own luck. You approach every task with a single-minded certainty. You have no choice, you *have to* succeed, perfectly. The flowers that have to be arranged just so, the dessert that must melt in your mouth, and the clothes that must be impeccable—these are all expected, demanded. Don't misunderstand; it's not all work. Perfectionists do get to enjoy their moments of glory and accomplishment, but they're fleeting moments at best. The next challenge is already knocking at the door, with another not far behind, and another after that.

All That Glitters Is Not Gold

Generally speaking, Perfectionists tend to be quite successful. Because of their many and varied accomplishments, they are often admired, even envied by others. When I was in graduate school, my wife and I were friendly with another couple who could only be described as a supercouple. Both husband and wife were Perfectionists whose lives, by any standard, seemed extraordinary. Aside from having three kids, they had an immaculate house, ever-shiny cars, always-blooming perennials, weedless grass, and (my envy) a garage where every nail, screw, and tool was not only hung and in its place, but also labeled. The husband, who held a challenging position at the university, somehow managed to be at every Little League game, volleyball match, and parent-teacher conference. The wife, who worked part-time, was a class mother, the Parent-Teacher Association president three years running, a world-class cook, and a black belt in karate. My wife and I felt our lives paled in comparison.

The supercouple seemed to possess an energy and ability far beyond our reach. Years after we lost contact with them, my wife and I would occasionally lament our disordered lives and wonder why we couldn't be more like this supercouple. My garage (to this day) is an obstacle course, my lawn supports a nation of grubs, and our home rarely approaches perfection. For many years, we just assumed it was because we were less motivated, less perfect.

My wife and I have matured, and now we have a different perspective on our so-called shortcomings. Our epiphany came a few years after I

217

finished graduate school and we moved back east from California. I got a call from one of our superfriends' teenage daughters wanting to know if I could do anything to help. It seems that the husband had been drinking heavily and the wife had slipped into a depression. I spoke to the husband, and he admitted that both he and his wife were burnt out, that they didn't want to go on together any longer.

They seemed so perfect. Regrettably, maintaining their illusion of perfection took too much out of them. They were perfect but got too tired staying perfect. Yes, it's possible to maintain an illusion of perfection, success, competence, or omnipotence if you desire. All it takes is effort, vigilance, maintenance, tenacity, fear, compulsion, stress, and complete dedication—twenty-four hours a day, seven days a week. Are you sure it's worth it?

What may be confusing is that not only are you convinced it's possible to have it all, but you've proven over and over again that you *can* have it all. So what's a little effort? This conclusion is dangerously short-sighted. Sustaining these unnatural efforts (in other words, living flawlessly) will eventually bring you face to face with a more important reality—you can never be happy unless you're perfect. It's a scary world where one glitch, one faux pas, one stumble leaves you depressed and anxious, scurrying to reclaim your throne. It's unnatural to live with such demands. Rather than focusing on being perfect, ask yourself why you need to be so perfect. If being imperfect causes you to feel anxious, suspect that your life is being ruled by your Reflexive Thinking.

Three Expressions of Perfection

Perfectionists fall into three major groups: the Star, the Fanatic, and the Control Freak. Each of these types behaves with a perfectionistic style of black-and-white, tunnel-visioned rigidity. Because of this similarity, there is overlap among groups, but there are also some interesting differences:

- *The Star*—Stars want one thing: to be applauded. If people are impressed with you (and what you do), they're not going to hurt you. This is control. The Star is convinced that everyone loves a winner. Stars are usually in successful, spotlighted positions. They are typically leaders, not followers, and are always trying to impress the world.

- *The Fanatic*—Fanatics are what we think of as the classic Perfectionist. Fanatics may enjoy the applause of others, but unlike the Star, approval is only a secondary pursuit. For them, the primary objective of their fanatical way is to rise above vulnerability by eliminating all flaws. (If someone happens to applaud this effort, that's a bonus, not an essential.) Fanatics are typically obsessive and compulsive about some or all aspects of their lives, such as keeping fanatically neat closets, cars, or personal appearance. Sometimes, Fanatics become fanatical about their pursuits, hobbies, clubs, religions, or exercise. They are typical overdoers who can't do anything halfway.

- *The Control Freak*—Control Freaks differ from Stars and Fanatics in one essential way: they are socially oblivious. Whereas Stars insist on winning the acclaim of others, and Fanatics are often (although not exclusively) driven by their image and what others may think, Control Freaks are only concerned with absolute control, rather than with being liked. Whether it be controlling others, things, or events, the Control Freak leaves nothing to fate. Everything must be controlled.

The Star

Stars are leaders, presidents of clubs and organizations, winners, high rollers, and risk takers. They work hard to keep the spotlight on themselves. As long as everyone is applauding, the Star is content. Because Stars believe "Everyone loves a winner," they are driven to succeed, whatever the cost. Losing ground, fading into the background, and not being noticed is a frightening loss of control. It's one step away from being forgotten and rejected. The Star's Child-Reflex creates a fragile self-image that constantly needs to be shored up by everyone's admiration.

Sometimes, the Star's perfectionism is diffuse and hard to detect. Gary, a twenty-four-year-old man I was working with, was shocked to hear that his Star efforts were hurting him. He had the following (abridged) list of accomplishments to report: "I don't understand why I don't make a better impression on women. I'm a college graduate, I play the piano and trumpet, I'm well read, I have a good job, I'm an athlete, I'm a photographer, an artist, a writer. . . . What's wrong with me? I think I'm a pretty good catch. I'm even thinking about going back to school." Gary was trying to be everything. He wanted to become the perfect person. His Child-Reflex had him convinced that the more accomplished he became, the more irresistible he would become.

What Gary needed wasn't more school, or another accomplishment; he needed some Self-Coaching. First, he had to stop listening to his Child-Reflex's insistence that in order to be appreciated, loved, liked, and valued, he had to be better than everyone else. According to Gary's Child, the equation was simple: the more you're admired, the better you are. If you're better than other people, then you're controlling how people feel about you. A + B = C, where C, of course, stands for control.

Using the Follow-Through part of his training program, Gary was quickly able to hit the mark. In his words, "I have a 'little man' complex." Although this admission wasn't buried too deeply, it was nevertheless very upsetting for him to discuss. Actually, he sounded and acted more like a man confessing a murder. After all, it had been Gary's deep, dark secret for many years.

"Everyone thinks I'm the most secure, positive person they know," he said. "They wouldn't believe how messed up I am." He seemed to have made a pact with the devil: "Let me be a Star, then people won't notice how short I am." His Child-Reflex left him hopelessly trapped in an adolescent struggle for power, potency, and virility. Because he was doomed to be a "little man," no matter what he did, he would never be—nor could he ever be—enough of a man. This was Gary's life sentence, and it depressed him.

When Gary started his Self-Coaching program, he didn't have to look far to discover his Child's influence. He was constantly finding fault with himself, or trying to tear himself down. His Child-Reflex provided ample opportunity for practice. If, for example, someone were nice to Gary, showed him some respect, or applauded his accomplishments, rather than feeling a sense of relief, Gary's Child would grow anxious. After all, success was temporary, and he couldn't rest on his laurels.

Gary was on a treadmill, powered by the belief that unless he maintained his stellar performance, he would be minimized (pun intended). Once, early on, I asked what was actually so terrible about being short. Gary, reacting with his Child-Reflex as if I'd just punched him in the gut, winced. "If you really want to know, I feel like I'm only half a man!" I almost jumped out of my seat, "That's absurd! You're acting like half a man if you allow your Child to get away with this farce. Enough is enough! It's time to become a whole man."

For the first time it became clear to Gary that he was *allowing* himself to be victimized by his knee-jerk, reflexive thoughts. When his Child talked, Gary would hang his head and, as he put it, "accept my fate." Eventually, it dawned on him that he was buying his Child-Reflex's "half-man" notion without so much as a whimper. He tried to get motivated by recalling my words, "Enough is enough!" He was enthralled by the notion that if he could fight off his Child, he might feel okay about himself—enthralled, but far from convinced. He met stiff resistance from his Child, who kicked, screamed, and threw tantrums for weeks. The harder Gary came back with some directed Self-Talk, the more his Child-Reflex would throw up a barrage of insecurity, "I can't change. Who am I kidding, nothing's going to change the fact that I'm a shrimp. All the therapy in the world isn't going to add an inch to my height."

Gary, however, quickly developed enough muscle to not let his Child-Reflex have the last word. On a page in his training log, Gary wrote, "It's not me, it's my Child who's hung up on my height. I

221

think I really understand this now. My choice is to go along with this view and hate myself or fight. I choose to fight! I've got to see that I'm more than my height. That sounds so stupid when I write it—of course I'm more than my height! Somehow I've got to own this insight. I think if I could say, 'I'm tall enough,' I'd be cured—say it and believe it!"

It was imperative that Gary continue to be tough with his Child-Reflex. Typically, the Child will intensify its sabotage when fighting for its life. I helped Gary realize that this was an indication that he was getting to his Child. "Don't let up," I encouraged. "You have absolutely nothing to lose except your insecurity." He didn't give up. Working on his motivation, Gary developed his own pep-talk slogan: "I don't need to grow taller, I need to grow up!" He would use this affirmation every time he confronted his Child-Reflex.

Gary's perfectionistic lifestyle was an attempt to overshadow his insecurity by molding the perfect persona. His truth could be stated simply: I don't have to be perfect, I just have to become more secure. This wasn't security from the outside in (that is, through accomplishments), but from the inside out: "I don't need to grow taller to be okay. I need to grow up." There was no rational reason why he had to go on looking at the world from an adolescent, Child-Reflex point of view.

Self-Coaching Reflection

It's useful to try to assess the age of your Child.
A tantrumy attitude, for example, may suggest a very regressed Child whose style is reminiscent of a two- or three-year-old: "No, just leave me alone. I won't say a word!" One tip-off that you're dealing with an adolescent Child is a hypersensitive focus on physical concerns. It's during adolescence that physical attractiveness becomes all-encompassing. It's what teenagers obsess about.

The Fanatic

Fanatics are your archetypal perfectionists. They can be fanatical about anything: work, clothes, shopping, eating, cleanliness, exercise, you name it. I ran into a prototypical Fanatic while pursuing my hobby as an astronomy buff. The club I belong to has viewing parties, where the public can come and enjoy an evening under the stars. The first time I went to one of these star parties, I was amazed to see the guy next to me setting up. Talk about bells and whistles: this guy's telescope was equipped with a steel-reinforced tripod, dew shield, eyepieces, cameras, light-pollution filters, star charts, even computer-assisted tracking. He wore battery-powered socks, gloves, and a headband with a red flashlight for night vision. A card table and adjustable folding chair were the last to materialize from the back of his station wagon. He proudly let me know that he was fanatical about his telescope.

I'd like to think that my nocturnal friend at the star party was driven more by passion rather than a compulsive need to control. When fanaticism is driven by enthusiasm, rather than a compulsive "have-to" insecurity, it's usually constructive and often quite restorative. The opposite is also true, whether you've run into the Fanatic at the gym, at the club you belong to, or at your job: when fanaticism is driven by insecurity, then it becomes destructive and depleting.

You've been to their houses, seen their manicured lawns, or marveled at their elaborate, carefully maintained worlds. It's hard to tell at first if it's legitimate passion or insecurity that's steering these achievements. Although this important distinction will be more fully explained later in this chapter, for now, if you suspect that you're a Fanatic, simply ask yourself how happy you are. If your lifestyle is driven by enthusiasm and passion, you'll have no problem recognizing the end result—a life filled with happiness and contentment. If, on the other hand, your life reflects frustration, stress, anxiety, and depression, then it's time to recognize that a fanatical lifestyle has become part of your problem.

Like the couple my wife and I knew in graduate school, however, perfection puts enormous pressure on your resources. Like a sprinter, you may look great for the first hundred meters, but you're not going to keep it up for long. You can't—not without serious consequences.

Jack was an anxious and depressed patient of mine who struggled to maintain his healthy lifestyle. He refused to accept the fact that his fifty-year-old body was going to age, sag, or fail him in any way. His waist was a solid thirty-two inches, he bragged about not having had a cold in two years, and he was convinced that for him, aging was "a myth!" He lifted weights and jogged, and he was a fixture at his neighborhood health-food store. He was also an avid chef whose tofu dishes, freshly juiced beverages, and organic veggies were worthy of a gourmet restaurant. Jack was indeed fanatical about his health.

When left to pursue his rigorous schedule, Jack felt great. The problem that brought him to therapy was that his wife, kids, boss, bills, and obligations were all competing and conflicting with his ambition to remain forever young. Jack never had enough time. He could never afford to take an afternoon off or stay out late. No one understood his frustrations. Jack also began to become anxious. After a couple of full-blown panic attacks, he gave me a call.

The problem was that Jack, rather than trying to juggle the situation and reduce the anxiety, kept adding more to an already choked life. Just prior to our first meeting, for example, he decided that flexibility was the key to the fountain of youth and immediately signed up for yoga lessons (which he attended after his nightly workouts at the gym). Jack was fanatical, tunnel-visioned, obsessed, and compulsive about one thing—control. He couldn't tolerate losing his grip to age.

Jack died of a brain tumor, but there was one consolation to this tragedy. In the months before his death, he came to realize the foolishness of his ways. He could have remained fanatical: at one point, he thought of flying to Mexico for an exotic cancer cure. Instead, however, he chose to open himself to the time he had left with his family and his friends.

I can't say Jack died a happy man, but I can say he died courageously. Perfectionism had wasted much of his life. In dying, Jack learned that life wasn't about control; it was about letting go.

The Control Freak

Control Freaks are easy to spot. They're always directing, organizing, steering, and meddling in everyone's business, and typically are seen as royal pains in the ass!

Clair is a Control Freak whose confrontations with her teenage son led her to therapy. Tony, her beleaguered sixteen-year-old, had the following complaints about his mother:

She refuses to give me any space. I have no privacy. Is it wrong to want to close my door? What does she think I'm doing in there? I've never been in any trouble, I don't smoke, I'm not into drugs. Why is she so suspicious? She's always on my back. No matter what I do, she has to correct it. She has to know where I am, who I'm with, what we're doing. If I forget to call home, I'm grounded. If I'm five minutes late on my curfew, I'm grounded. I'm already grounded for the next two months! She insists she has the right to go through my things, read my notes and mail, and even insists that I give her my AOL password. I'm not stupid. I know parents have to monitor their kids, but she's insane!

Clair, after biting her tongue as long as she could, finally exploded:

Look, you're the kid, and I'm the parent. If I say your door has to stay opened, it stays open. I don't need to give you a reason. Whose house is it anyway? And don't think you're so perfect. Your attitude stinks. You haven't been doing your chores, and you're disrupting my house.

Clair was obviously tough on her son, but her control wasn't confined to him. She divorced Tony's father because, as he told me in an earlier interview, he couldn't stand being pushed around by her. When talking with Tony's guidance counselor, I was told—off the record—how impossible Clair was at Tony's school. She was constantly complaining, always snooping around, and never hesitant to cause trouble. For example, when Tony's counselor forgot to call her back one afternoon, Clair reported her to the principal. Clair demanded—and got—a formal apology.

At first, Clair was impenetrable. She did, however, have enough insight to recognize one twisted perception. "I know it's probably neurotic, but I feel that if I relax my grip on Tony, I'm going to lose him." She was terrorized by the thought that he would wind up in a pit of illegal drugs and alcohol. She was convinced, not because of Tony's behavior, but because her Child-Reflex told her so—and she listened. It never occurred to her that she might be frustrating Tony to the point where he might begin acting out, that her fears could become a self-fulfilling prophecy. Nor did it occur to her that her marriage, her reception at Tony's school, and even her friendships all suffered under the strain of her constant demands.

One opening came when Clair admitted she might be losing Tony. This turned out to be her Achilles' heel. It backed her off from her bullheaded arrogance and created a different kind of anxiety. Clair was used to feeling anxious most of the time, but this was because her demands caused conflict. Losing Tony was different. It was one of the few times she felt powerless. After all, she was used to controlling everything and everyone. Anyone she couldn't control, she eliminated (such as her husband and Tony's counselor). Now she was backed up against the wall. She couldn't control Tony and couldn't bear the thought of losing him. Finally, humbled by her anxiety, she realized she would have to change.

Clair and I had a few sessions together without Tony. She

recognized that underneath all her fears and doubts about Tony was a profound sense of insecurity that went as far back as her early childhood. Growing up with a volatile, alcoholic father who was always threatening divorce and abandonment, Clair looked for any opportunity to feel more in control. She had to do something, and she did. She began to take charge. As a child, she became bossy, aggressive, and tunnel-visioned. It worked. Where she was powerless and weak, she now became tough, powerful, and insensitive. Her motto was: "Don't tread on me!"

Realizing the connection between her past vulnerability and her present Control Freak nature was enough to get the ball rolling. To be really secure, she knew she was going to have to risk letting go, or at least relaxing the reins. Security, as Clair found out, begins with a willingness to believe in yourself. Sure it took effort, but she finally appreciated what was at stake if she didn't make the effort.

Self-Coaching Reflection
A willingness to believe in yourself promotes healing and security.

Clair's efforts to apply Self-Coaching were met with enthusiasm by Tony. Life at home quickly improved. Claire stumbled along for a while, but Tony realized she was trying, and that was enough for him. Clair did well.

Telling the Difference between *Want-Tos* and *Have-Tos*

If you suspect that your Reflexive Thinking is pushing you into a perfectionistic lifestyle, it's time for Self-Coaching. How can you tell whether your desire to sing in the choir, to decorate your living room, or to run a marathon is driven by a legitimate or a neurotic ambition? In order to make this distinction, you'll need to learn to distinguish between your *want tos* and your *have-tos*. The essential difference can be stated thus:

- *Want-tos* are driven by a desire for self-satisfaction, not for any ulterior, control-driven motive.

- *Have-tos* are driven by insecurity. They are compulsive, rigid attempts to use whatever you're doing to feel more in control.

If what you want to do is driven by a legitimate and sincere desire, it's going to feel like a *want-to.* If, on the other hand, Reflexive Thinking is involved, then it's going to feel much more compulsive—a *have-to.* *Want-tos* can be intense and passionate experiences, but they're not perfectionistic because your motive isn't control. That's reserved for *have-tos.* You'll need to decide: "Do I feel I *want to,* or do I *have to?*"

Don't be surprised if at first *want to* and *have to* seem identical. You may, for example, hear yourself saying, "I *want to* keep my house spotless." Upon closer examination, however, you may detect your Child-Reflex convincing you that unless your house is spotless, you can't relax and enjoy it—or worse, you won't be seen as perfect. In this case, the truth would be that in order to feel in control you *have to* keep your house spotless. Be patient, and use all your Self-Coaching tools to help you differentiate between whether you *want to* or you *have to* do something.

Self-Coaching Reflection
The perfectionism rule of thumb: If what you engage in restores and rejuvenates you, consider it healthy. If what you engage in depletes you, stresses you, or makes you anxious or depressed, consider it unhealthy.

Larry's Love-Hate Relationship with His BMW

My friend Larry is at the cusp of understanding this *have-to/want-to* dilemma. He's a car fanatic, and he knows it. It's not uncommon for him to wash and wax his BMW daily. He has a camel-hair brush for cleaning the air conditioner louvers, and he gets upset whenever he has to use the car because the freshly vacuumed nap on his rugs will be ruined. He knows he's a fanatic with his cars, but he loves the process. Is this a *have-to* or a *want-to*?

For Larry, it's both.

Larry does love cars, always has. He enjoys every aspect of detailing his car. This clearly is a *want-to* aspect—self-satisfaction without ulterior motive. Where Larry's *want-to* crosses the line and becomes a *have-to* is the point where control seeps into the picture. Keeping the car perfect, not allowing it to get smudged or to have the rugs stepped on is both excessive and rigid (that is, perfectionistic). When, because of a smudge, love can become hate (black-and-white thinking), we're no longer talking about enjoyment. We're talking compulsive, all-or-nothing control.

Larry will be the first to tell you, if it rains and his car's beautiful black paint is showing water spots, not only is he stressed and unable to enjoy his car, he *can't* enjoy it—not until he washes and waxes it again.

Larry is a perfect (pun intended) example of one of perfectionism's most common by-products: stress. Stress is the single most common complaint of all Perfectionists, "I'm so stressed, I need a vacation," or "I don't remember being this stressed out before. What's happened to my life?" What about you: is stress your constant companion?

Are you working too hard for all the wrong reasons? Are your *want-tos* beginning to turn into *have-tos*? Has your life already become a life sentence? What are you waiting for?

❖ ❖ ❖
TRAINING SUGGESTION

In the left-hand column of the chart on page 230, under "Perfectionistic Tendencies," list any Star, Fanatic, or Control Freak tendencies. Using the scale to the right, circle the number that corresponds to the intensity of any tendency you've noted (see the example) within the past three months.

If you've listed any perfectionistic tendencies, include this self-assessment in your training log, and then retake the quiz on a monthly basis in order to evaluate your Self-Coaching progress. Scoring is simply a tally of the numbers you've circled. Your total score should be decreasing with your training.

Perfectionistic Tendencies			Intensity Scale		
Example:	Weak		Moderate		Strong
1. I know I'm fanatical about my appearance. I just can't not care!	1	2	3	4	5

	Weak		Moderate		Strong
1.	1	2	3	4	5
2.	1	2	3	4	5
3.	1	2	3	4	5

PART V

Self-Coaching for Life

17

Saying Good-Bye to Anxiety and Depression

In the introduction, I mentioned that I had been on a high school football team. My decision to join the team wasn't an easy one. I was 102 pounds and scared to death. If you recall, the only reason I joined was to give the impression that I was a tough kind of guy. In spite of my trepidation about playing, however, something quite remarkable happened. This "something" is important for you to understand, and it has nothing to do with football and everything to do with self-liberation.

The first day of practice, I was handed my equipment: shoulder pads, hip pads, thigh pads, knee pads, helmet, mouthpiece. Never before had I seen such paraphernalia. Coming from a neighborhood where old baseballs were typically wrapped in electrical tape, I thought this was impressive stuff! I sat in the locker room, mesmerized. As I began adjusting the massive array of plastic, rubber, and foam armor onto my body, a strange feeling began to emerge, one I had never experienced before. I can only describe it as a profound serenity, tranquility. Considering the horsing around and general mayhem of the locker room, my mood was certainly curious.

Completely dressed, I stood in front of the locker-room mirror. I saw not a skinny kid, but someone transformed. I was gigantic. Not only were my shoulders as big as a house and my legs bulging with foam pads, but I had grown a full inch and a half taller, due to my cleats—this was definitely good. Walking onto the field, I realized that I was completely protected and insulated from harm. My skinny body was no longer vulnerable. I was encased in an exoskeleton that left me feeling confident and secure. What was really startling, however, was that for the first time I didn't have any doubts or fears. Absolutely none! This was an amazing awakening. No one could hurt me. I truly believed this, and this is what set me free. For the first time in my life, I felt liberated from insecurity.

I came to love football, and for four years I played with reckless abandon. It never occurred to me (in spite of my teammates' injuries) that I could get hurt. Here's my point: it wasn't my pads that made me invulnerable; it was my willingness to believe in those strategically placed pieces of armor that allowed me to let go of all my fears. Put simply, I trusted those pads.

Before you run out and purchase shoulder pads, recognize that if you can learn to trust—yourself, your world—then you're free to discard insecurity, anxiety, and depression. Self-Coaching can teach you to trust again, perhaps for the first time. Once you believe in yourself, once you trust your natural resources to handle life rather than to control it, then you're ready to experience that almost transcendent feeling of serenity, the one I first tasted in that locker room many years ago.

Reflexive Hot-Buttons

Now that you've come to understand how Reflexive Thinking can twist your perceptions, thoughts, and emotions in so many ways, it's important that you're not caught off guard by insecurity's wily efforts to throw you off balance. Whether it be a 911 panic or an apocalyptic feeling of doom, regardless of the intensity or power of any challenge, your Self-Coaching response remains the same: building self-trust by starving (using each of your Self-Talk steps) rather than feeding insecurity.

Sometimes, especially when you encounter a particularly powerful reflexive reaction—what I call a Reflexive Hot-Button—the effort to pull yourself off of, and out of, a destructive reaction can be substantial. No matter how significant the challenge, you need to know that now you have the tools to prevail. Let me tell you about one of my Reflexive Hot-Buttons.

When I was a child, no more than five or six, I came across half of a lemon lying in the gutter in front of a grocery store. Scooping up my treasure, I ran all the way down my block to deliver this wonderful treasure to my mother. Handing her my gift, I immediately sensed something was awry. She looked at the lemon and decided that I had stolen it and needed to be taught a lesson. Ignoring my violent protests, she dragged me to the grocery store to apologize to the owner. I was devastated! What was to be a simple gift of love turned into a traumatic incident that paved the way for a Reflexive Hot-Button reaction to any perceived unfairness.

Fast-forward five decades. I was pulling innocently into a parking space a few weeks ago when a car to the right of the spot I was pulling into began to back out, obviously not seeing me. I tapped my horn (honest, just a warning tap) and proceeded to pull into my spot. This elderly guy jumps out of his car and starts screaming, "You animal, you animal! . . . You're just like all the other animals around here. You're a [expletive deleted] animal!" The guy was screaming so violently that a small, curious crowd had gathered. I tried to calm him with a little assurance that I had no intention of doing anything other than pull safely into my empty spot. My calm, rational attempt to defuse the situation only made things worse. Fearing the guy might have a heart attack, I had no choice but to eventually walk away.

Here was my Reflexive Hot-Button lemon experience all over again—getting yelled at, being accused of doing something wrong when I had done nothing. In past situations like this, my lifelong habit, my reflex, had always been to leap to a defensive posture: "How dare this lout yell at me this way! I'm not going to stand for this." Sure, I'll admit, I felt a tidal wave of emotion tugging me toward a defensive/aggressive response. Who wouldn't when confronted with such an outrageous assault? My Child-Reflex was quite evident, clearly wanting to take control of the situation by putting this guy in his place. Fortunately, I've learned my Self-Coaching lessons well, and in spite of the intensity of my feelings that day, I was well aware of the fact that reflexive reacting as well as Reflexive Thinking is always a slippery slope, and I wasn't about to slide down it.

Whenever a Child-Reflex—especially a Hot-Button one—is engaged in the fray, you invariably pay a price. Instead of capitulating to reflexive responding, I pulled (more like yanked) myself away from my desire to combat this fellow. Years ago, if I had been confronted with a similar situation, my reflexive need to control the situation would surely have led to some type of emotional meltdown, inevitably followed by lingering anxious, depressive, self-loathing thoughts: "I'm so embarrassed. Why did I lower myself to his level? I acted like such a lunatic." Fortunately, I am no longer a victim of my reflexive insecurity; my Child-Reflex can no longer turn my world inside out.

My parking lot experience also confirmed another rather important point. Some Hot-Buttons, because of their traumatic significance and early imprinting, may never fully go away. From time to time, given a resonate situation (one that mimics the original trauma), a Reflexive Hot-Button can rear its ugly head to challenge you. Challenge you it might, but once you understand and employ Self-Coaching in your life, you'll understand that your reflexes—even the Hot-Button type—can't hurt you, not once you understand that you have a choice.

"What?" you may ask. "Self-Coaching can't erase my past and all my reflexes?" No, not completely. But fortunately this isn't necessary, because Self-Coaching can neutralize any reflex and render it harmless. As annoying as a Hot-Button (or, for that matter, any other type of reflexive reaction to life) can be, the goal of Self-Coaching isn't to purge your past completely; it's to eliminate anxiety and depression. Pep talks, Self-Talk, and your systematic daily training efforts are all necessary components designed to at least neutralize, if not eliminate, any habit of insecurity—no matter how hot.

Self-Coaching Reflection
It isn't necessary for Self-Coaching to eliminate all Reflexive
Thinking from your repertoire, only to neutralize it.

Habits Were Made to Be Broken

So often, patients want me to know how screwed up they are, how "mental" they are, or how crazy they are. I never accept these dire perceptions. From the beginning I insist, "The only thing wrong with you is that you have a bad habit, a habit of insecurity." As with any habit, whether nail biting or cigarette smoking, your habits won't be easy to break, but they are breakable. Your Reflexive Thinking has gained habit strength—it has become your nicotine, your booze, your weakness.

Self-talk is your tool to dislodge your destructive Child-Reflex habit and replace it with a life-sustaining capacity for natural, instinctual functioning. Don't be deterred by the tenacity of your insecurity habits; expect a struggle. Habits, by their very nature, resist change. Mark Twain, referring to his smoking habit, said that smoking was the easiest habit in the world to break; after all, according to Twain, "I've stopped thousands of times!" Breaking old habits requires an ongoing effort. Your Child-Reflex must be challenged, not just today but every day, until you're liberated from all anxiety and depression. As mentioned earlier, pep talks, Self-Talk, Follow-Through, and your systematic daily training efforts are all necessary components designed to help you kick the habit of insecurity.

I've mentioned that it's up to you to develop your own positive affirmations. After many years of helping and coaching patients to shed the skin of anxiety and depression, I've found one positive affirmation (derived from Self-Coaching healing principle 5) I use more than any other, and I want you to add it to your list. Whenever I'm with a patient who's starting to overly dramatize his or her struggle, I make sure I point out, "It's just a habit!"

I want you to repeat this often: It's just a habit. I want to remind you, again and again, you're not up against anything supernatural, demonic, or mysterious—it's just a habit, nothing else. You've probably given your symptoms too much respect. As my patient Ira once told me, "You don't understand, Doc, this is a depression I'm talking about!" Ira was totally awed by his depression. He wasn't seeing it as just a habit. For Ira, it was a matter of deflating his depression, seeing it for what it was, and then, using Self-Coaching, breaking the habit of depression and insecurity.

Perhaps you're a bit like Ira, looking at your problems as being more than you can handle. As long as your abilities to function and to feel safe aren't in jeopardy, however, it's up to you to stand nose to nose with your struggles and decide that you're going to trust your Self-Coaching program (remember what my football pads did for my confidence).

Trust is a willingness to believe. Don't take my word for it. You decide. Review the chapters in this book, and ask yourself, "Does this program really make sense of why I'm suffering? Does understanding my Reflexive Thinking need for control explain my anxiety and depression?" If your anxiety and depression can be explained, if you can actually see the effects of your Child-Reflex and its many nefarious strategies for control, then why not take that next and last leap of faith? Why not admit the one thing that will start you on the path of true liberation? Why not admit that what you're suffering from is just a habit, a habit of insecurity? While you're at it, you might as well admit another truth: *Habits can be broken.*

Some Realities

I remember running a marathon when I was forty-five years old. For much of the race, I kept thinking, "I'm getting too old for this." I'm sure these thoughts eroded my efforts and diminished my performance. That night, while I was sitting at home watching the local news coverage of the marathon, three old men were being interviewed. These old men had finished the marathon. These old men were each over ninety years old. On my next marathon, I didn't feel too old.

What does this have to do with you? Just be careful with negatives. Realize that negatives, as rational as they may seem, can always be challenged. Negatives are part of your Child-Reflex's habit of keeping you off balance and perpetually insecure. At forty-five, I wasn't too old. People twice my age were competing. I was listening to my Child. Now, more than a decade later, I'm still planning my next marathon. Sometimes the truth becomes even more obvious with time.

I don't have much more to tell you about beating anxiety and depression. You're going to need to be patient and realistic about your goals and expectations. Impatience will bury you just as well as negativity; both are poisons. If you were quitting cigarettes, you'd have no problem telling yourself that a destructive attitude was "just the nicotine talking." When it comes to negativity, impatience, laziness, doubt, or distrust, do the same as you would with nicotine: "That's just my Child-Reflex talking."

Muscle Building

You need to stick with this program long enough to develop positive and healthy emotional muscle. Your muscle-bound Child-Reflex has weakened you. In order to change the balance, you'll need to exercise your mental muscle every day, through your training program. There's no shortcut. To break a habit, you're going to have to reshape your thinking and perceptions, especially about yourself. As you develop your muscle for self-trust, everything else will follow. Stick with the truths laid out in these seven Self-Coaching healing principles:

1. Everyone has a legacy of insecurity.
2. Thoughts precede feelings, anxieties, and depressions.
3. Anxiety and depression are misguided attempts to control life.
4. Control is an illusion, not an answer.
5. Insecurity is a habit, and any habit can be broken.
6. Healthy thinking is a choice.
7. A good coach is a good motivator.

Now that you've had an opportunity to digest the essence and power of Self-Coaching, you'll understand why I waited until now to add three final truths to this list. Together these ten principles will work to eliminate anxiety, depression, and panic from your life:

8. You must challenge the myth that anyone can rescue you.
9. You must accept responsibility for change.
10. You must be convinced that you really have a choice.

The Importance of Letting Go

Self-Coaching is a program composed of many interwoven components, but if I were to single out the single most important variable to your success, it would be Self-Talk's third step: letting go, coupled with its follow-through component, reactive living. I'd like to emphasize this all-important point with an experience I had recently when my wife and I decided to take a few dance lessons.

Tango, salsa, and merengue dancing sound like lots of fun, right? I was shocked to find out that instead of it being an enjoyable experience, learning to dance was frustrating, draining, and rather discouraging. Try as I might, I just couldn't seem to remember the patterns and variations. The struggle went on for a while, until inexplicably one night everything changed. To my surprise, my feet just seemed to know where to go—no effort, no struggle. But what really amazed me was that in that moment, it was the first time I actually heard the music! I had been so focused and intent on doing the right thing, I never realized I wasn't hearing (or enjoying) the music that was playing in the background. I had finally reached a place where I could *let go* of my efforts and allow the music to move me.

You may find yourself with similar feelings of frustration as you attempt to derail Reflexive Thinking using Self-Talk's first two steps. As with learning to dance, these steps require a similar focus, attention, and practice. It's important for you to appreciate that you're learning a new psychological dance, one consisting of new patterns and perceptions. The operative word is *patience*, because whether it's dancing or Self-Coaching, the goal isn't to be doing steps, the goal is to get to a place where you can let go and embrace the moment—to hear the music.

The single best way of letting go is to be in the moment. One of my favorite Zen Buddhist stories is of a monk who, walking along a mountain path, encounters a tiger. Seeing a vine growing on the cliff face just below his path, the monk leaps off the edge, grabbing hold of the vine. The vine begins to loosen, and in the frozen moment before his fall and death, the monk notices a strawberry growing on the vine. The last words the monk speaks before his death are, "What a magnificent strawberry. I think I'll eat it."

This story illustrates being totally in the moment. For the monk, there was no past, no future, no tigers, no cliffs; there was only that pristine moment filled with an appreciation of that magnificent strawberry. As you become more proficient at separating from your Child-Reflex, you will think less and feel more. You will let go of your doubts, fears, and negatives to be with the wonderful strawberries that populate your world.

Letting go takes practice and patience, especially because much of your training has been a cognitive effort to free yourself from your Child-Reflex's distortions. Nonetheless, you'll find that as your Child's influence diminishes, your capacity to let go increases. You will begin to grow in confidence and self-trust. Once you're no longer living in chronic fear, you can risk letting go of any struggle and become totally engrossed in watching a sunset, listening to an opera, playing with your children, or soaking in a warm bath.

How do you let go? There's only one way. First, through your Self-Coaching efforts, you lessen your Child-Reflex's compulsive grip on your life. Then, periodically you begin to practice being in the moment, staying reactive to life. You let go of thoughts as you become immersed in whatever activity you're involved in. It doesn't matter what activity it is; while you're raking leaves or eating supper, practice being totally in that moment, experiencing the sensations, impressions, sounds, tastes, and sights, not your thoughts. This is letting go. In time, you will experience more and more of your life outside of your head. Anxiety and depression don't exist outside of your head, so remember to take a break once in a while and eat a strawberry.

Ready, Coach?

That's all I have to say. It's all I need to say. You have everything you need to insist on a life free from anxiety and depression. If I had one wish, it would be for you to find out just how simple all this really is. It's never been that complicated; it only felt that way. Your days of struggle are numbered as you prepare to live the life you were meant to live. Remember that Self-Coaching isn't just for your acute pain; it's also a way of life. Just as I get up and jog every day, you can adopt Self-Coaching as a way of maintaining balance, clarity, and spontaneity throughout your life. There will always be challenges, anxieties, and depressions; that's life. With Self-Coaching, however, you'll always have a way to get back to your center.

Training Log Format

Designing Your Training Log

There is no right or wrong way to set up a training log. It's up to you to be as elaborate or as simple as you want. One thing I can promise: your efforts will not be wasted. Experience has demonstrated that the feedback, insights, and reinforcement you get from a training log cannot be duplicated in any other way. It's the single best method to provide an ongoing, objective, and systematic way of beating anxiety and depression.

Although any suitable notebook will do, I suggest a three-ring binder. The advantage of a three-ring binder is that you can make copies of the exercises presented in this appendix and insert them as needed, or pull them out for comparison. You can reproduce the exercises exactly as I've presented them, or (where applicable) you can just record the scores from each, with an attached note of explanation. Either way, you'll have a means of evaluating the effects of your training program over time.

Remember, it's your Training Log—make it personal. It's up to you to personalize and use your log in whatever way you can to motivate and instruct yourself.

I suggest that your training log contain the following four sections:

1. A section for Self-Talk efforts

2. A section for Follow-Through

3. A section for specific incidents, insights, or daily observations

4. A section for pertinent exercises reproduced from this book

Section 1: Self-Talk

Self-Talk Review
Self-Talk Step 1. Separate Fact from Fiction, Learn to Listen

Step 1 isn't complicated; it just takes practice to
cultivate a skill for listening to your inner dialogue.
Start by asking a simple question: Are the thoughts
I'm reacting to facts or fictions?

Self-Talk Step 2. Stop Reflexive Thinking

When you realize that your Child-Reflex is steering
your thoughts, use the visuals suggested in chapter 9
as an aid to stop listening.

Self-Talk Step 3. Letting Go

Do something by doing nothing. When it comes to Reflexive
Thinking, turning away, distracting yourself, or just plain
ignoring thoughts of insecurity is the ultimate goal necessary
for liberating yourself from anxiety and depression.

Describe any encounters with Reflexive Thinking, including a step-by-
step analysis of your Self-Talk efforts:

_____

_____

_____

_____

_____

_____

_____

_____

_____

_____

_____

Section 2: Follow-Through

These expressions of control contaminate my life:

_____

_____

_____

_____

Relevant, historical connections I can make to shed light on my struggle:

_____

_____

_____

_____

Trends or hooks I notice connected to my anxiety or depression:

_____

_____

_____

_____

Proactive or passive thoughts I have been aware of lately:

_____

_____

_____

_____

Clues I was able to catch by shifting my perspective and learning from my struggle:

_____

_____

_____

_____

Section 3: Daily Observations

Insights, feelings, incidents, and observations:

_____

_____

_____

_____

_____

_____

_____

_____

_____

_____

_____

_____

_____

_____

_____

_____

_____

_____

_____

_____

_____

_____

_____

Section 4: Exercises

Include in this section any or all of the training suggestions listed at the end of each chapter. I've divided these exercises into three categories:

1. *Daily.* Make every effort to include these exercises as part of your daily log entries.

2. *Monthly.* Use this category mainly to help you monitor your Self-Coaching progress over time. It should be periodically included in your log.

3. *As needed.* Use this category at your own discretion.

Here is a list of all the Self-Coaching exercises and assessments available. You will find these listed at the end of each chapter, as indicated.

Daily

1. Experiences where you felt a loss of control (chapter 6)
2. Thinking traps (chapter 6)
3. Charting Follow-Through efforts (chapter 10)

Monthly

1. Assessing depressive symptoms and their severity (chapter 4)
2. Assessing natural and destructive anxiety symptoms (chapter 5)
3. Assessing Turtle tendencies (chapter 14)
4. Assessing Chameleon tendencies (chapter 15)
5. Assessing Perfectionist tendencies (chapter 16)

As Needed

1. Inner–outer experience: learning to get out of your head (chapter 1)
2. Determining whether your struggles are rooted in anxiety or depression or a combination of the two (chapter 3)
3. Healthy versus insecurity-driven need for control—telling the difference (chapter 7)
4. Differentiating among directed Self-Talk, undirected thoughts driven by insecurity, and neutral undirected thoughts (chapter 8)
5. Assessing your Self-Talk reactions (chapter 9)
6. Changing channels (chapter 9)
7. Looking for hook experiences (chapter 10)
8. Working with proactive and passive thinking (chapter 10)
9. Using pep talks (chapter 11)
10. Determining how and why you worry (chapter 12)

Index